Fieldnotes from Celtic Palestine

Fieldnotes from Celtic Palestine

Diarmait Mac Giolla Chríost

UNIVERSITY OF WALES PRESS
2025

© Diarmait Mac Giolla Chríost, 2025

All rights reserved. No part of this book may be reproduced in any material form (including photocopying or storing it in any medium by electronic means and whether or not transiently or incidentally to some other use of this publication) without the written permission of the copyright owner except in accordance with the provisions of the Copyright, Designs and Patents Act. Applications for the copyright owner's written permission to reproduce any part of this publication should be addressed to the University of Wales Press, University Registry, King Edward VII Avenue, Cardiff CF10 3NS.

www.uwp.co.uk

British Library Cataloguing-in-Publication Data
A catalogue record for this book is available from the British Library.

ISBN 978-1-83772-189-4
eISBN 978-1-83772-190-0

The right of Diarmait Mac Giolla Chríost to be identified as author of this work has been asserted in accordance with sections 77 and 79 of the Copyright, Designs and Patents Act 1988.

For GPSR enquiries please contact:
Easy Access System Europe Oü, 16879218. Mustamäe tee 50, 10621, Tallinn, Estonia. *gpsr.requests@easproject.com*

Typeset by Marie Doherty

Printed and bound by CPI Group (UK) Ltd, Croydon, CR0 4YY

Contents

	Chronology of Events	vii
	Glossary of Acronyms	xi
	List of Photographs	xiii
	List of Illustrations	xv
	Acknowledgements	xvii
	Epigram	xix
1	Introduction	1
2	A Time for Saying	31
3	Making the Witness	63
4	Taking up Form	89
5	The Seeing Places	121
6	The Suffering Subject	149
7	Conclusions	175
	Select Bibliography	211
	Index	227

Chronology of Events

1916	Sykes–Picot Agreement
1917	Balfour Declaration
1920–48	Mandatory Palestine
1948	Declaration of the Establishment of the State of Israel
1948	Arab-Israeli War
1959	Fatah
1964	Palestine Liberation Organisation (PLO)
1967	Six Day War
1970–1	Black September (Jordanian Civil War)
1973	Yom Kippur War
1975–90	Lebanese Civil War
1978	Camp David Accords
1979	Iranian Revolution
1981	Palestinian Islamic Jihad
1982	Operation Peace for Galilee (Lebanon)
1982	Hezbollah
1983–92	Islamic Jihad Organisation
1987	Hamas
1987–93	First Intifada
1991	End of Cold War
1992	*An Evil Cradling*
1993	Oslo I Accord
1994	Palestinian (National) Authority (PNA/PA)
1995	Oslo II Accord
2000–5	Second Intifada
2001	World Conference Against Racism (Durban I)
2002	Operation Defensive Shield (West Bank)
2002	Quartet on the Middle East
2002	Separation Barrier[1] (West Bank)
2003	Roadmap
2004	Operation Rainbow (Gaza)
2004	Operation Days of Penitence (Gaza)

2005	Disengagement Plan Implementation Law (Gaza)
2005	Boycott, Divestment, Sanctions (BDS)
2006	Operation Summer Rains (Gaza)
2006	Operation Autumn Clouds (Gaza)
2006	Second Palestinian Legislative Council Elections
2006	Israel–Hezbollah War (Lebanon)
2007	Battle of Gaza
2008	Operation Hot Winter (Gaza)
2008–9	Operation Cast Lead (Gaza)
2009	*Ymateb/Response*
2012	Operation Returning Echo (Gaza)
2012	Operation Pillar of Defence (Gaza)
2013	*A Month by the Sea*
2014	Operation Protective Edge (Gaza)
2015–16	Jerusalem Intifada
2018	Control of Economic Activity (Occupied Territories) Bill
2018–19	Great March of Return (Gaza)
2020	*Apeirogon*
2021	A Threshold Crossed, Human Rights Watch
2021	Operation Guardian of the Walls (Gaza)
2022	Operation Breaking Dawn (Gaza)
2023	Operation Shield and Arrow (Gaza)
2023	International Court of Justice (ICJ), Request for Advisory Opinion on Legal Consequences arising from the Policies and Practices of Israel in the Occupied Palestinian Territory, including East Jerusalem[2]
2023	Operation Al-Aqsa Flood
2023–Present	Israel–Hamas War (Gaza)
2023–Present	Israel–Hezbollah Conflict (Lebanon)
2024	ICJ, Order on the Application of the Convention on the Prevention and Punishment of the Crime of Genocide in the Gaza Strip (South Africa v Israel)[3]
2024	Integrated Food Security Phase Classification (IPC), Special Brief, Gaza Strip Acute Food Insecurity[4]
2024	Anatomy of a Genocide, UN Special Rapporteur on the Situation of Human Rights in the Palestinian Territory Occupied since 1967[5]

2024	Commitment by Ireland to Declaration of Intervention on Order on the Application of the Convention on the Prevention and Punishment of the Crime of Genocide in the Gaza Strip (South Africa v Israel) at ICJ[6]
2024	UN General Assembly, Resolution on Illegal Israeli Actions in Occupied East Jerusalem and the Rest of the Occupied Palestinian Territory,[7] Co-sponsored by Ireland[8]
2024	International Criminal Court (ICC), Applications for Arrest Warrants[9] in the Situation in the State of Palestine[10]
2024	Welsh Parliament (Senedd Cymru) Statement of Opinion on Recognising the State of Palestine[11]
2024	Recognition of the State of Palestine by Ireland[12]

Notes

1. B'Tselem. The Israeli Information Center for Human Rights in the Occupied Territories, *The Separation Barrier*, 11 November 2017: https://www.btselem.org/separation_barrier (accessed 10 March 2024).

2. ICJ, *Request for Advisory Opinion Transmitted to the Court Pursuant to General Assembly Resolution 77/247 of 30 December 2022 on the Legal Consequences Arising from the Policies and Practices of Israel in the Occupied Palestinian Territory, including East Jerusalem*, 17 January 2023: https://www.icj-cij.org/sites/default/files/case-related/186/186-20230117-REQ-01-00-EN.pdf (accessed 23 April 2024).

3. ICJ, *Application on the Convention on the Prevention and Punishment of the Crime of Genocide in the Gaza Strip (South Africa v Israel)*, 26 January 2024: https://icj-cij.org/sites/default/files/case-related/192/192-20240126-ord-01-00-en.pdf (accessed 23 April 2024).

4. IPC Global Initiative, *Special Brief. The Gaza Strip. Famine is Imminent as 1.1 Million People, Half of Gaza, Experience Catastrophic Food Insecurity*, 18 March 2024: https://www.un.org/unispal/wp-content/uploads/2024/03/IPC_Gaza_Strip_Acute_Food_Insecurity_Feb_July2024_Special_Brief.pdf (accessed 20 March 2024).

5. Human Rights Council, *Anatomy of a Genocide. Report of the Special Rapporteur on the Situation of Human Rights in the Palestinian Territories Occupied since 1967*, Francesca Albanese, 25 March 2024: https://www.ohchr.org/sites/default/files/documents/hrbodies/hrcouncil/sessions-regular/session55/advance-versions/a-hrc-55-73-auv.pdf (accessed 26 March 2024).

6. Department of Foreign Affairs, Government of Ireland, *Statement by the Tánaiste on the South Africa vs Israel case at the International Court of Justice*, 27 March 2024: *https://www.gov.ie/en/press-release/4e9a7-statement-by-the-tanaiste-on-the-south-africa-vs-israel-case-at-the-international-court-of-justice/* (accessed 23 April 2024).
7. Draft Resolution A/ES-10/L.30/Rev.1, 10 May 2024: *https://www.un.org/en/ga/* and *https://documents.un.org/doc/undoc/ltd/n24/129/97/pdf/n2412997.pdf?token=oBA7BR88DcBqhkYpTa&fe=true* (accessed 10 May 2024).
8. Ireland's Deputy Prime Minister, Micheál Martin, welcomed the passing of the resolution by declaring that 'it is time for Palestine to take its rightful place amongst the nations of the world': *https://twitter.com/MichealMartinTD/status/1788958448626905589?ref_src=twsrc%5Egoogle%7Ctwcamp%5Eserp%7Ctwgr%5Etweet* (accessed 10 May 2024).
9. The warrants are for Benjamin Netanyahu (Prime Minister of Israel), Yoav Gallant (Minister of Defence of Israel), Yahya Sinwar (Hamas), Mohammed Diab Ibrahim Al-Masri (Hamas) and Ismail Haniyeh (Hamas).
10. *https://www.icc-cpi.int/news/statement-icc-prosecutor-karim-aa-khan-kc-applications-arrest-warrants-situation-state* (accessed 20 May 2024).
11. A cross-party declaration of support made in Senedd Cymru, the Welsh Parliament, on 16 May 2024: *https://record.assembly.wales/StatementOfOpinion/387* (accessed 28 May 2024).
12. Effective from 28 May 2024: *https://www.gov.ie/en/press-release/1b086-ireland-recognises-the-state-of-palestine/* (accessed 22 May 2024) and *https://www.gov.ie/en/press-release/71936-ireland-recognises-the-state-of-palestine/* (accessed 28 May 2024).

Glossary of Acronyms

ALFA	A Land for All
BBC	British Broadcasting Corporation
BDS	Boycott, Divestment, Sanctions
C4	Channel 4
CIA	Central Intelligence Agency
CND	Campaign for Nuclear Disarmament
CNN	Cable News Network
CRSV	Conflict-Related Sexual Violence
ECHR	European Convention on Human Rights and Fundamental Freedoms
ETA	Euskadi Ta Askatasuna, meaning Basque Homeland and Liberty
EU	European Union
FATAH	Harakat al-Tahrīr al-Watanī al-Filastīnī, meaning Palestine National Liberation Movement
GBV	Gender-Based Violence
HAMAS	Ḥarakat al-Muqāwamah al-Islāmiyyah, meaning Islamic Resistance Movement
HET	Historical Enquiries Team (NI)
HRW	Human Rights Watch
ICC	International Criminal Court
ICJ	International Court of Justice
IDF	Israel Defense Forces
IPC	Integrated Food Security Phase Classification
IQB	Izz al-Din al-Qassam Brigades
IRA	Irish Republican Army
KJV	King James Version
MAGAV	Israeli Border Police
MFA	Ministry of Foreign Affairs (Israel)
NGO	Non-Governmental Organisation
NI	Northern Ireland
OPT	Occupied Palestinian Territories/Territory

OTR	On The Run
PA	Palestinian Authority
PLO	Palestine Liberation Organisation
PNA	Palestinian National Authority
PSNI	Police Service of Northern Ireland
PTSD	Post-Traumatic Stress Disorder
RUC	Royal Ulster Constabulary
S4C	Sianel 4 Cymru, meaning Channel 4 Wales
SAS	Special Air Service
SDLP	Social Democratic Labour Party
TG4	formerly Teilifís na Gaeilge
TOM	Troops Out Movement
TUV	Traditional Unionist Voice
UDA	Ulster Defence Association
UDR	Ulster Defence Regiment
UFF	Ulster Freedom Fighters
UK	United Kingdom
UN	United Nations
UNHCR	United Nations High Commissioner for Refugees
UNRWA	United Nations Relief and Works Agency for Palestinian Refugees in the Near East
USA	United States of America
USSR	Union of Soviet Socialist Republics
UWTSD	University of Wales Trinity Saint David
WAFA	Wikalat al-Anba al-Filastiniya, meaning Palestine News Agency
ZAKA	Zihuy Korbanot Ason, meaning Disaster Victim Identification

List of Photographs

1	The distaff grave, Llanfihangel Abercywyn	44
2	Figures on an unnamed street in Qalandiya refugee camp (April 2017)	129
3	Irish language political graffito on the West Bank separation barrier, Abu Dis (April 2017)	131
4	Haredi demonstration, Sarei Yisrael Street, Jerusalem (July 2019)	133
5	Chagall windows – Asher, Naphtali, Joseph and Benjamin, Abbell Synagogue, Hadassah Hospital, Ein Kerem (July 2019)	137
6	Children, the Old City, Jerusalem (July 2019)	138

List of Illustrations

all by Osi Rhys Osmond

Cover Image	Gwystl Glas/Blue Hostage	
1	Operation Cast Lead	127
2	Clwyf/Wound	152
3	Hostage 1	156
4	Hostage 2	156
5	Hostage 3	157
6	Hostage 4	157
7	Eglwys-fach	159
8	Aftermath	167
9	Gaza	178
10	Rhyfelwr/Warrior	188

Acknowledgements

The making of this book would not have been possible without the engagement and support of very many individuals based in Israel and Palestine, all of whom, for various reasons, shall remain anonymous. Nonetheless, my sincere thanks to them. I am also very grateful for the support of an Isaiah Berlin Israel Travel Award which enabled some of the fieldwork. I am wholly indebted also to Hilary Rhys Osmond for supplying the images of the works by the late Osi Rhys Osmond that are reproduced in this book, and for her permission to use these images. These comprise the cover image, entitled 'Gwystl Glas/Blue Hostage' as well as Illustrations 1 to 10, entitled as follows: 'Operation Cast Lead', 'Clwyf/Wound', 'Hostage 1', 'Hostage 2', 'Hostage 3', 'Hostage 4', 'Eglwys-fach', 'Aftermath', 'Gaza' and 'Rhyfelwr/Warrior'. In addition, I would like to record my thanks to the Hay Festival of Literature and Arts 2024 for the opportunity to talk about the book while it was still in the process of being written. Finally, I would like to thank the editorial staff of the University of Wales Press for their support and guidance in bringing the book to press, along with the various suggestions and comments put to me by their anonymous, scholarly readers.

Three of the Triads of Ireland

    Number 174   Three doors through which truth is recognised: a patient answer, a firm pleading, an appeal to witnesses.

    Number 201   Three candles that illumine every darkness: truth, nature, knowledge.

    Number 249   Three darknesses of the world: custody, surety, oblation.[1]

                                             Trecheng breth Féne

The Second Branch of the Mabinogi

    And when he looked, every loss they had ever suffered, and every kinsman and companion they had lost, and every ill that had befallen them was as clear as if they had encountered it in that very place …[2]

                                             Heilyn fab Gwyn

Síle Nic Chonaonaigh, TG4

    I know that the people of Ireland feel a kinship with the people of Palestine. We understand that story. We have our own history. And I came here with that story in my head.

                      An Balla: Iosrael/An Phalaistín, 20 October 2019

Cen Llwyd, Cymdeithas yr Iaith Gymraeg

    We, as an organisation, have, since our foundation, seen the struggle for rights and freedom for the Welsh language as part of a wider international struggle. We stand in solidarity with the Palestinian people, another nation without a state. The people of Palestine are subjected to horrific mistreatment by the Israeli state. It is from these principles in favour of rights and freedom that we as a movement have adopted BDS. In response to this call emerges a truly global movement against the subjugation of Palestine of which Cymdeithas is now a part.

            BDS in support of the Palestinian People, 27 December 2014

Notes

1 This triad is rendered in the original, late ninth-century Old Irish as 'Trí dorcha in betha: aithne, ráthaiges, altrom' (pp. x–xi in Kuno Meyer, *The Triads of Ireland* (Dublin: Hodges, Figgis and Company Ltd, 1906)). The term 'altrom' is usually translated as 'fosterage', but in the historical period to which the term applies the concept of fosterage contrasts with the modern usage of the term. In the medieval period, infant or child fosterage is a type of tribute, bound by contract, aimed at ensuring patronal and cliental allegiance (e.g. Peter Parkes, 'Celtic fosterage: adoptive kingship and clientage in northwest Europe', *Comparative Studies in Society and History*, 48/2 (April 2006), 359–95).
2 Sioned Davies, *The Mabinogion* (Oxford: Oxford University Press, 2007), p. 34.

CHAPTER 1

Introduction

I am six years old. I am not at home. Home is social housing. Home is a housing estate that is Protestant by faith, loyal to the English crown, and British by nationality. I am not at home. But I am not far from home. I am on an ordinary city-centre street in Derry.[1] I see a dead soldier for the first time. I see him where he lies in the back of a military ambulance. Its rear door is still open as it drives from the scene. I see his breast, smothered in a plume of scarlet. I think my mother asks me to look away. It is a clear autumn day, and it is a Saturday. He has been shot by an IRA[2] sniper. I hear my father's voice now. I can hear the jeers of the rioters as the ambulance departs. Later, I can't remember if we continue shopping after that.[3] Later, I remember stopping speaking for a long time after that. I am silent; I am mute. Then, it's two years later, perhaps even to the very day, that I first see a dead soldier on television. It's in a neighbours' home, for we have no television set of our own. He lies dead in his tank in the Sinai Desert.[4] This time, there is no colour. But it is the same. And it's normal. I am eight years old, and there's another place out there in the world that's just like our place, like Derry. Writing now, many years hence, while the soldiers are long dead, I find the trauma not raw but yet still immediate. The two scenes elicited contrasting emotional responses: the first, a sense of dread and a need to look away; the second, a compulsion to look. Certain words of E. Valentine Daniel on the civil war in Sri Lanka[5] come to mind, as if not merely explanatory but comforting also:

> Violence ... is an event that is traumatic, and interpretation is an attempt at mastering that trauma ... those of us who are either forced or called upon to witness the event's excess flee in terror or are appeased into believing that this excess can be assimilated into culture, made, in a sense, our own. Regardless of who the witness is ... the violent event persists like crushed

glass in one's eyes. The light it generates, rather than helping us see, is blinding.[6]

As I contemplate this damage, I am sensitive to certain complexities related to the task of giving an account of violence, such as some described by Daniel: how to write such an account while avoiding 'giving in to a desire to shock',[7] how to write such an account without it becoming 'a pornography of violence',[8] how to write such an account so that it be 'true' to 'not only the experience of violence as an event but (also) complex agendas … demands for justice, revenge, forgiveness, freedom and relief'.[9] I find a way forward in the testimony of the creative practitioner. First of all, I find myself identifying with the philosopher Agnes Callard, who asserts that 'art is for seeing evil', evil being 'the whole range of negative human experience (including) hunger, fear, injury, pain, anxiety, injustice, loss, catastrophe, misunderstanding, failure, betrayal, cruelty, boredom, frustration, loneliness, despair, downfall, annihilation', and that she finds herself 'in awe of the poets and their power to reveal'.[10]

Then I find myself in concurrence with philosopher Anastasia Berg's particular reading of Callard as she addresses the question, what is art for. This reading turns upon Callard's claim that she would respond in one way to the sight of a dead body on the street in the real world while she would respond in another very different way to the sight of a dead body on a screen, whether television, film, computer or other such device. I feel that it is necessary to quote from Berg fully here:

> Callard, who ostensibly puts the question of pleasure to the side, pauses to consider the infamous tale of Leontius in Plato's *Republic*,[11] who could not help but stare at corpses strewn outside the walls of the city. Disgusted, he is at the same time overpowered by the 'appetite' to look. Were she to see a corpse in real life, Callard assures us, she would be compelled to turn away. Things are different, however, when she sees one on the screen. There, she feels her eyes are invited to 'take their fill of the "beautiful" sight'. But no one can entice you with what you do not already crave. If this is right, to truly turn toward art and beauty is not to reach out to some external object or special form of experience, but rather to reach into ourselves—and

what we end up finding there may just be the most alien and unruly discovery of all. 'Beauty is nothing but the beginning of terror,' Rilke wrote in the *Duino Elegies*, 'which we are barely able to endure, and it amazes us so, because it serenely disdains to destroy us'.[12]

However, my question of art is a little different: it is not to ask what it is for but rather, what can it do, what are its latent possibilities. I attempt to do more, therefore, than reflect upon Daniel's crushed glass. I am invested in understanding to what extent art is useful, capable of helping us not only to better recognise the challenges we face but to overcome them too. In this vein, writing in response to 'dark ethnographies' of violence and its effects,[13] the anthropologist Joel Robbins argues that to only 'offer accounts of trauma that make us and our readers feel in our bones the vulnerability we as human beings all share'[14] is insufficient and that a moral ethnographic testimony ought to be made in such a way as to help identify how to address real-world injustice.[15] It is in this vein, therefore, I conclude that an account of violence invites, perhaps even requires, an inward and as well as an outward gaze, an insight both to the damage and to its remedies. This book is such an account.

Methodology, questions, ethics

Fieldnotes from Celtic Palestine may be said to be an example of sociography, a new type of writing that has emerged in the field of contemporary sociology, for and about which 'there is an urgency'[16] both in that field and beyond it. It is an approach to 'writing differently' that embodies 'unconventional literary forms, styles and devices' as well as engaging with various 'artistic/literary modes'.[17] For writers such as Rita Felski, sociographic writing implies a 'more literary sociology'[18] or, drawing from the work of Andrew Abbott,[19] a 'lyrical sociology'[20] that is 'attuned to … mood and disposition as well as argument'.[21] It is an approach to social scientific writing that engages 'emotionally as well as intellectually'[22] in paying attention to 'poetic detail', to those 'transitory, self-contained and affectively powerful moments'.[23] A common feature of this sociographic writing is the blending of autobiography or autoethnography with other sorts of methodologies, sources and evidence. One of Felski's very specific examples of books written in the sociographic vein is *Retour à Reims* by Didier Eribon, first published in French in 2009 and subsequently published in English as *Returning to Reims* in 2018, and it is wholly significant that she presents the work as 'a compelling blend of literary memoir and sociological essay'.[24] Another of the examples that Felski notes is the similarly autobiographical or autoethnographic *Landscape for a Good Woman: A Story of Two Lives* by Carolyn Steedman (1986), in which 'fragments of theory, history, biography, and fiction' are artfully juxtaposed.[25] For Felski, this is a very particular type of sociological writing 'that strives to be both public and literary, that does not see reason and politics as opposed to art or feeling'.[26] I too write in that spirit.

More particularly again, in foregrounding and juxtaposing ethnographic and autoethnographic 'fieldnotes', this book has been shaped by *Ordinary Notes* by Christina Sharpe (2023) during the process of its rewriting, reimagining, and reworking. Sharpe's 'genre-defying'[27] book, 'assembling memories and observations, artifacts and artworks',[28] has at its heart a 'kaleidoscope'[29] of 248 'discursive notes'[30] or 'fragmentary dispatches'[31] that 'look beyond the formal disciplinary constraints of the academy and into the realm of the felt, the subjective, the conjectural'.[32] Sharpe thereby presents, in a form that is 'episodic, fragmented, intimate',[33] 'a multidimensional picture of Blackness in America'[34] that 'should', according to Omari Weekes, 'prompt us to action'.[35] Take, for example, Note 240 from *Ordinary Notes*:

> I am twelve years old and walking by myself to the Tredyffrin[36] Public Library on suburban roads that are meant for driving and not for walking. But it is only a quarter of a mile from my house to the library and I go there almost every day in the summer. On this bright morning, I am halfway there when a car filled with whiteboys drives by and calls me [******]. As the epithet leaves their mouths, they slow down, reach out through the open windows, and push me hard into the hedges that line the road. / This is the unsafety of 'white spaces'. This is the violence of maintaining a space as white.[37]

In other places in the book there are images of such 'whiteboys'. *Fieldnotes from Celtic Palestine* is similarly comprised of a carefully constructed assemblage of notes and images that speak to one another as well as indicating how art calls us to action.

Sociography, for Nayanika Mookherjee, is an intertextual approach to writing that has the potential to be both 'evocative and compelling'.[38] Mookherjee describes her use of visual imagery in her writing as 'graphic ethnography' whereby sociography is conceived of as 'a representational and aesthetic practice'.[39] The interweaving of image and text is indispensable in helping, says Mookherjee, 'to configure how we can ethically elucidate experiences of sexual violence which are inherently felt as incoherent, non-linear and fragmented'[40] and in helping also 'make sense of the traces of the unrepresentable, unbearable witnessing that individuals and communities carry out on a daily basis'.[41] *Fieldnotes from Celtic Palestine* is written with that also very much in mind, hence the illustrations and photos embedded in this book and hence also the choice of creative practitioners presented here – three writers and one visual artist. Finally with regard to sociography, for the moment at least, Kilby and Gilloch point out that both Greg Smith[42] and also Ash Watson[43] argue that fiction has a role to play in sociological writing as an 'alternative' to but not a 'substitute' for 'academic "explanation, exposition and argument"' and that fiction may be used 'to inform and illustrate an argument'.[44] Importantly for this book, Watson herself says that '(t)hrough writing sociological fiction, we distil our disciplinary attunement – we strip down and refine the many concepts and findings of our work – to craft scenes which unsettle "common sense" and the notion that there is a natural way of things' and that '[b]y making the familiar strange (authors of sociological fiction) unsettle common sense and can disintegrate boundaries between common feeling'.[45]

It is the case, as far as I am aware, that I first developed a serious interest in Palestine when Belfast native Brian Keenan was kidnapped by members of Islamic Jihad[46] in Beirut in 1986. At that stage, my political antennae had already long since been finely honed by events in Northern Ireland (NI) and in particular by being caught up in the street conflicts caused by the Irish republican hunger strike of 1981 during a much-disrupted school career. But by now a university student in Belfast, it also happened to be the case that Keenan's local drinking den in the western part of that city was a place that I too had begun to regularly frequent, it being a public house renowned as a venue for traditional Irish music and where speaking Irish was welcome. It helped too that Keenan was also Protestant by background. I already knew too of the invasion of Lebanon by the IDF[47] and of the massacres at Sabra and Shatila Palestinian refugee camps by the Phalange[48] working in tandem with the IDF, and I knew also of the suicide bombing attack, also by Islamic Jihad, on the barracks of the US Marine Corps that killed almost 300 soldiers at a stroke. The mission of the IDF was to rid Lebanon of the PLO,[49] which had ensconced itself there during the late 1970s, eventually moving its headquarters there following expulsion from Jordan in 1971. In a series of violent confrontations known as Black September, the PLO had attempted, unsuccessfully, to overthrow the Hashemite monarchy in Jordan. The immediate result of this failure was the forcible ejection of the PLO from there. Despite Keenan's very public assertions as to his Irish identity, some of the most popular sources on the Lebanon hostage crisis, of which his kidnapping was a part, still list him simply as a British citizen.[50] I identify with that too. At the time, however, I did wonder at what had drawn Keenan to Beirut in the first place, especially so given the brutal nature of Lebanon's then ongoing civil war.

It may well be the case that I was, myself, drawn to Palestine because of Keenan, at least in part. Although, it is also a fact that I first went there, in 2016, in order to develop field contacts, gatekeepers,[51] that would allow me to conduct research into the experiences of learning Hebrew whilst suffering politicised incarceration, by two distinctive groups of people, namely (1) Jewish refuseniks held in the gulags of the USSR, and (2) Arab Palestinians held as security prisoners in the Israeli prison system.[52] This study visit was for a project that I had provisionally entitled *Captive Tongue*,[53] of which more later. Successive years of fieldwork in Palestine followed, and during that fieldwork my Irish identity was foregrounded by those whom I encountered in almost every interaction. If such ethnographic encounters are co-constructed by the researcher and the research subject, it follows that this foregrounding has an effect on how I might see Palestine. Keenan once claimed that as a native of Belfast he would be in a better position than his fellow hostages to know 'the terrorist mind'[54] and, by implication, be able to better understand the conflict in Palestine than most. I am not so sure that natives of the conflict in NI have a special or privileged insight to such a place as Palestine, not even those of us who have lived it 'bomb by bomb'.⁵⁵ While I am such a native, as with Keenan, I also have, by now, a Welsh sensibility having lived the greater part of my life in Wales and, moreover, done so through the medium of the Welsh language.⁵⁶ Some might say that I am, as a result, peculiarly Celtic, and not merely Irish. When in Palestine, therefore, I ask of myself how the Irish and Welsh sensibilities interact.

A few short months after Keenan was kidnapped in Beirut, an 'extraordinary'⁵⁷ Welsh artist by the name Osi Rhys Osmond was on a field visit in Palestine. In his fieldnotes, which may indeed be read as a Welsh perspective on Palestine and Beirut and Ireland, he records the following in an entry dated 14 August 1986: 'News full of riot police and people protest but are harshly treated. The news contains also vivid film of bomb blasts in Beirut. Military manoeuvres off the coast and on Galilee near Tiberius ... News of N. Ireland. Cloudy skies ... News is strange, just the picture'.⁵⁸ On that day a Mercedes car packed with a 200-pound bomb exploded in the Christian quarter of north-east Beirut killing twenty people. That the car was a Mercedes was wholly unsurprising, yet still noteworthy, for limousines of that make were the preferred vehicle of the car bomber. The Mercedes thereby became known as the car of death in Lebanon.⁵⁹ The Irish news came from Dublin, where the High Court had ordered the release of John Gerard O'Reilly, a member of the IRA. The UK government had been seeking the extradition of O'Reilly from the Republic of Ireland on charges of 'conspiracy to murder and explosive charges' and the collapse of the case was a very substantial political problem for the two governments.⁶⁰ Despite these events and this political awareness, Osmond's 1987 exhibition arising out of that fieldwork, *Cymru a'r Wlad Sanctaidd/ Wales and the Holy Land*, was pointedly apolitical in the sense that the exhibition does not attend to the conflict in Palestine. The exhibition is instead a meditation on how the identities of the two countries connect through shared place-names: that matter, one could argue, has its own politics. As Crispin Sartwell puts it, 'All art has a political context. But not all art has a political message'.⁶¹ By his 2009 exhibition, entitled *Ymateb/Response*, however, this had changed. That exhibition was directly addressed the political violence in Gaza by calling for peace and calling upon his audience to take action in order to try to bring that about: the artist had become a rhetorician. What had brought about this metamorphosis?⁶²

Being a near neighbour of Osmond's when I began my own work on Palestine, then living on the same street in the small, west Wales village of Llansteffan, I was following in his wake. And yet, over the course of my periods of fieldwork, conducted over several years, it was the visits of Irish writers to Palestine that would arise in conversation in the field there. In these ethnographic encounters, I seemed to be following in their immediate wake. My ethnographic subjects were framing Palestine for me, and in so doing I was obligated to pay attention to the content of their framing as well as to the hinterland of that process. Colm Tóibín, Eimear McBride and Colum McCann were to the fore, having been to the West Bank in 2016, along with Dervla Murphy, subsequent to her extended visits to both the West Bank and Gaza between 2008 and 2011. Such writers are the most articulate of practitioners but artistic too in how they present their perspectives on the conflict in Palestine as a type of suasory writing. As I read their works on Palestine, in Palestine, I found myself caught in the thorns of that oft-set puzzle: 'what responsibility does the artist have to society?'[63]

Writing now, I call to mind this warning regarding *artistes engagés*, convincing in both style and content: 'When the "power (of art) as a mode of redress ... as agent for proclaiming and correcting injustices" precludes its autonomously self-creating character, the survival of art itself is at stake'.[64] Art must stand its own ground. Nonetheless, I question here the extent to which the creative works at hand are art alone, but that they are works of rhetoric also. By rhetoric, I mean 'the ways symbolic action influences subsequent (symbolic) actions – the properties of an utterance in context that can make a social, pragmatic or ideational difference'.[65] Along with this, in considering their effectiveness as rhetoric, I ask too whether the artist is able to change the world qua artist. Sartwell seems to suggest such a potential certainly exists when he argues that '[t]he aesthetic embodiments of political positions are material transformations and interventions, with concrete effects'.[66] Thus, my question here is this: does it fall to the creative witness to find, on our behalf, the language for the dreadful thing that is become Palestine?

These issues I approach through certain works by four creative practitioners comprised of triad of Irish writers and a lone Welsh visual artist. The piece of work made by each of them represents a different, distinctive type of rhetoric afforded by the specific genre within which their work is situated along the form their work takes. Here, genres may be understood as categories of both communicative action and of social action; they may be conceived of as 'sociological concepts' that mediate 'textual and social ways of knowing, being, and interacting in particular contexts'.[67] Also, different types of genres provide different affordances,[68] that is to say that they allow for different sorts of rhetorical opportunities that in turn may facilitate or constrain certain modes of engagement by the intended audience, of understanding the problem at hand, and of mobilisation of support for the argument being made.[69] Writing in the context of literary theory, and of form in particular, Caroline Levine describes affordances as relating to the latent potentiality provided by a given form – its possibilities and its constraints, its capacities and its limitations.[70] As regards form, I follow Caroline Levine in how she differentiates between that and genre:

> Genres, then, can be defined as customary constellations of elements into historically recognizable groupings of artistic objects, bringing together forms with themes, styles and situations of reception, while forms are organizations or arrangements that afford repetition and portability across materials and contexts.[71]

While the affordances of form and genre specific to the four creative practitioners and their pieces of work will be explored in detail in the chapters to follow, some very brief signposting here serves the purpose of opening up this study.

Taking each of Keenan, Murphy, McCann and Osmond in turn, a number of points are highlighted here. First, *An Evil Cradling* by Keenan has epideictic qualities. Written as an 'abreaction in art form',[72] the aim of the book is to 'reveal men in extremis'[73] in the shape of an exploration of both 'hostage and captor'.[74] Moreover, Keenan finds parallels in these lives and their sharing of a psychology born of 'a world laden with … divisions … in their most extreme and confused forms on the streets of Belfast and Beirut',[75] forms that include 'extremes of language'.[76] Secondly, Murphy's travelogue, *A Month by the Sea*, is the closest of the works to the contentious rhetoric of polemic. It is a book 'bursting with political engagement' and 'underlying the book is (the) determination to try to understand how Arab Palestinians and Israeli Jews might forge a solution and ultimately live in peace'.[77] Murphy makes explicit her advocacy of 'the one-state solution' and the book points to her own activist sympathy and engagement on the part of Arab Palestinians in realising that result.[78]

Next, McCann's novel, *Apeirogon*, has features akin to parrēsia, a 'highly rhetorical' mode of truth-telling in the classical rhetorical tradition according to Arthur E. Walzer.[79] The work takes the form of counsel given, under circumstances of grave risk, to a friend. As with Murphy, McCann too hints at activist engagement in his book: 'Thanks also to everyone associated with Pal Fest and the Jerusalem Book Fair. We get our voices from others: it is, yes, a community of feeling'.[80] Pal Fest, elsewhere described more fully as the Palestine Festival of Literature,[81] is an event that directly addresses the politics of the conflict in Palestine. For example, Pal Fest set the following question for its 2020 gathering: 'Do we believe that what we are doing can liberate Gaza? Can liberate all of Palestine?'[82] McCann, in the acknowledgements section to the novel, describes his book as 'a work of storytelling'[83] that is derived from his initial introduction to 'Israel and Palestine' through two organisations, namely Narrative 4 and Telos.[84] Significantly, Telos believes that 'a viable two-state solution remains the solution to the conflict'.[85] Fourth and finally, the Welsh artist I have in mind is, of course, Osi Rhys Osmond. I have said much about him already, but suffice to add here that he is significant not only as a creative practitioner but also as a Welsh language activist[86] and campaigner for universal pacifism.[87] The specific piece of work is his collection of pictorial narrative art entitled *Ymateb/Response*, based upon events in Gaza in 2008–9.[88]

During the course of researching and writing this book I had encounters with various politicians, diplomats, political activists, members of terrorist organisations, political prisoners, members of the security services, journalists, and academics. Amongst these are Presidents and convicted killers, Ambassadors and survived suicide bombers, Nobel Prize Laureates, foot soldiers and journeymen freedom fighters, and numerous victims of some of the most upsetting and shocking political violence. The different field visits to Israel and the Occupied Palestinian Territories were subject to gaining the appropriate ethical, security and safety approvals. Also, due attention was paid to the travel warnings and advice of the Department of State (USA) (as I planned at some times to travel with a citizen of the USA), the Foreign

Introduction

and Commonwealth Office (UK) (as I am a citizen of the UK), and the Department of Foreign Affairs and Trade (Republic of Ireland) (as I am an Irish national and travel on an Irish passport). In addition, given that my travelling companions included Israeli Jews, Palestinian Arabs and Arab Israelis, close attention was similarly paid to Israeli law, in particular as pertains to the legal restrictions governing the movement of Israeli citizens in Judea and Samaria, a territory more familiar to much of the rest of the world as the Occupied Palestinian Territories, as well as governing also the ability of Palestinian Arabs to gain access to the State of Israel and to Jewish settlements situated beyond the boundaries of Israel.

The fieldwork also included several archival sallies to repositories in London, Oxford, New York, Jerusalem and Belfast. The text was written and rewritten in a number of different locations over the course of several years. Some of it was written in the Nassau Inn in Princeton, New Jersey, during a feral snowstorm: the ocean crashed upon the Jersey Shore with a rabid ferocity, and over the white horizon the wind barrelled the concrete canyons of Manhattan. Other parts were made in the Bodleian Library in Oxford during the spring of another year, and in the evenings there the light of the dying sun would turn the Headington limestone of the colleges round and about to gold before the yellowed amber of the street lights enveloped the city for the night.

Structure

The first thematic chapter (Chapter 2, 'A Time for Saying') comprises an analysis of the circumstances and conditions in which the witnesses created their testimonies, their literary and visual texts. It begins with a concise explanation of the evolution of the research of the authorial I into how language, including in the form of visual rhetoric, is implicated in ethno-political conflict, signalled by three milestone monographs – *Language, Identity and Conflict* (2003),[89] *Jailtacht* (2012)[90] and *Branwen's Starling* (2013),[91] leading up to my most recent fieldwork on the experiences of learning Hebrew by the refuseniks of the Soviet gulag and by the security prisoners of the Israeli prison system, a project entitled *Captive Tongue*, and upon which the book is partly based. It is explained here also the way in which a series of ethnographic encounters that occurred during the course of this fieldwork called into question how certain distinctively Irish and Welsh accounts of the Palestinian conflict are constructed and communicated in the form of literary and visual texts. It is in the context of addressing these issues together that the concept of witnessing as understood in the fields both of ethnography and of rhetorical analysis is foregrounded, as illustrated respectively by Deborah Reed-Danahay[92] and Bradford Vivian.[93] Here too the imperative of artistic creation is called into question: why narrate that story then, and there? What caused their witness testimony to be felt to be necessary, to be urgent, at that moment of saying?

Each work in turn – *An Evil Cradling* (1992), *A Month by the Sea* (2013), *Apeirogon* (2020), *Ymateb/Response* (2009) – is temporally contextualised in relation to both the particular situation of the witness and also the chronology of events in Palestine, Ireland and Wales. In terms of rhetorical analysis, this chapter is concerned with the extent to which the individual witnesses perceive of the act of creating their texts as an appropriate, well-measured and artfully crafted response to a sense of the decisive, opportune moment having arrived. The rhetorical concept of kairos, 'denoting both a sense of "adaptation and accommodation to convention" and, conversely, "the uniquely timely, the spontaneous, the radically particular"', as Joanne Paul puts it,[94] is applied to each of these acts of creativity. Making use of unfettered access to the personal, and wholly unarchived, papers of Osi Rhys Osmond, including his fieldnotes and sketchbooks from Palestine, I construct an outline of the conditions under which he created his art on this subject.

Similarly, drawing upon interviews with each of Keenan, Murphy and McCann, as well as upon various other types of reflection upon their creative practices, portraits of the personal circumstances of their writing are also analytically constructed. Under this analysis, the kairos of their creative practice is related to not only their personal circumstances but also to the broader social and political conditions of contemporaneous events in Palestine. These events too are set in historical context. In this way kairos, as it pertains to each of Keenan, *An Evil Cradling* (1992), Murphy, *A Month by the Sea* (2013), McCann, *Apeirogon* (2020) and Osi Rhys Osmond, *Ymateb/Response* (2009) is shown to be contingent upon the variable personal circumstances of the four witnesses as well as their judgement of the significance of events in Palestine in the immediate circumstances of their creative practice but also upon their sense of their work in context as an artistic intervention in conversation with other such interventions in temporal context.

Building upon the assertion of Reed-Danahay that we remain in 'the era of the witness',[95] a term first coined by Wieviorka in 2002,[96] a central aim of this book is to examine how Keenan, Murphy, McCann and Osmond construct their identities as witnesses, and to explain why they do so in the manner that they do. In other words, the text may be considered a type of 'meta-testimonial discourse', as Givoni puts it, concerned with 'the incisive preoccupations with the conditions of witnessing and testimony, their risks, and the keys to their effective performance'.[97] Chapter 3, therefore, entitled 'Making the Witness', is interested in the Aristotelian concept of ethos, that is the way in which rhetors present themselves to their audiences. The rhetorical analysis of the ethos of Keenan, Murphy, McCann and Osmond asks how each of them presents themselves as authoritative and credible witnesses. The characteristics subjected to critical examination include their self-ascribed ethnicity or nationality, their gender and sexuality, their professional competence and status, their social activism, as well as their age at the time of the specific creative practice at hand here. Certain qualities, it is shown, are written in to these characteristics, such as the creative artists' objectivity or neutrality, their empathy and their degree of engagement, their authority and expertise. This chapter illustrates how these characteristics and qualities are mobilised and deployed by these creative artists. The analysis here also identifies the potential of the creative artists as witnesses along with their limitations, demonstrating how the authenticity of their moral knowledge as witnesses to Palestine is dependent upon their individual ethos.

A further feature of this analysis is that the four witnesses are situated in a distinctive genealogy of witnessing and a particular sort of regime of witness, as creative practitioners that are a part of a community of practice, which may be styled as the arts industry. Thus, even as their professional autonomy is bound to certain institutional platforms, the creative artists use this to insert themselves into the political field. In this context, the creative artists' ethea variously correspond to that of 'spokesperson of a public',[98] of 'defiant truth-tell(er)' per Michal Givoni,[99] and of practitioner of non-governmental politics as critical practice per Judith Butler.[100] A final concern of this chapter is how the ethos may be shaped by the very act of witnessing whereby the witness herself, or himself, undergoes subjective transformation. This, it is argued, may happen in one of two ways: first, in that 'Acts of witnessing ... are not concerned with the exposure and reaffirmation of a pre-existing identity but rather with the creation of ethical and political subjectivities that did not exist prior to them',[101] thus the witness too may be reinvented; second, when the act of witnessing is repeated over a long period of time (1992 to 2020 in this case), it begins to lose its power. As Givoni puts it, '[the] testimonies keep piling up and yet somehow refuse to accumulate'[102] : in other words, witnesses to the conflict come and go; yet it remains unresolved. In these circumstances, the ethos of the witness, if not transformed, is vulnerable to presenting as despairing and alienated.

Chapter 3 shows how the ethea of the Irish and Welsh witness of Palestine relate to his insight of Givoni and consideration is given to the extent to which their testimonies conform to it. In terms of reflexive ethnography, the chapter relates to the others in which the author is shown to also undergo the type of subjective change referred to by Givoni whereby his identity as a witness is shaped by formative experiences in NI as well as by various ethnographic encounters that he experiences in the field during the course of the project *Captive Tongue*. In this sense, therefore, the chapter explains the ethnographic self that is variously articulated in the book as a whole. It confirms also that while the book is not a memoir, it includes 'personal narrative'.[103] Therefore, as the author I present memoir-style fragments for the purpose of examining the meaning of the testimonies of the creative practitioners as witnesses to the conflict in Palestine. As Vivian Gornick puts it, the author's persona here serves 'to explore a subject other than (himself)'.[104]

Chapter 4, entitled 'Taking up Form', engages in the analysis of the four testimonies, of each work of creative endeavour, as, in rhetorical terms, artistic proofs, while also offering a reflection upon the ethnographic encounter as a form. Of particular interest here is the effect of this meeting between, or, to paraphrase Caroline Levine, this overlap or collision between different forms, literary and social.[105] In this context I depend also upon Levine's definition of form as something 'much broader in its ordinary usage in literary or cultural studies'; being '*any arrangement of elements – any ordering, patterning, or shaping*' (her italics), given that form is 'as much the stuff of the sociopolitical world as (it is) of art'.[106] The three works by Keenan, Murphy and McCann are thereby studied in terms of their literary form, along with their internal arrangement, or *dispositio*. The latter includes the writers' use of features such as the epigram, preface, acknowledgements, named chapters, numbered sections, illustrations, timelines, and maps. The key question posed here is this: why choose these forms? And, following from that, how do the forms differ in enabling the writers to effectively articulate their rhetorical appeals?

The extent to which each of Keenan, Murphy and McCann react to the imperative to write in relation to an audience, and the manner in which they do so, is an important consideration in Chapter 4. In analysing the texts as rhetorical performances, the readerships of *An Evil Cradling*, *A Month by the Sea* and *Apeirogon* constitute a particular type of audience. Through applying the connected concepts of the implied, intended and actual audience to how the three writers construct and approach their readerships in their own distinct way, and by analysing the various responses of the works' actual audience, the reception of the testimonies is problematised. In particular, the effect of the texts as testimonies of persuasion upon public discourse and activism, or social action, is gauged. The chapter examines how *An Evil Cradling* takes the form of an autobiographical prosimetrum, allowing Keenan to both narrate the story of his captivity and establish his credentials as a serious creative writer. The rhetorical analysis of the text interrogates it as a retrospective narrative, a work of psychological introspection, in which the outline of Keenan's own personal development is a work of 'textual self-fashioning', as Helga Schwalm puts it.[107] It is shown here how the triadic complication of the narrative logic of the autobiographical form, as described by Philippe Lejeune,[108] whereby Keenan is author, narrator and protagonist, shapes the rhetorical efficacy of the work. The rhetorical analysis of *A Month by the Sea* sees Murphy, already an internationally renowned travel writer with a well-established readership, as self-consciously adding her travelogue to an extensive body of western travelogues of Palestine. In this context, it can be said the impact of Edward Said's critique of Orientalism upon Murphy's travelogue is profound. It is polemical travel writing, an exemplar of despair but also a call to social action. Also, more than mere travel, it is shown to self-consciously present as a work of ethnographic encounter.

The analysis of *Apeirogon* challenges McCann's claim that the work is a novel. Instead, it is revealed as dual biography somewhat in the style of Plutarch's *Parallel Lives*, and an exemplar, as Louis van den Hengel would say,[109] of aesthetic practice that has turned two lives into art. In Chapter 4, the corpus of the critical reviews of *An Evil Cradling*, *A Month by the Sea* and *Apeirogon* are subjected to rhetorical analysis as, following Jeanne Fahnestock and Marie Secor, a body of material that is designed to 'do the work of epideictic discourse',[110] with the critics cohering as a discourse community in the manner outlined by Laura Wilder.[111] The topoi of despair and of social justice identified in the field of literary studies by Fahnestock and Secor and by Wilder are shown to also apply to the three Irish testimonies. However, the rhetorical analysis made here also identifies an epistemological problem pertinent to literary testimony: despite the commitment to address injustices in the real world, including Palestine, as epitomised by academics such as Barbara Harlow,[112] complexity is still understood to be a value that transcends all other topoi and that serious literature remains characterised by 'unresolvable tensions and shadows'.[113] In other words, were it operating in isolation from other forms, the literary form at hand would limit the rhetorical case that the writer may convincingly make. Similar such limitations could be said to apply to the work of Osmond. But, when analysed in terms of an encounter between aesthetic form and the form of visual rhetoric, in line with the approach taken to this by Marcel Danesi[114] and by Gunther Kress and Theo van Leeuwen,[115] other possibilities open up. Rather than mere propaganda, it is shown how, in the context Osmond's approach to composition, rendering of form, and use of colour in the body of work for *Ymateb/Response*, as exemplified in pieces such as in the *Hostage* series, affords him considerable latitude of expression, thereby actifying certain connotative senses in the visually literate audience.

Sense of place, or the topos of a place apart, is the focal point of Chapter 5, 'The Seeing Places'. Here we examine how Keenan, McCann, Murphy and Osmond each invoke certain qualities or sensibilities as they speak of the locations that are of particular significance to their testimonies. One of the rhetorical devices used by all of the creative practitioners in this context is analogy. Each of Keenan, Murphy and McCann draws an analogy with Ireland and its twentieth-century ethno-political conflict. For example, Beirut becomes Belfast for Keenan, and for McCann the Interface Barriers of Belfast become the Separation Wall of the West Bank. For Osmond, the beach of

Llansteffan evokes that of Gaza, thereby signalling in turn the trauma of Operation Cast Lead. I ask here why the analogy is drawn, how it is drawn, and also, how effective it is. In addressing these questions, I explore the way in which the creative practitioners transform a variety of places (that is, sites such as Beirut, Gaza, Jerusalem and Nablus, as well as specific locations within those sites, such as the Chagall windows in Hadassah Medical Centre at Ein Kerem, Rafah Gate, or Qalandiya refugee camp) from inartistic into artistic proofs, in rhetorical terms.

In developing an understanding of the effectiveness of the rhetorical invention of the creative practitioners, this analysis makes use of the geographical concept of fourth space, or place-space, superseding Lefebvre's triad of (1) spatial practice, (2) representations of space, and (3) representational space.[116] In this context, place may be conceived of as 'the process whereby spaces are ordered in ways that open up affective and other embodied potentials'.[117] It is the expressive quality of place, the idea of place as an actor that impacts upon the nature of ethnographic encounters and thereby shapes the affective connections made there, which is at the core of this analytical approach. It is in this context too that different, particular forms of presence in the aforementioned sites and locations in Palestine on the part of the creative practitioners are shown to be key to understanding the extent of rhetorical effectiveness. Very briefly, a significant part of this involves the creative practitioners showing how they are involved in the co-production of the place-space of Palestine.

As a work of reflexive ethnography, the authorial I too is implicated in constructing this sense of place. The approach taken here could also be said to involve not merely ethnographic engagement with multiple sites in the manner of Ulf Hannerz,[118] for example, but also several different ways of 'being there', in the ethnographic sense. For John Postill[119] there are four such ways: physically, remotely, virtually and imaginatively. In a broadly similar vein, Nina Grønlykke Mollerup describes this combination of different types of being there as 'thick presence'.[120] I thereby create the ethnographic field of Palestine in the process of undertaking fieldwork there for *Captive Tongue* but construct it also through virtual encounter.[121] National governments too are shown to play an important role in shaping this field through the author. That I was, in different ways, subject to the travel advice and restrictions of the governments of the UK, Ireland, the USA and Israel during the conduct of fieldwork becomes a significant feature of sense of place in the context of my autobiography, in the sense defined by Reed-Danahay,[122] both northern Irish (frequenting the same local tavern in Belfast as Keenan) and west Welsh (living on the same Llansteffan village street as Osmond). Thus, it is shown that the seeing places of Palestine are not so much specific physical sites but are rather moments: the highly problematic products of a series of unequal and temporary encounters. And in their turn too, the three writers, by invoking moments in Ireland as analogous, along with the visual artist, by drawing places in Wales as analogous, in effect make the rhetorical case for alternative and more durable senses of place in Palestine.

In Chapter 6, 'The Suffering Subject', I develop the idea of the embodied potentials that are inherent to fourth space through identifying the ethnographic macro-trope of the suffering subject, as introduced and refined by E. Valentine Daniel, Bruce Knauft, Joel Robbins and Alan Rumsey, amongst others,[123] as a crucial topos in the work of each of Keenan, Murphy, McCann and Osmond whereby the suffering subject is a most important vehicle for articulating the affective quality of space in their literary and visual texts. While none of the creative practitioners have an identifiable fictional character as suffering subject, not even McCann in his novel, each of them, in their different ways, construct embodied performances of suffering in their works with the quality of rhetorical suasion. They do so, it is argued here, in line with the ethnographic insight that, as the twentieth century closed, 'the human being suffering from trauma ... became the very embodiment of our common humanity'.[124] In their texts, various types or characterisations of the suffering subject, such as hostage, martyr, refugee, victim, prisoner, are transformed by the creative practitioners into artistic proofs. And the appeal of these proofs, in rhetorical terms, is founded upon both pathos and logos. One of the key questions in the chapter is to ask what is meant by the suffering subject as an embodied potential. In this context the body is not conceived of as simply an autonomous, flesh and blood container. Rather, this work is concerned with the sense of the body in place. Embodiment therefore entails the affective connectedness of physical presence – voice, smell, energy, taste – the full range of bodily sensibilities. In this context too the subject suffers both corporeally and incorporeally, as an individual and as part of a collective, directly and indirectly.

Certain scenes from the testimonies of the three writers and certain pieces from the body of testimony that is *Ymateb/Response* are examined in detail so as to demonstrate the rhetorical effect of the suffering subject as constructed by them. The episodes in which the hostage Keenan has his nails clipped by one of his keepers or is presented with fruit for the first time in several months are cases in point: 'He would not let me cut my own nails, for fear that I might attempt to injure myself with the clippers. He held my hands and cut my nails and I sat in silence wondering what thoughts were running through his head ...'[125]; 'I lift an orange into the flat filthy palm of my hand and feel and smell and lick it. The colour orange, the colour, the colour, my God the colour orange ... I cannot, I will not eat this fruit'.[126] For Murphy it is the gendered body that is of interest, and in particular that of the female in Islamic Gaza, including her own transgressive presence. As regards McCann, the testimonial evidence is to be found in the fatal injuries to two young females: one, Abir, killed by an Israeli Border Police officer and the other, Smadar, by a Palestinian suicide bomber. It is found too in the mental anguish of the fathers of Abir and Smadar; and it is to be found also in the fraught geography of the suicide bombers:

> They arrived disguised as women ... Witnesses said that the bombers made eye contact with each other from under their veils when they reached the area around Hillel Street ... The apartments above. The shop awnings below. The fruit stalls, the juice joints, the fashion stores ... The girls swaying arm in arm down the street. The laughter from a café ... The plimp of the bombers' soft-soled shoes.[127]

And, for Osmond, the *Hostage* series is especially rich, fertile for semiotic analysis as visual rhetoric upon the suffering subject. In reflexive ethnographic terms, the authorial I is implicated here too. Drawing upon encounters in the field, some of which are necessarily serendipitous, as Alice Tilche and Edward Simpson point out,[128] my own act of witness is that of being served shay bil maramiya by the daughter of survived Hamas suicide bomber in his PNA[129]-funded apartment on a nameless street in Ramallah. In these ways, therefore, the suffering subject is become the biopolitics[130] of fourth space.

In the closing chapter (Chapter 7, 'Conclusions') the threads of the argument that are laid out in the different chapters of the book, and the various insights that arise from them, are drawn together. First of all, one of the implications of the three Irish writers and the Welsh artist presenting themselves as witnesses to Palestine is that their texts, whether literary fiction, travel writing, autobiography or visual art, are necessarily open to rhetorical analysis because each of them sets out to say something about the state of the world and how it ought to be changed. It is also argued here that, while their texts are limited in their potential as sources of knowledge and understanding of right action, given the contingency of the individual artist, the affordances of their art form, and the irreducible and unresolvable complexity of works of art, they nonetheless stand, authoritatively, as revelations of moral conscience. They demonstrate that serious art may indeed enter into the realm of informed social activism and yet remain art. Moreover, it is concluded that such art is, indeed, necessary as it invents the language by which the resolution to the conundrum that is Palestine will be imagined.

Keenan, Murphy, McCann and Osmond each offer their own prescription for the conflict in Palestine, respectively:

i. the coloniser discovering sympathy for the native;
ii. a one-state solution;
iii. a two-state solution;
iv. pacifism, understood as a deeply held commitment to the power of peace.

None of these are easy choices. Indeed, part of the complication that I address in this book is the extent to which Murphy and McCann prioritise a particular concept of justice for Palestine in their intimate portraits of the non-fictional characters who are at the heart of their writings as they set about the reconstruction of morality in their everyday lives in the aftermath of violently irruptive events – a suicide bombing, a fatal military intervention. The same applies to Keenan in relation to his autobiographical self-examination and to Osmond's treatment of Gaza.

Introduction

I show in this book, therefore, how such witnesses can, as Joel Robbins puts it, 'do justice to the different ways people live for the good'.[131] As regards how this work might be said to speak to moral theory, my readings of *An Evil Cradling*, *A Month by the Sea*, *Apeirogon* and *Ymateb/ Response* are shaped by what I see as the affinity of these testimonies with Charles Larmore's claim that 'the task of moral theory … can only be to explicate what we already know in our conscience'.[132] And we know, of course, that an injustice has been at work in Palestine for very many years now.

Notes

1. The city of Derry, or Londonderry, is the second largest city in Northern Ireland and it is regarded as a cockpit of the Troubles in Northern Ireland. See, for example, Robin Sheeran, 'The Troubles: when Belfast children fled the city', *BBC News*, 30 August 2021: https://www.bbc.co.uk/news/uk-northern-ireland-58193536 (accessed 18 January 2024). In my childhood, it appears to me that all natives call the city 'Derry', even though its official name is Londonderry. That is, until the official name of the city's governing body was changed by its nationalist administration from 'Londonderry City Council' to 'Derry City Council' in 1983: then, colloquial usage becomes highly politicised and contentious. This is affirmed by Vincent Quinn, 'On the borders of allegiance: identity politics in Ulster', in R. Phillips, D. Shuttleton and D. Watt (eds), *De-centring Sexualities: Politics and Representations Beyond the Metropolis* (London: Routledge, 2000), pp. 258–77. Since 1613, the city was officially entitled as 'Londonderry' under an amendment to the Royal Charter of 1603 by which the historical urban settlement 'Derry' was rebuilt by a consortium of London investors following the Elizabethan conquest and colonisation of Ireland.
2. The Provisional IRA, generally known also as the Provos.
3. David McKittrick, Seamus Kelters, Brian Feeney and Chris Thornton, *Lost Lives. The Stories of the Men, Women and Children Who Died as a Result of the Northern Ireland Troubles* (Edinburgh and London: Mainstream Publishing, 1999), entry number 145, p. 106.
4. The Yom Kippur War, October 1973.
5. 1983–2009.
6. Errol Valentine Daniel, *Charred Lullabies: Chapters in an Anthropography of Violence* (Princeton NJ: Princeton University Press, 1996), p. 208.
7. Daniel, *Charred Lullabies*, p. 3.
8. Daniel, *Charred Lullabies*, p. 4.

9 Daniel, *Charred Lullabies*, p. 5.
10 Agnes Callard, 'Art is for seeing evil', *The Point*, 15 July 2022): *https://thepointmag.com/examined-life/art-is-for-seeing-evil/* (accessed 27 January 2024).
11 I add here that the story of Leontius is soon told: 'I once heard a story which I believe, that Leontius the son of Aglaion, on his way up from the Peiraeus under the outer side of the northern wall, becoming aware of dead bodies that lay at the place of public execution at the same time felt a desire to see them and a repugnance and aversion, and that for some time he resisted and veiled his head, but overpowered in despite of all by his desire, with wide staring eyes he rushed up to the corpses and cried, "There, ye wretches, take your fill of the fine spectacle!"' Plato, *Republic*, 4.439e: *http://data.perseus.org/citations/urn:cts:greekLit:tlg0059.tlg030.perseus-eng1:4.439e* and Plato, *Republic*, 4.440a: *http://data.perseus.org/citations/urn:cts:greekLit:tlg0059.tlg030.perseus-eng1:4.440a* (accessed 2 January 2024).
12 Anastasia Berg, 'On the aesthetic turn', *The Point*, 30 (19 July 2023): *https://thepointmag.com/criticism/on-the-aesthetic-turn/* (accessed 27 January 2024).
13 Sherry Ortner, 'Dark anthropology and its others: theory since the eighties', *Hau: Journal of Ethnographic Theory*, 6/1 (2016), 47–73.
14 Joel Robbins, 'Beyond the suffering subject: toward an anthropology of the good', *Journal of the Royal Anthropological Institute*, 19/3 (2013), 447–62, at 455.
15 Robbins characterises this in terms of the philosophical concept of 'right action'. See, for example, Michael Slote, 'Right action', in T. Honderich (ed.), *The Oxford Companion to Philosophy* (Oxford: Oxford University Press, 1995), pp. 774–6.
16 Jane Kilby and Graeme Gilloch, 'Sociography: writing differently', *The Sociological Review*, 70/4 (2022), 635–55, at 638.
17 Kilby and Gilloch, 'Sociography', p. 636.
18 Rita Felski, 'Sociological writing as resonant writing', *The Sociological Review*, 70/4 (2022), 656–65, at 656.
19 Andrew Abbott, 'Against narrative: a preface to lyrical sociology', *Sociological Theory*, 25/1 (2007), 67–99.
20 Felski, *Sociological Writing*, p. 658.
21 Felski, *Sociological Writing*, p. 658.
22 Felski, *Sociological Writing*, p. 657.
23 Felski, *Sociological Writing*, p. 661.
24 Felski, *Sociological Writing*, p. 659.
25 Felski, *Sociological Writing*, p. 661.
26 Felski, *Sociological Writing*, p. 664.
27 Publishers Weekly, '*Ordinary Notes*. Christina Sharpe', 24 January 2023: *https://www.publishersweekly.com/9780374604486* (accessed 16 January 2024).

Introduction

28 Jennifer Szalai, 'In "Ordinary notes", a radical reading of Black life', *The New York Times*, 19 April 2023: https://www.nytimes.com/2023/04/19/books/review/ordinary-notes-christina-sharpe.html (accessed 16 January 2024).
29 Megin Jimenez, 'Seeing through the kaleidoscope of "Ordinary Notes"', *Chicago Review of Books*, 5 May 2023: https://chireviewofbooks.com/2023/05/05/ordinary-notes-christina-sharpe/ (accessed 16 January 2024).
30 Neil Price, 'Ordinary notes by Christina Sharpe', *Quill & Quire*, 14 June 2023: *https://quillandquire.com/review/ordinary-notes/* (accessed 18 January 2024).
31 Publishers Weekly, *Ordinary Notes*.
32 Omari Weekes, 'What about Black life? The art of everyday Black experience', *The Nation*, 13 December 2023: *https://www.thenation.com/article/culture/christina-sharpe-ordinary-notes/* (accessed 18 January 2024).
33 Gustav Parker Hibbett, 'Ordinary notes by Christina Sharpe', *Criticism*, 27 September 2023: *https://stingingfly.org/review/ordinary-notes/* (accessed 16 January 2024).
34 Kirkus Reviews, 'Ordinary Notes by Christina Sharpe. An Exquisitely Original Celebration of American Blackness', 18 January 2023: *https://www.kirkusreviews.com/book-reviews/christina-sharpe/ordinary-notes/* (accessed 16 January 2024).
35 Weekes, 'What About Black Life?'
36 Given the extent to which this book is in a sense Welsh, it seems necessary to point out here that the Tredyffrin Township of Chester County in Pennsylvania is a part of the historical Welsh Tract granted by William Penn specifically for settlement by Welsh-speaking Quakers in 1684. The placename pertains to the Welsh language terms /tre/, meaning 'town', and /dyffryn/, meaning 'vale'.
37 Christina Sharpe, *Ordinary Notes* (London: Daunt Books, 2023), Note 240.
38 Nayanika Mookherjee, 'Aurality of images in graphic ethnographies: sexual violence during wars and memories of the feelings of fear', *The Sociological Review*, 70/4 (2022), 686–99, at 687.
39 Mookherjee, 'Aurality of Images', p. 687.
40 Mookherjee, 'Aurality of Images', p. 687.
41 Mookherjee, 'Aurality of Images', p. 687.
42 Greg Smith, 'Fiction in Goffman', *The Sociological Review*, 70/4 (2022), 711–22.
43 Ash Watson, 'The familiar strange of sociological fiction', *The Sociological Review*, 70/4 (2022), 723–32.
44 Kilby and Gilloch, 'Sociography', p. 647.
45 Watson, 'The familiar strange', p. 730.

46 This group, properly known as Islamic Jihad Organisation, is believed by some to have been a cover for Hezbollah, or perhaps to be the direct precursor of it, or even to be a cover for the Islamic Revolutionary Guard Corps of Iran.
47 IDF = Israel Defense Forces.
48 Also known as the Lebanese Phalange or Kataeb. It is understood to represent the political interests of Lebanon's Maronite Christian clans.
49 PLO = Palestine Liberation Organisation.
50 *htttps://en.wikipedia.org/wiki/Lebanon_hostage_crisis* (accessed 1 June 2023).
51 In sociological or ethnographic fieldwork, gatekeepers are understood in the following terms. 'Gatekeepers are individuals, groups, or organisations who have control or influence over a researcher's access to participants … Gatekeepers are often conceptualised as "barriers" to access, something researchers must "get over" or through, but they are also considered as helpful mediators, sources of knowledge, and critical influencers of research design, especially of recruitment strategies': Julie Latchem-Hastings, 'Gatekeepers in ethnography', in P. Atkinson, S. Delamont, A. Cernat, J. W. Sakshaug and R. A. Williams (eds), *Sage Research Methods Foundations* (London: SAGE Publications, 2020), published online at *https://methods-sagepub-com.abc.cardiff.ac.uk/foundations/gatekeepers-in-ethnography* (accessed 19 September 2024). Also, 'Gatekeepers are essential mediators for accessing study settings and participants within social research. They may be persons within organisations who have the power to grant or withhold access to people or situations during research into organisations … They can fill both obstructionist and facilitative roles': Johnny Andoh-Arthur, 'Gatekeepers in qualitative research', in P. Atkinson, S. Delamont, A. Cernat, J. W. Sakshaug and R. A. Williams (eds), *Sage Research Methods Foundations* (London: SAGE Publications, 2020), published online at *https://methods-sagepub-com.abc.cardiff.ac.uk/foundations/gatekeepers-in-qualitative-research* (accessed 19 September 2024).
52 I later found out that the phenomenon has its own prehistory. I learned the following from reading a certain book from Osi Rhys Osmond's archive relating to his visits to Palestine: 'David Shaltiel. Commander of Jerusalem's Haganah, received his military training in the French Foreign Legion. Arrested by the Gestapo while on a secret mission to his native Germany before World War II, he kept his sanity during long weeks of torture and confinement by teaching himself Hebrew.' The extract is from Larry Collins and Dominique Lapierre, *O Jerusalem!* (London: The History Book Club, 1972), Illustration 48.
53 Part supported by the award of an Academic Study Group on Israel and the Middle East Isaiah Berlin Travel Scholarship.
54 Brian Keenan, *An Evil Cradling* (London: Hutchison, 1992), p. xii.

55 Derek Mahon, 'Afterlives', *Collected Poems* (Dublin: The Gallery Press, 1975/1999), line 4, stanza 4, part 2: But the hills are still the same / Grey-blue above Belfast. / Perhaps if I'd stayed behind / And lived it bomb by bomb / I might have grown up at last / And learnt what is meant by home./ *http://www.troublesarchive.com/artforms/poetry/piece/afterlives* (accessed 1 June 2023).

56 I learned Welsh upon moving to Wales after graduating from university in Belfast.

57 Short Films Matter, *My Brief Eternity. Review*, 8 July 2023: *https://shortfilmsmatter.com/4040/my-brief-eternity* (accessed 10 July 2023).

58 Osi Rhys Osmond, *1986 Fieldnotes. Cymru a'r Wlad Sanctaidd* (Wales and the Holy Land) (unpublished fieldnotes, 1986).

59 Ihsan A. Hijazi, 'Car bombs deal new blow to shattered Lebanon', *The New York Times*, 18 August 1986, section A, p. 3: *https://www.nytimes.com/1986/08/18/world/car-bombs-deal-new-blow-to-shattered-lebanon.html* (accessed 1 June 2023).

60 Department of the Taoiseach, *Letter from the Department of Justice to the Department of the Taoiseach*, 2 December 1987: *https://cain.ulster.ac.uk/nai/1987/nai_TSCH-2017-10-19_1987-12-02a.pdf* (accessed 1 June 2023).

61 Crispin Sartwell, *Political Aesthetics* (Ithaca NY: Cornell University Press, 2010), p. 64. One might add here that Sartwell finds the question of whether all art is political to be inherently ambiguous. For example, he explains (at p. 63) as follows:

> The question of whether all art is political picks out a central dilemma in political aesthetics. I think the question is too general as it stands: certainly there is no style that may not reveal political implications, and certainly all art reflects the experience and social resources of its maker, which are partly fixed by political factors. Modes of artistic production, such as handcraft or industrial manufacturing, have political as well as aesthetic entailments. But while no art should be eliminated as possible datum, I think we should acknowledge that aesthetic objects are often made with no political or economic program in mind, and we should take with some seriousness their demand to be considered as something other than political statements.

62 Osmond's work on Palestine ought, by now, merit featuring in any survey of the connections between Wales, Israel and Palestine on its own terms. See, in particular, Jasmine Donahaye, *Whose People? Wales, Israel, Palestine* (Cardiff: University of Wales Press, 2012).

63 Here, the question is posed by Robert Huddleston, 'Arts in society "Poetry makes nothing happen". W. H. Auden's struggle with politics', *Boston Review*,

25 February 2015: *http://bostonreview.net/poetry/robert-huddleston-wh-auden-struggle-politics* (accessed 1 June 2023).
64 Huddleston, 'Poetry makes nothing happen'.
65 Tommy Bruhn and Joanna Doona, 'Serious grappling with satire: rhetorical genre affordances and invitations to participation in public controversy', *Javnost – The Public. Journal of the European Institute for Communication and Culture*, 29/3 (2022), 284–300, at 285.
66 Sartwell, *Political Aesthetics*, p. 2.
67 Anis S. Bawarshi and Mary Jo Reiff, *Genre: An Introduction to History, Theory, Research, and Pedagogy* (West Lafayette, Indiana: Parlor Press, 2010), p. 59.
68 The term 'affordance' is widely used in a range of disciplines, such as social media research: Alexander Ronzhyn, Ana Sofia Cardenal and Albert Batlle Rubio, 'Defining affordances in social media research: a literature review', *New Media & Society*, 25/11 (2023), 3163–88. There, affordances are described as being relational, perceptional, contextual and discrete, noting also that they are both 'potentials for action' and also 'constrain action'.
69 See, for example, George Kamberelis, 'Genre as institutional informed social practice', *Journal of Contemporary Legal Studies*, 6 (1995), 117–71 and also Carolyn R. Miller, 'Genre as social action', *Quarterly Journal of Speech*, 70/2 (1984), 151–67.
70 See pp. 6–11 especially in Caroline Levine, *Forms: Whole, Rhythm, Hierarchy, Network* (Princeton, NJ: Princeton University Press, 2015).
71 Levine, *Forms*, pp. 13–14.
72 Keenan, *An Evil Cradling*, p. xi.
73 Keenan, *An Evil Cradling*, p. xi.
74 Keenan, *An Evil Cradling*, p. xiii.
75 Keenan, *An Evil Cradling*, p. xiv.
76 Keenan, *An Evil Cradling*, p. xi.
77 Dervla Murphy, *A Month by the Sea: Encounters in Gaza* (London: Eland, 2013), cover page.
78 Murphy, *A Month by the Sea*, pp. 238–9.
79 Arthur E. Walzer, 'Parrēsia, Foucault, and the classical rhetorical tradition', *Rhetoric Society Quarterly*, 43/1 (2013), 1–21.
80 Colum McCann, *Apeirogon: A Novel* (London: Bloomsbury, 2020), p. 463.
81 *https://www.palfest.org* (accessed 1 June 2023).
82 *https://www.palfest.org/globalsouthvolumeone* (accessed 1 June 2023).
83 McCann, *Apeirogon*, p. 461.
84 Narrative 4 self-describes as follows: 'Narrative 4 is a global organization driven by artists, shaped by educators and led by students. Our core methodology, the story exchange, is designed to help students understand that their voices, stories, actions and lives matter, and that they have the

power to change, rebuild and revolutionize systems': *https://narrative4.com* (accessed 1 June 2023). It is in the context of his work with Narrative 4 that McCann claims that storytelling is 'the one true democracy': McCann quoted at *https://narrative4.com* (accessed 1 June 2023), implying that there are false democracies. Telos, the second organisation referred to by McCann, is an American (USA) non-governmental organisation. It describes its mission as 'radical peacemaking' aimed at reconciling 'seeming intractable conflicts' such as Israel–Palestine by 'taking influential Americans from across the political and theological spectra on high-touch, multi-narrative pilgrimages to the Holy Land' in order to help Telos with realising their vision 'to effectively and relentlessly wage peace': *https://www.telosgroup.org/who-we-are/* (accessed 1 June 2023).

85 *https://www.telosgroup.org/who-we-are/* (accessed 1 June 2023).
86 On the occasion of his elevation in 2006 to membership of the Orsedd (Gorsedd Cymru, in the Welsh language: *http://www.gorsedd.cymru*), amongst his virtues were listed the following: 'Mae'n wlatgarwr brwd, a dysgodd Gymraeg nodedig o dda' (He's an enthusiastic patriot, and he has learned the Welsh language notably well) and 'Mae'n genhadwr effeithiol dros Gymru a Chymreictod ymhlith y di-Gymraeg, ac ar y llwyfan rhyngwladol' (He's an effective missionary on behalf of Wales and Welshness among those that do not speak Welsh, and on the international stage): *http://www.gorsedd.cymru/anrhydeddau-2006/* (accessed 1 June 2023). While Osmond was motivated to learn Welsh by nationalist ideology, I was moved to do so by its relationship to Irish as a Celtic language.
87 Lansio llyfr Osi ar Ddiwrnod Heddwch y Byd. Codi baner er mwyn galw am heddwch a lansio llyfr newydd yr artist diweddar (Launch of Osi's book on International Day of Peace. Raising a flag in order to call for peace and to launch a new book on the late artist), *Golwg 360*, 21 September 2015: *https://golwg.360.cymru/newyddion/cymru/200395-lansio-llyfr-osi-ar-ddiwrnod-heddwch-y-byd* (accessed 1 June 2023); Ymgyrchwyr heddwch yn Epynt. Dynnu sylw at y bobl sy'n cael eu lladd gan awyrenau di-beilot (Peace campaigners in Epynt. Drawing attention to the people who are being killed by drones), *Golwg 360*, 26 June 2011: *https://golwg.360.cymru/newyddion/cymru/42119-ymgyrchwyr-heddwch-yn-epynt* (accessed 1 June 2023).
88 *Ymateb/Response* by Osi Rhys Osmond was exhibited in Oriel Q in Narberth, Pembrokeshire, in west Wales, in June 2009. See, for example, 'Powerful paintings in Oriel Q', *The Western Telegraph*, 9 June 2009: *https://www.westerntelegraph.co.uk/leisure/localentertainmentnews/4427945.powerful-paintings-in-oriel-q/* (accessed 1 June 2023).
89 Diarmait Mac Giolla Chríost, *Language, Identity and Conflict: A Comparative Study of Language in Ethnic Conflict in Europe and Eurasia* (London: Routledge, 2003).

90 Diarmait Mac Giolla Chríost, *Jailtacht: The Irish Language, Symbolic Power and Political Violence in Northern Ireland 1972–2008* (Cardiff: University of Wales Press, 2012).
91 Diarmait Mac Giolla Chríost, *Welsh Writing, Political Action and Incarceration. Branwen's Starling* (Basingstoke: Palgrave Macmillan, 2013).
92 Deborah Reed-Danahay, 'Participating, observing, witnessing', in S. Coleman, S. B. Hyatt and A. Kingsolver (eds), *The Routledge Companion to Contemporary Anthropology* (London: Routledge, 2016), pp. 57–71.
93 Bradford Vivian, *Commonplace Witnessing: Rhetorical Invention, Historical Remembrance, and Public Culture* (Oxford: Oxford University Press, 2017).
94 Joanne Paul, 'The use of kairos in Renaissance political philosophy', *Renaissance Quarterly*, 67/1 (2014), 43–78, at 43.
95 Reed-Danahay, 'Participating, observing, witnessing', p. 62.
96 Annette Wieviorka, *L'ère du Témoin* (Paris: Hachette Littératures, 2002).
97 Michal Givoni, *The Care of the Witness: A Contemporary History of Testimony in Crises* (Cambridge: Cambridge University Press, 2016), p. 9.
98 Michal Givoni, 'The ethics of witnessing and the politics of the governed', *Theory, Culture and Society*, 31/1 (2013), 123–42, at 139.
99 Givoni, 'The ethics of witnessing', p. 128.
100 Judith Butler, 'What is critique? An essay on Foucault's virtue', in D. Ingram (ed.), *The Political: Blackwell Readings in Continental Philosophy* (Malden, MA: Blackwell, 2002), pp. 212–26.
101 Givoni, 'The ethics of witnessing', p. 139.
102 Michal Givoni, 'Indifference and repetition: occupation testimonies and left-wing despair', *Journal of Cultural Studies*, 33/4 (2019), 595–631, at 602.
103 Vivian Gornick, *The Situation and the Story: The Art of Personal Narrative* (New York: Farrar, Straus and Giroux, 2001), p. 85.
104 Gornick, *The Situation and the Story*, p. 77.
105 Caroline Levine, 'Forms, literary and social', *Dibur Literary Journal*, 2/Spring (2016), 75–9: https://arcade.stanford.edu/sites/default/files/article_pdfs/Dibur-v02i01-article07-Levine.pdf (accessed 1 June 2023).
106 Levine, 'Forms, literary and social', p. 75.
107 Helga Schwalm, 'Autobiography', in P. Hühn et al (eds), *The Living Handbook of Narratology* (Hamburg: Hamburg University, 2014), p. 1: https://www.lhn.uni-hamburg.de/node/129.html (accessed 1 June 2023).
108 Philippe Lejeune, *On Autobiography* (Minneapolis, MN: University of Minnesota Press, 1988).
109 Louis van den Hengel, 'Zoegraphy: per/forming posthuman lives', *Biography*, 35 (2012), 1–20.
110 Jeanne Fahnestock and Marie Secor, 'The rhetoric of literary criticism', in C. Bazerman and J. Paradis (eds), *Textual Dynamics of the Professions: Historical and*

Contemporary Studies of Writing in Professional Communities (Madison: University of Wisconsin Press, 1991), pp. 77–96, at p. 94.

111 Laura Wilder, '"The rhetoric of literary criticism" revisited: mistaken critics, complex contexts, and social justice', *Written Communication*, 22/1 (2005), 76–119.

112 Barbara Harlow, '"Be it resolved …": Referenda on recent scholarship in the Israel–Palestine conflict', *Cultural Critique*, 91/Fall (2015), 190–205.

113 Fahnestock and Secor, 'The rhetoric of literary criticism', p. 88; Wilder, '"The rhetoric of literary criticism" revisited', p. 85.

114 Marcel Danesi, 'Visual rhetoric and semiotic', in *Oxford Research Encyclopedia of Communication* (published online, 2017): https://oxfordre.com/communication/view/10.1093/acrefore/9780190228613.001.0001/acrefore-9780190228613-e-43 (accessed 1 June 2023).

115 Gunther Kress and Theo van Leeuwen, *Reading Images: The Grammar of Visual Design* (New York: Routledge, 1996).

116 Henri Lefebvre, *The Production of Space* (Oxford: Blackwell, 1974, trans. D. Nicholson-Smith, 1991).

117 Nigel Thrift, 'Space: the fundamental stuff of human geography', in N. Clifford, S. Holloway, S. P. Price and G. Valentine (eds), *Key Concepts in Geography* (London: SAGE Publications, 2008), pp. 95–107, at p. 105.

118 Ulf Hannerz, 'Being there… and there… and there! Reflections on multi-site ethnography', *Ethnography*, 4/2 (2003), 201–216.

119 John Postill, *Digital Ethnography: 'Being There' Physically, Remotely, Virtually and Imaginatively* (published online, 2015): https://johnpostill.wordpress.com/2015/02/25/digital-ethnography-being-there-physically-remotely-virtually-and-imaginatively/ (accessed 1 June 2023) and see also Sarah Pink, Heather Horst, John Postill, Larissa Hjorth, Tania Lewis and Jo Tacchi, *Digital Ethnography: Principles and Practice* (London: SAGE Publishing, 2015).

120 Nina Grønlykke Mollerup, *'Being There', Phone in Hand: Thick Presence and Anthropological Fieldwork with Media* (EASA Media Anthropology Network E-Seminar Series, 2017): https://comm.ku.dk/staff/?pure=en%2Fpublications%2Fbeing-there-phone-in-hand(58d7d7f1-e042-4006-95d4-30bcc2d4d116)%2Fexport.html (accessed 1 June 2023). See also Anne Beaulieu, 'From co-location to co-presence: shifts in the use of ethnography to the study of knowledge', *Social Studies of Science*, 49/3 (2010), 453–70.

121 Roger Sanjek and Susan W. Tratner (eds), *eFieldnotes: The Makings of Anthropology in the Digital World* (Philadelphia, PA: University of Pennsylvania Press, 2016).

122 Deborah Reed-Danahay (ed.), *Auto/ethnography: Rewriting the Self and the Social* (Oxford: Berg, 1997) and Reed-Danahay, 'Participating, observing, witnessing'.

123 Daniel, *Charred Lullabies*; Bruce Knauft, 'Good anthropology in dark times: critical appraisal and ethnographic application', *The Australian Journal of Anthropology* (2018), 1–15; Robbins, 'Beyond the suffering subject'; Alan Rumsey, 'Ethnographic macro-tropes and anthropological theory', *Anthropological Theory*, 4/3 (2004), 267–98.
124 Didier Fassin and Richard Rechtman, *The Empire of Trauma: An Inquiry into the Condition of Victimhood* (Princeton, NJ: Princeton University Press, 2009).
125 Keenan, *An Evil Cradling*, p. 75.
126 Keenan, *An Evil Cradling*, p. 68.
127 McCann, *Apeirogon*, p. 270.
128 Alice Tilche and Edward Simpson, 'On trusting ethnography: serendipity and the reflexive return to the fields of Gujarat', *Journal of the Royal Anthropological Institute*, 23 (2017), 690–708.
129 PNA = Palestinian National Authority, or Palestinian Authority. The former is the preferred term of Palestinians.
130 Michel Foucault, *The Birth of Biopolitics* (Basingstoke: Palgrave Macmillan, 2008).
131 Robbins, 'Beyond the suffering subject', p. 459.
132 Charles Larmore, 'The right and the good', *Philosophia*, 20/1–2 (1990), 15–32, at 24.

CHAPTER 2

A Time for Saying

Being born and raised in a society of profound and fatalistic religiosity, in which political violence is endemic, one knows when a moment of grave intent has arrived. After all, it is written in the language of the tribe of my deceased mother's mother:[1] 'To every thing there is a season, and a time to every purpose under the heaven: a time to be born, and a time to die; ... a time to kill, and a time to heal; ... a time to keep silence, and a time to speak'.[2] A body is summoned to speak by circumstance, and in so speaking becomes the witness. In terms of rhetoric, such circumstance is called kairos, the 'qualitative aspect of time'.[3] It captures 'both a sense of "adaptation and accommodation to convention" and, conversely, "the uniquely timely, the spontaneous, the radically particular"'.[4] Indeed, kairos, ever 'elusive',[5] invokes the witness statement as much more than simply 'saying the right thing at the right time',[6] for in that text that is also an action converge each of the ethical, the epistemological, the aesthetic and the social.[7] Thus, the rhetorical imperative of artistic creation is interrogated in this chapter: for what reason, at that given time, was such testimony felt essential? Why was it that the moment is now?

'writing just after an encounter'[8]

For such a long time my silence was not voluntary. It was the kind of silence that was not a matter of choice, not a matter of refusing to speak. I found a label for it much later.[9] As with many children growing up in conflict zones,[10] PTSD was an inevitable feature of my psychology, and speech withdrawal a symptom of that. Thereby, of necessity, I bore muted witness to my world, and my testimony, as Ronit Lentin might put, was one of silence.[11] But since, and all the while, I shape[12] myself to speak. And I do so with the exhortation to bear witness made by Seamus Heaney in 1975 still in mind. His poetic criticism of NI as a society of inchoate witnesses yet resonates: 'Smoke-signals are loud-mouthed compared with us'.[13] By now, that poem's title is long-established as a part of the northern Irish lexicon of saying what you see: 'Whatever you say, say nothing'. I am able, therefore, to say that I might bear witness to the Troubles[14] of NI in the conventional sense. More than a child of that place, I am made from it; therefore, I qualify, and I suppose I must accept this, as one of those who may claim, as Bradford Vivian puts it, 'an especially proximate relationship with the evils or tragedies of human history so as to speak with an elevated sense of moral responsibility from the ground of that relatively rare, embodied and traumatic, experience'.[15] So deeply internalised is that experience for me that excavating the vocabulary of witness from within has been a long drawn-out process.

Much of the necessary language surfaced when it seemed that the long war in the north had finally come to an end, and both of my parents had died, fairly young and within a few, very short years of each other: they were invested in the conflict. I made a book of it.[16] Although that book, *Jailtacht*, is about other things, it says, 'Here I am. I was there. I saw it happen. It happened to me'. Published in 2012, *Jailtacht* is about Irish republican prisoners and their complicated relationship with the Irish language. Whilst I met with many of them during the conduct of fieldwork, I first encountered such prisoners, however, as a child fetching cigarettes for my mother from the local supermarket. We lived, at that time, in another place on the edge of the city, in a staunchly Irish nationalist and republican stronghold, for we had been cleansed from our loyalist, Protestant estate for liking the Irish language too much, too publicly. I recall that it that was most probably sometime early in the new year of 1976 and internment, aka Operation Demetrius, had only recently been brought to an end.[17] Why Demetrius? Only now do I ask.

In ending internment, many young Catholics who had been incarcerated without trial, without charges being laid before them, were released from prison. Politics: they were to be sent home by Christmas. He walked into the shop, streetwise and confident in his denim uniform. He was a soldier of the people, said one of the younger daughters of the shop, yet halfway through primary school. There he was, for real, fresh from the set of a Joe McCann photograph, the Che Guevara of the IRA.[18] He, Joe McCann, was familiar to me for his image adorned the streets of Derry in various forms. Sometimes his armed silhouette was on a fly poster on the boarded-up window of an abandoned house;

other times it was on a crude mural, or a placard at an IRA checkpoint in the Bogside.[19] Holding always the M1 carbine in his right hand, resting its butt upon his right knee, he sits hunkered, casual, gazing into the bright white heat of Belfast burning. The figure then before me in the shop seemed unscathed by anything that might have happened to him, or by anything that he might have done. But Joe McCann himself was, by that stage, long dead, shot by British soldiers from the Parachute Regiment on Joy Street in the Markets in Belfast in 1972. He is entry number 334 in *Lost Lives*.[20] That's the thing about this place; no one here gets out alive.[21] He had such bravado. He really was like a rock star, but there, with us, in the supermarket. Of course, none of us knew then how it would all end for him. Demetrius: a devotee of Demeter of the 'beautiful hair',[22] the goddess of the cycle of life and death, mother of the 'dread'[23] Persephone. Persephone: goddess of destruction, bringer of death. Persephone: bride of the labyrinth, wed by rape. What legacy culminates inexorably in that womb?[24]

Half a dozen or so years later, a long time in a short life, I had a very different encounter with some other Irish republican prisoners. I was by then living between two worlds, profoundly conflicted. That is to say that while we, as a family, still lived in that same staunchly Irish nationalist and republican stronghold, I attended a secondary school in the very heart of the city that was loyalist, Protestant and British in its values. I was, therefore, subjected to being institutionalised, directly and indirectly, by the school. That process included assorted loyalist, Protestant and British organisations in society that were connected with the school, both formally and informally. My loyalist, Protestant and British institutionalisation included involvement with the RUC and the British Army and familiarity with paramilitary organisations. On that day, a Sunday, late afternoon, I travelled, a member of a team (not quite children but not yet adults) on its way back from a rifle-shooting competition at Ballykinler Barracks in County Down. Those very barracks served as a holding centre for prisoners interned under Operation Demetrius.[25] We were in transit in an unmarked white minibus. With us was a set of L96 sniper rifles, brand new to the British Army. They were locked away in secure cases. Before that day we practised our shooting in Shackleton Barracks, in County Derry. Those very barracks served as a holding centre too for the internees of Demetrius. There they were subjected to 'inhuman and degrading' interrogation.[26] We were first stopped by an ad hoc RUC and UDR checkpoint only a few minutes, a short mile or two, up the road. They redirected us, without explanation. We took another road. A short time later we were stopped once more and further redirected. We found a different road. A mile or so along that way, another checkpoint. We took another route. Another checkpoint. They sent us back to a road that we had already been sent from. Checkpoint. What's the story? We've got rifles in the back. The driver revealed his ID. Wait here. Do not get out of the van. Stay there. We'll get somebody for you. Sunday, 25 September 1983. What's the story? There's been a breakout from the Maze. H-7. IRA. On the loose. Thirty-eight of them. IRA. Armed with guns and knives. Hijacked cars. Prison officers killed. Complete mayhem on the roads. We're all out. Massive operation. Everybody's out. Big chiefs. Total panic stations. In the rear of the van, one of us decided that we would use the rifles if they caught us. Maybe we admired his bravado. Stay here. We'll get somebody for you. British Army Land Rovers came for us. In the small, dark hours of Monday morning we journeyed the contorted roads homeward. Say prayers for Demeter.

Then, much later, I deliberately set up encounters with Irish republican prisoners for *Jailtacht* (2012). In researching for that book, and in the course of fieldwork too, my attention was distractedly drawn to Palestine. Prisoners there, it is true, developed a dialogue with their incarcerated peers in Ireland during the Irish republican hunger strike of 1981.[27] The support was reciprocated in 2012[28] and again in 2017.[29] I was in Palestine conducting fieldwork during the hunger strike of 2017, led by Marwan Barghouti of Fatah. A leader of the First Intifada, he was 'schooled in Hebrew',[30] or 'learned Hebrew',[31] between 1978 and 1983 during one of his substantial periods in prison, to the extent that some commentators claim for him the following: 'Of all of the men who would be leaders of the nation and would be Palestine, he is the most popular, his personal story the most compelling, his command of Hebrew and understanding of Israelis the most sophisticated'.[32] I was puzzled as to whether Irish republican prisoners were unique in the politicised learning of language during incarceration. I began to come across, with increasing frequency, references in the print and online media to former Palestinian 'security' prisoners having learned English and Hebrew whilst held in the Israeli prison system. A security prisoner is, according to the Israeli Prison Service, defined as follows:

> A prisoner who was convicted and sentenced for committing a crime, or who is imprisoned on suspicion of committing a crime, which due to its nature or circumstances was defined as a security offense or whose motive was nationalistic ... Most of these prisoners are also connected to terror organisations and this connection poses special dangers to order and discipline in the prison, as well as to the security of the state. The anticipated security threat from the 'security' prisoners requires that they be confined separately from criminal prisoners and be subjected to special restrictions in all things related to connection with the outside.[33]

Amongst those who were such prisoners is Jibril Rajoub, once the National Security Adviser to Yasser Arafat and Head of the Palestinian Preventive Security Force:

> Jailed for life at fifteen for throwing a grenade at an IDF convoy; spent 17 years in Israeli prison (1968–85), where he learned fluent Hebrew and passable English, and translated into Arabic former PM Menachem Begin's 'The Revolt'. Released as part of a prisoner exchange in 1985, but expelled from West Bank to Lebanon in 1988, during the first intifada.[34]

Another is Khalil Wishah, who teaches Hebrew to young Palestinians at the Nafha Center for Prisoner Studies and Israeli Affairs in Gaza. The building in which the centre is located was destroyed[35] by the IDF during Operation Guardian of the Walls[36] in 2021:

> Now in his early 60s, Wishah learned the language during the 1980s. He and other prisoners effectively set up their own school behind Israeli bars. He felt that he had a firm grasp of Hebrew after studying the language intensely for six months. 'I didn't realize when I lay back against the dank walls of Bir al-Saba (Beersheba) prison in 1982 that the place would transform me into a professional Hebrew teacher,' he said ... 'I want my people to educate themselves about the Israeli community more and more,' he said. 'For me, it's a national duty to understand your enemy, to analyze it and to know how it thinks

through reading or following its media.' / 'Resistance is not always about holding a gun, it might be about understanding your enemy,' he added.[37]

And another is Yahya Sinwar, the leader of Hamas in Gaza since 2017 and 'mastermind' and 'architect' of 7 October 2023, and 'dead man walking' as a result according to the IDF.[38] During his time in Israeli prisons, twenty-four years in total,[39] he 'spent much of his spare time studying what he could about his Israeli enemies, reading Israeli newspapers and becoming fluent in Hebrew in the process':[40]

> He was convicted in 1988 of playing a role in the murder of two Israeli soldiers and four Palestinians suspected of collaboration with Israel, and spent more than two decades in Israeli prison. Sinwar later said that he spent those years studying his enemy, including learning to speak Hebrew.[41]

> Yaari (a journalist who interviewed Sinwar in prison several times) says that Sinwar always preferred to speak Hebrew with him, even though Yaari was fluent in Arabic. 'He sought to improve his Hebrew,' Yaari says. 'I think he wanted to benefit from somebody who spoke higher Hebrew than the prison wardens.[42]

According to local news media, Hamas consider the learning of Hebrew to be a tactical priority in the armed struggle against Israel: 'The leadership of the Izz al-Din al-Qassam Brigades (IQB), Hamas' military wing, views mastering Hebrew as one of the most important criteria for fighters seeking to join the elite unit. They are required to learn the language to improve the outcome of military confrontation with Israeli soldiers, according to Al-Majd, an al-Qassam Brigades affiliated website'.[43] And according to the Israeli Ministry of Foreign Affairs, Hamas recommend in their training booklet entitled 'The Kidnapper's Handbook' that Hamas activists 'should learn Hebrew until they speak it fluently' so as to better effect their abduction of 'Zionist soldiers' who would be traded at some point in exchange for Palestinian prisoners.[44]

When I began writing this book prior to 7 October 2023 I asked myself the following: why is the moment now? My response then was as follows: there is a developing sense of foreboding interlude, of interregna. The landscape is shifting at subterranean level, with tremors felt at the surface. Jerusalem is declared capital by President Trump, 'reversing nearly seven decades of American foreign policy',[45] and drawing international condemnation.[46] Hamas makes a dramatic call to action but the immediate response by Palestinians is subdued.[47] New elections announced for the Palestinian Legislative Council for 2021 following agreement between Fatah and Hamas[48] are indefinitely postponed by Mahmoud Abbas[49] of Fatah and President of the PNA in April 2021, shortly before they are due to be held.[50] Some are saying that Fatah is afraid of the popularity of Hamas being given democratic expression. Gaza erupts: it gets its own page on Wikipedia within hours.[51] Ireland, after coming within a whisper of adopting BDS[52] as state policy in 2020 via the Occupied Territories Bill,[53] is the first nation-state in the EU to declare, through its parliament, that Israeli policy in Palestine is 'de facto annexation'.[54] Benjamin Netanyahu may finally fall from the political pinnacle in Israel.[55] Human Rights Watch (HRW) publish their report declaring Israel guilty of 'the crimes against humanity of apartheid and persecution': it is *A Threshold Crossed*, they claim.[56] If that is the case, then we have indeed crossed the Rubicon, it would appear. However, the claim is aggressively contested by some.[57]

Now, as I write after 7 October 2023, the issue has become clearer again. The assertion made in plain and simple language by HRW that 'the three elements of the crime of apartheid all come together in the OPT (Occupied Palestinian Territory)'[58] seems to hold true ever more so now. The aftermath of 7 October 2023 is, it seems to me, the 'tipping point' anticipated by John Dugard and John Reynolds in their authoritative article on the topic of apartheid, international law and the OPT.[59] I feel compelled to quote at length from their concluding remarks:

> As happened in South Africa, what begins as segregation is liable to evolve into an institutionalized system of racial domination. Such separateness cannot be sustained without spawning suffering and cycles of violence. The US underwent a process of racial reckoning to confront this incongruity in the 1960s. South Africa underwent its own transformation in the 1990s. Both nations are the better for it, despite tensions persisting and gross socio-economic inequalities continuing

to plague society. With the dual system of law that currently prevails in the occupied Palestinian territory best understood as the derivative of an ongoing settler colonial process, logic dictates that Israel will inevitably reach the tipping point at which it is forced to confront its own racial realities *vis-à-vis* the Palestinians. While the shape that such a transformation ultimately takes will depend primarily on social attitudes and political craft, international law may retain a role through the light that it shines on the normative issues to be resolved in this context.[60]

Indeed, a darkness has descended upon Israel. It is one that is shaped by the outrageous discourse of a range of very significant political figures in Israel subsequent to 7 October 2023, revealing an ugly truth. That ugly truth is that Bezalel Smotrich, Finance Minister in the Israeli government, together with Itamar Ben-Gvir, National Security Minister, have called for the relocation of the Palestinian population of Gaza thereby creating the space for its settlement by Israeli Jews, saying, respectively:

> What needs to be done in the Gaza Strip is to encourage emigration … If there are 100,000 or 200,000 Arabs in Gaza and not 2 million Arabs, the entire discussion on the day after will be totally different … Let's make the desert bloom,[61] it doesn't come at anyone's expense.[62]

> [The war is an] opportunity to concentrate on encouraging the migration of the residents of Gaza … We cannot withdraw from any territory we are in in the Gaza Strip. Not only do I not rule out Jewish settlement there, I believe it is also an important thing.[63]

Francesca Albanese, the UN Special Rapporteur on the Occupied Palestinian Territories, describes the language of voluntary migration used by Israeli politicians as a 'cynical' cloak disguising what is the actual plan, namely 'forced displacement', an act that is 'utterly illegal' tantamount to a 'crime against humanity'.[64] This appears to confirm the thesis of Ilan Pappé, political scientist, historian of Israel, and former

IDF soldier, that the forced migration, or ethnic cleansing, of Palestinian Arabs has been a foundational goal of the Zionist state-building project from the outset.[65] The Israeli government has published in outline form its vision for Gaza 'the day after', and it is no less ugly than the state of affairs that led up to the Israel–Hamas War. In simple terms, the two-state solution for the conflict in Palestine is hereby defunct: the Prime Minister Benjamin Netanyahu is clear that there shall be 'no Palestinian state'[66] because the 'security needs' of Israel leave 'no space for a sovereign Palestinian state'.[67] The plan says, 'Israel would retain operational freedom in Gaza in terms of defense and security'.[68] In other words, it is a licence for the military occupation of Gaza, and the construction by the IDF in March 2024 of Highway 749,[69] running east–west through the strip just to the south of Gaza City all the way to the Mediterranean Sea, is purposefully designed to enable that goal. Moreover, part of the solution under this regime, according to the Israeli Ambassador to the UK is the 're-education' of Palestinians, to redeem them from 'evil'.[70] Where to go from here? Let us be reminded here of Joel Robbins's argument that to provide accounts of violence and do no more than invoke in us a sense of the vulnerability we share as human beings[71] is not enough. Rather, one of the tasks of ethnographic testimony is to consider how to address injustice as directly as possible.[72] For Ilan Pappé, 7 October 2023 and its aftermath is the harbinger of something wholly transformative: 'we are witnessing the beginning of the end of this project (of Israel as a settler-colonialist state)'.[73] Such a development would be momentous, monumental, epoch-making: a paradigm shift. For the ethnographer, according to Robbins (quoting Max Weber), the mood of that is as follows:

> [T]here comes a moment when the atmosphere changes. The significance of the unreflectively utilized viewpoints becomes uncertain and the road is lost in the twilight. The light of the great cultural problems moves on. Then science too prepares to change its standpoint and its analytical apparatus and to view the streams of events from the heights of thought.[74]

More recently, again, even as the full extent of the horrendous humanitarian catastrophe in Gaza was becoming ever clearer to the rest of the world, the Minister for Social Equality and for the Advancement of the

Status of Women in the Government of Israel, May Golan, declared that she was 'proud of the ruins in Gaza'.[75] This is the moment we are in. This is why now.

'all the King's horses'[76]

What of the timing of Brian Keenan? In his review of *An Evil Cradling*, Sebastian Faulks says that the book was written in 'worryingly' short space of time:

> Having been detained for four and a half years, Brian Keenan completed his account of his captivity in little more than 18 months after his release. This is worryingly quick work. It would take a remarkable person to assimilate this hellish experience so quickly and to develop a way of writing that could describe the outer edges of human experience.[77]

Despite this, he finds the work 'colossal' and 'a moving and remarkable triumph'.[78] In retrospect, the timetable that concerned Faulks seems to be the norm for the publication of such autobiographical accounts of Lebanese hostages. For example, Keenan was released on 24 August 1990, *An Evil Cradling* was published in 1992; Terry Anderson was released on 4 December 1991, *Den of Lions* was published in 1993; Terry Waite was released on 18 November 1991, *Taken on Trust* was published in 1993; Joseph Cicippio was released on 2 December 1991, *Chains to Roses*, written with Richard W. Hope, was published in 1993. As a result, these books were sometimes reviewed together as a body of work, such as with *The Los Angeles Times* and *The New York Times*.[79]

Similarly, John McCarthy, Brian Keenan's companion hostage, was released 8 August 1991 and *Some Other Rainbow*, written together with Jill Morrell, was published in 1993; Thomas Sutherland, released on 18 November 1991, published *At Your Own Risk* in 1996; Charles Glass, held as a hostage during 1987, published *Tribes with Flags* in 1991, and Benjamin Weir who was released on 14 September 1985 published *Hostage Bound, Hostage Free* in 1987. David Jacobsen, released on 2 November 1986, published *Hostage* in 1991. And Sis Levine, wife of hostage Jerry Levine who was released on 14 February 1985, wrote *Beirut Diary* in 1989. Marie Seurat, wife of Michel Seurat who died in captivity on 5 March 1986, published *Les Corbeaux d'Alep* in 1988. This book was subsequently translated by Dorothy S. Blair in 1990 as *Birds of Ill Omen*. Roger Auque, released on 28 November 1987, published, with Patrick Forestier, *Un Otage à Beyrouth* in 1988. Point of note: these two books caused considerable disruption to the French presidential election of 1988. Indeed, the tone of the campaign was set by the negotiated release of the last of the French hostages, namely Marcel Fontaine, Marcel Carton and Jean-Paul Kauffmann, at the outset of the campaign, on 4 May 1988.

Thus, one could say that hostage memoirs were very much in vogue in the publishing industry in the period between 1987 and 1996. This coincides not merely with the release of the hostages but also with political events in Palestine too having particularly high news value. The First Intifada began in 1987 and was covered extensively by the international broadcast and print media at the time. The fact that this ended with the political processes that led to the Oslo I and II Accords in 1993 and 1995, respectively, along with the creation of the PNA in 1994 meant that the news agenda remained with Palestine and, more to the point in publishing terms, that there remained an audience for the testimonies of the international hostages of Beirut. The most notable exception to this chronology is *La Maison du Retour* by Jean-Paul Kauffmann. That book was not published until almost twenty years after his release, which was in 1988. One should note that Kauffmann had been abducted and held with Michel Seurat, who died in captivity in 1986 and whose remains were not recovered until 2006.[80] That the book was published in 2007 is no coincidence, surely.

Nor is it a coincidence either that Kauffmann, on the occasion of the recovery of the body of Michel Seurat in 2006, talks of writing a book such as that written by Marie Seurat as something cathartic because Keenan had been there already in 1992:

> I think it was D. H. Lawrence, speaking about the act of writing, who said that writers throw up their sickness in books. So it is with this work. It is the process of abreaction in art form, both a therapy and an exploration. I once wrote in an article about the process of re-adjustment that we are our own self-healers. The writing of this book has been part of that healing.[81]

And in a further coincidence, it is during the second half of the 1980s, by way of preface to the genre of hostage memoirs, that science too discovers expressive writing as therapy.[82]

It could be said that the publication of *An Evil Cradling* was timely in the political context in some ways. Keenan's portrait of 'men in extremis', his efforts at finding parallels between 'hostage and captor',[83] makes his captors human, and victims too, trapped by circumstance. He makes the terrorist more approachable. Reaching by governments to those whom they regard as terrorists was very much in the air in both NI and Palestine during the early 1990s. In the case of the former, the UK government made it known in 1990 that it had 'no selfish economic or strategic interest' in its relationship with NI, a public signal of the incipient peace process.[84] Then, in 1992, Sinn Féin published the document *Towards a Lasting Peace*,[85] indicating a shift in emphasis in Irish republican ideology away from the armed struggle and towards greater engagement with democratic processes and political institutions, and the Hume–Adams statement of April 1993 brought the 'embryonic' peace process into the public sphere.[86] The significance of these events was confirmed by the end of that calendar year in the shape of the Downing Street Declaration,[87] a joint commitment by the UK and Irish governments to reach a durable peace in the region.

Similarly, also underlying *An Evil Cradling* is an urge to develop better mutual understanding between Israeli Jews and Palestinian Arabs. Efforts to find peace seem to be in the air in this political context too. The First Intifada ends in 1993 and under the Oslo I Accord the Israeli government for the first time recognises the PLO as a legitimate negotiating partner while at the same time the PLO recognises Israel. But, in retrospect, this was an illusion. Hamas had already overtaken the PLO together with its dominant faction, Fatah, on the ground in the West Bank and on the Gaza Strip.[88] The PLO had been ejected from the West Bank by the Jordanian government in 1971 and forced into exile to Lebanon. In turn, the PLO was ejected from Lebanon in 1982 and further forced into exile to the city of Tunis, the capital of Tunisia. Thus, when the First Intifada erupted in 1987 the PLO had no substantive nor meaningful presence on the ground in Palestine. The Oslo Accords of 1993 and 1995 may well be the high-water mark of the secular, Palestinian nationalism that defined the PLO. Indeed, in Palestine the geo-political meaning of the end of the Cold War in 1991 was the retreat of the USSR (or, subsequently, Russia or the Russian Federation) as a supporter of such ideology in practice. Moreover, it was an opportunity for post-revolutionary Iran to further its own geo-political aims in the region as the sponsor of organisations such as Hezbollah. It is in this context that suicide attacks become a prevalent feature of Palestinian resistance, reaching a peak during the Second Intifada.[89] What was once exceptional and extraneous to Israel itself, such as the bombing of the IDF headquarters' building in Tyre, Lebanon, in 1982[90] and 1983[91] and the bombing, also in 1983, of the Beirut barracks of the multinational force comprised of US marines and French paratroops,[92] became a usual terror on the very streets of the towns and cities of Israel. Suicide attacks only began to decline around 2002, after the construction of the physical barriers dividing the West Bank from Israel.[93]

'the coastline and water that I see from my garden'[94]

The coastal headland of Wharley Point[95] rises to a height of 109 metres above sea level, from where it overlooks the confluence of three rivers: Tâf, Tywi and Gwendraeth. Ferries would traverse the waters here, in all seasons, once, summoned back and forth by wayfarers who would strike the ferry bell in its small stone-built tower sitting squat on the banks of the river. Osi Rhys Osmond would walk to there from Bristol House in Llansteffan, where he lived, in less than an hour. During the last months of his life, and his long battle with cancer, he would abide in that place each day, and there he would paint the sun as it fell over the horizon in the west.[96] Of that same setting, he produced a series of watercolour paintings, and of which no two are alike, each a unique moment: 'What I have left is evidence ... The evidence is what will speak.[97] ... These watercolours of the sunset are my way of holding on to the beauty of the earth and to the wonder of life itself', he explained, just before the end.[98] He had his own language for that place, according to Clare Sturges: yr Awyr-Le, the Sky-Place.[99]

Beneath lies the river Tâf, languid and grey. On the far bank sits Laugharne, and the empty boathouse of Dylan Thomas. Laugharne: Treflan Lacharn in the Welsh language, where feudal bonds still tie,[100] and a thousand years pass in the blink of an eye.[101] The bell tolls. The ferry crosses. The tide turns. Upriver, along the pilgrims' path, lies a pair of churchyards: Llanfihangel Abercywyn and Llandeilo Abercywyn.

Photograph 1 *The distaff grave, Llanfihangel Abercywyn*

They face each other across the Cywyn, a modest tributary of the Tâf. There, the Pilgrim's Rest is to be found.[102] In the burial ground of St Michael's Church is the distaff grave (Photograph 1).[103] Medieval in age, a body was exhumed from there once and found sharing the space of the grave were the cockleshells of the penitent and of the pilgrim. The gravestone is feminine: she holds in her right hand a distaff rod, a tool used in spinning, especially flax, to hold unspun fibres. Whatever she had held in her left hand is now gone. Upon her breast is a Maltese cross, and at either side of her head rest two creatures, perhaps hounds: Cŵn Ebrill?[104] The dogs of April: searchers of lost souls.

As the sun falls, the earth darkens from the east, and the people and places that the artist knows descend into shadow. Osmond would call Thomas to mind there often. He says it to himself as the poet-serf once wrote: 'Time held me green and dying / Though I sang in my chains like the sea'.[105] He would gaze over at Laugharne and see himself directing *Under Milk Wood*[106] in the streets of that ancient borough, dense and labyrinthine. 'He is buried there', he says. He would think of where he too will be buried. Such a small place. So of course it was there, along the two salt-marsh banks of the Tâf, that the English language literature of Wales was invented: Jones and Roberts and Thomas and Lewis; Cwm Celyn and Llanybri, Laques and Mwche, Rhooks and Heol Down. Literary critic Nerys Williams points out the immediate relevance of this to Osmond when she addresses that 'intractable question' of 'where might war be found' in art. While her principal concern is Welsh war poetry, by way of approaching her subject she notes of Osmond that his 'late paintings offer a complex negotiation of how ideas of home are inscribed by war'.[107] Amongst the poets is Lynette Roberts,[108] and surely she wrote what Osmond later painted. Alan Tucker frames it thus:

> The Roberts selection includes 'The Circle of C', included in *Poems*, which has the line: 'As a curlew stabbed the sand.' In a note the poet writes '…curlews crying at night are said to hunt for souls of the dead. I have used this image as an interpretation of the raiders droning over the estuary and the hill.'
> The most striking of her bird poems, 'Curlew:'
>
> > A curlew hovers and haunts the room
> > On bare boards creak its filleted feet:
> > For freedom intones four notes of doom,
> >
> > Crept, slept, wept, kept, under aerial gloom:
> > With Europe restless in his wing beat,
> > A curlew hovers and haunts the room:
>
> demonstrates the metaphysical dimension common to all Robert's best verse.[109]

Osmond too saw that 'curlews haunt' this landscape of 'neither air, nor earth, nor water',[110] where, nature and warfare collide. And similarly, Charles Mundye frames the image as follows:

> In an explanatory note to this poem appended to Faber's edition of her Poems (1944) she makes the same associations between the dogs of Annwn, Cwmcelyn, and the hoarstone,

or border stone, that she points out to Graves,[111] adding some further connections:

> The legend (of the Dogs of Annwn) is no doubt associated with Sirius and the third sea-track of the Phoenicians which may have guided those people to our shore: with Kerberos: and later to emerge as 'Cŵn Ebrill', when curlews crying at night are said to hunt for the souls of the dead. I have used this image as an interpretation of the raiders droning over estuary and hill; their stiff and ghostly flight barking terror into the hearts of the villagers.

This extends the poem text, connecting the dogs of Annwn to Cerberus at the gates of hell, and to the curlews whose eerie cry gives rise in Welsh folklore to the 'Cŵn Ebrill', the dogs of April.[112]

Mundye adds the following, by way of further framing, a little later in the same piece:

> But with the note there is a further resonance: the dogs of Annwn become the German bomber planes that had been active in South Wales through November and December 1940, and on 4 December the Manchester Guardian reported a Ministries of Air and Home Security communiqué which identified that on the previous night, the day upon which the poem was written, bombs were dropped on South Wales.[113]

Thus, Mundye concludes of the poems of Roberts that '[t]he metaphorical air is thick with the detritus of war's destruction'.[114] Or as Zoë Skoulding puts it elsewhere, simply, 'the cries of birds in her poems often morph into sounds of war', bringing 'the noise of conflict into local, domestic space'.[115]

This is the language too of Osmond, driven to speak in the moment by distant events felt local. The timetable for Osmond's witness to Operation Cast Lead in Gaza is remarkable in its alacrity. The war on Gaza, begun on 27 December 2008, concluded with a ceasefire on 18 January 2009. Osmond's work, *Ymateb/Response*, was on exhibition by the end of the month of May. His timetable was compelled by the immediacy of his emotional reaction to events on the ground, an immediacy that was manifest in the geography of Llansteffan, where he lived, as is clear from the reporting in the local press of the exhibition:

> In his highly emotive exhibition, he brings his personal experience of war and conflict quite literally onto our doorstep, with three drawings depicting large, chaotic scenes of war on Llansteffan beach and coastline. 'When they started bombing Gaza, I realised that the Gaza strip is about the same size as the coastline and water that I see from my garden in Llansteffan,' explained Osi. 'So I was struck by the image of a million-and-a-half people down there with bombs and rockets falling on them.' For Osi, this vision was further reinforced by the constant sound of bombing and machine gunning, which drifts over the water to Llansteffan from the military base in Pembrey. The exhibition, which consists of a body of paintings, three large drawings and several watercolours, takes the viewer on a series of emotional journeys and also reflects the artist's great love of poetry. Engraved within the three drawings are the words of the poets, Waldo Williams, Mahmoud Darwish and Frank Bidart.[116]

The militarisation of the beach at Llansteffan had been on his mind for a while, as is clear from his contribution to an edition of the BBC Radio 3 programme *Free Thinking* in 2008, where he says this of it: 'Here, a bombing range, jets scream in from the east, soar, climb and dive, tearing the sky apart ... On yellow sand ... small children play in the innocence of childhood. The bombs will fall in other times, on other people, in other places'.[117] He took up this theme again in 2010 in a series of paintings called *Hawk and Helicopter*, one of which, *Chinook*, was given as a gift by the Welsh government to the Flemish parliament in 2017.[118] While the art yet remained, the artist had passed by then and Israel and Gaza had been to war on three further occasions, in 2012 (twice) and 2014, and the Jerusalem Intifada too had been and gone.

★

Writing of kairos in its literary sense,[119] Daniel R. Schwarz notes that 'there are differences both in the duration and intensity of moments of kairos'.[120] This is most true for art as rhetoric. After all, *An Evil Cradling* is still read and *Ymateb/Response* still viewed. Of our witnesses, Colum McCann is the one who seems to bring this point most obviously to the fore. Writing in his essay from 2017, a text that anticipates his novel, the story ends as it begins, almost. McCann, along with the company of writers on their timely visit to Palestine, gather under a roof somewhere in the West Bank to hear the storytelling of the parallel lives of Rami Elhanan and Bassam Aramin. The scene is set: 'The darkness outside is descending'.[121] Stories told, the company departs: 'Outside the darkness has descended'.[122] But, the stories will be repeated, he asserts without any doubt whatsoever: 'They will be back again in a few days, to tell their stories again. Again and again and again. Until their dying days. Or until the days themselves are dead'.[123] Of course, McCann takes up the mantle of telling their stories in *Apeirogon*. And it seems likely that their stories will be further re-told by Steven Spielberg.[124] As with Keenan and Osmond, it is no coincidence that McCann makes clear the imperative of immediate witness. It is wholly purposeful of McCann to preface his essay from 2017 on the subject of his visit to the West Bank in that year with the following epigraph, attributed to Gaston Bachelard, French philosopher of poetics: '"What is the source of our first suffering?" It lies in the fact we hesitated to speak … It was born in the moment when we accumulated silent things within us'.[125]

Of course, it is obvious too that the timing of the book in which McCann's essay appears relates very straightforwardly to the occasion of the fiftieth anniversary of the Israeli occupation of the West Bank (1967–2017). Hence, the publishers of the volume describe it as 'a ground-breaking collection of essays by celebrated international writers bears witness to the human cost of fifty years of Israeli occupation of the West Bank and Gaza'.[126] Such anniversaries seem necessary. As with McCann, so also with Dervla Murphy. Upon returning from her visits to the West Bank in the period between November 2008 and December 2010, and in particular her visit to Gaza during the summer of 2011, Murphy writes in relation to drawing up her accounts of those experiences that 'on returning home I decided to write them at once'.[127]

The visit to Gaza was the earliest opportunity she had to travel there after the events of Operation Cast Lead. She had intended that her writings on this would form a part of a single book on Palestine but such was the impression left upon her by Gaza that during the process of writing up the material evolved into a whole, separate book. Hence, not only *Between River and Sea*[128] (2015)[129] but also *A Month by the Sea*. In actual fact, of course, it was the Gazan book that was written first. It is the fiftieth anniversary of the publication of her first book *Full Tilt*[130] and the year of the publication of *Between River and Sea* that frame the occasion of her 'evening in the company of' style event to speak on the case of Palestine. The event was supported by Pal Fest Ireland and the Ireland Palestine Solidarity Campaign, along with the Trade Union Friends of Palestine.[131] Also in 2015, on the occasion of the 'first anniversary of the last attack on Gaza', Murphy was the keynote speaker at a Q&A style session that followed the screening of the film *Tears of Gaza*.[132] As with Murphy, so with Keenan and *An Evil Cradling*: remembered and celebrated in 2015 on 'the 25th anniversary of his release from captivity in Beirut';[133] or in 2016, '30 years' after him being taken hostage;[134] or in 2009, on the occasion of the publication of his autobiographical text *I'll Tell Me Ma: A Belfast Memoir*, also noted as being twenty years after his release from captivity;[135] or the BBC documentary *Back to Beirut* of his return visit to Lebanon in 2007 televised 'eighteen years after he emerged blinking and bewildered from his evil cradling';[136] or drawn to comment with moral authority in the wake of the execution of hostage Kenneth Bigley in Iraq in 2004 by Jama'at al-Tawhid wal-Jihad, a paramilitary Jihadist group;[137] or, as recently as 2018, lending authenticity and humane dignity to performances of incarceration before an audience of the incarcerated.[138] Thus, immediacy but restatement too.

Notes

1 The reasoning behind adherence to this particular text is described as follows: 'Believing it to be the most reliable translation, the Free Presbyterian Church uses only the authorised Version (KJV) of the Bible.' Free Presbyterian Church of Ulster, *Distinctives of the Free Presbyterian Church of Ulster* (2014): https://www.freepresbyterian.org/distinctives/ (accessed 2 June 2023).
2 Ecclesiastes 3:1–8 (Authorised [King James] Version).
3 Ryan Patrick Kirby, 'A fourth rhetorical device: the role of kairos in narrative discourse', *Medium*, 27 April 2020: https://medium.com/age-of-awareness/a-fourth-rhetorical-device-the-role-of-kairos-in-narrative-discourse-6b78f2415e7f

4   Joanne Paul, 'The use of kairos in Renaissance political philosophy', *Renaissance Quarterly*, 67/1 (2014), 43–78, at 43.
5   Jane Sutton, 'Kairos', in Th. O. Sloan (ed.), *Encyclopedia of Rhetoric* (New York: Oxford University Press, 2001), pp. 413–7, at p. 413.
6   Michael Harker, 'The ethics of argument: rereading kairos and making sense in a timely fashion', *College Composition and Communication*, 59/1 (2007), 77–97, at 78.
7   See, for example, Kelly Pender, 'Kairos and the subject of expressive discourse', *Composition Studies*, 31/2 (2003), 91–106.
8   This is an extract from the first line of Seamus Heaney's poem 'Whatever you say, say nothing', *North* (London: Faber and Faber, 1975): *https://www.youtube.com/watch?v=OpDw5n_rb5I* (accessed 2 June 2023).
9   Selective mutism is 'a severe anxiety disorder where a person is unable to speak in certain social situations': *https://www.nhs.uk/mental-health/conditions/selective-mutism/* (accessed 2 June 2023).
10 The most authoritative single piece of research done on the extent of PTSD in NI is the following: Bamford Centre for Mental Health and Wellbeing, *Troubled Consequences: A Report on the Mental Health Impact of the Civil Conflict in Northern Ireland* (Belfast: Commission for Victims and Survivors, 2011). Amongst the results of this research is the insight that NI 'has the world's highest recorded rates of Post Traumatic Stress Disorder (PTSD), ahead of war-hit regions such as Israel and Lebanon' (The University of Ulster, *NI has World's Highest Rate of Post Traumatic Stress Disorder*, Press Release, 5 December 2011). For the literary expression of 'Northern Ireland's national PTSD' (Jim Ruland, 'The working-class Belfast-born author trying to reinvent the post-Troubles novel', *The Los Angeles Times*, 19 May 2023), see the debut novel by Michael Magee entitled *Close to Home*. For research on PTSD in conflicts in other parts of the world, see the following: Abdel Aziz Thabet, 'Post-traumatic stress reactions in children of war', *Journal of Child Psychology and Psychiatry*, 40/3 (1999), 385–91; Abdel Aziz Mousa Thabet, Yehia Abed and Panos Vostanis, 'Emotional problems in Palestinian children living in a war zone: a cross-sectional study', *Lancet*, 359/9320 (2002), 1801–4; Claudia Catani, 'Mental health of children living in war zones: a risk and protection perspective', *World Psychiatry*, 17/1 (2018), 104–5.
11 Ronit Lentin, 'Expected to live: women shoah survivors' testimonials of silence', *Women's Studies International Forum*, 23/6 (2000), 689–700.
12 Zoran Minderovic, *Shaping* (2021): *https://psychology.jrank.org/pages/581/Shaping.html* (accessed 2 June 2023).
13 Heaney, *Whatever You Say, Say Nothing*, Part III, Stanza 4, Line 1.
14 Whether the initial /t/ is capitalised or not varies from author to author: I use capita /t/, hence the Troubles.

15 Vivian, *Commonplace Witnessing*, p. 197.
16 Mac Giolla Chríost, *Jailtacht*.
17 CAIN Web Service, *Internment – A Chronology of the Main Events* (2021): https://cain.ulster.ac.uk/events/intern/chron.htm (accessed 2 June 2023).
18 John Mulqueen and Jim Smyth, '"The Che Guevara of the IRA": the legend of "Big Joe" McCann', *History Ireland*, 18/1 (2010): https://www.historyireland.com/troubles-in-ni/the-che-guevara-of-the-ira-the-legend-of-big-joe-mccann/ (accessed 2 June 2023).
19 Eamon Melaugh, 1972(?), *Official IRA 'Checkpoint' Lecky Road, Bogside, Derry*: https://cain.ulster.ac.uk/melaugh/portfolio3/f3p33.htm (accessed 2 June 2023).
20 McKittrick, Kelters, Feeney and Thornton, *Lost Lives*, p. 175.
21 The line is from the song 'Five to One' by the group *The Doors*, dating to 1968. I was reminded of it upon reading McCann's *Apeirogon* (p. 423, section 81): 'Eighteen years old: there are sometimes no ways out.'
22 Homeric Hymn 2, *To Demeter*, line 1: https://uh.edu/~cldue/texts/demeter.html (accessed 2 June 2023).
23 Homer, *The Odyssey*, Book 10, line 475: https://www.perseus.tufts.edu/hopper/text?doc=Perseus%3Atext%3A1999.01.0136%3Abook%3D10%3Acard%3D475 (accessed 2 June 2023) and Homer, *The Iliad*, Book 9, line 453: https://www.perseus.tufts.edu/hopper/text?doc=Perseus%3Atext%3A1999.01.0134%3Abook%3D9%3Acard%3D453 (accessed 2 June 2023).
24 This is to paraphrase lines 13–14, Part I, 'Act of Union' by Seamus Heaney, a sonnet also published in *North* (London: Faber and Faber, 1975).
25 The site is identified in the Compton report commissioned by the British government to investigate allegations of physical brutality against some of those interned: Edmund Compton, *Report of the Enquiry into Allegations Against the Security Forces of Physical Brutality in Northern Ireland Arising out of Events on the 9th August, 1971* (London: HMSO, 1971). Compton found evidence of 'ill treatment' but none of physical brutality: https://cain.ulster.ac.uk/hmso/compton.htm (accessed 2 June 2023).
26 The enquiry by Compton was followed in 1972 by a second inquiry, led by former Lord Chief Justice Hubert Parker: Lord Parker of Waddington, *Report of the Committee of Privy Counsellors Appointed to Consider Authorised Procedures for the Interrogation of Persons Suspected of Terrorism* (London: HMSO, 1972). In his report he found that, while some of the interrogation techniques used constituted criminal assault, they should continue, subject to the approval of a government minister and the oversight of a medical doctor with psychiatric training: https://cain.ulster.ac.uk/hmso/parker.htm (accessed 2 June 2023). The European Commission on Human Rights found the British government in breach of the European Convention on Human Rights in 1976, determining that the techniques constituted torture. The

European Court of Human Rights ruled in 1978 that, whilst in breach of the Convention, the techniques constituted inhuman and degrading treatment but not torture.

27 Samidoun. Palestinian prisoner solidarity network, *1981 Solidarity Message from Palestinian Prisoners to Irish Hunger Strikers*, 8 May 2012: https://samidoun.net/2012/05/1981-solidarity-message-from-palestinian-prisoners-to-irish-hunger-strikers/ (accessed 2 June 2023).

28 Samidoun. Palestinian prisoner solidarity network, *Solidarity to Bilal, Thaer and the Hunger Strikers from Irish Striker Laurence McKeown*, 7 May 2012: https://samidoun.net/2012/05/solidarity-to-bilal-thaer-and-the-hunger-strikers-from-irish-striker-laurence-mckeown/ (accessed 2 June 2023) and Noreen Sadik, 'Global solidarity for Palestinian hunger strikers', *New Internationalist*, 18 December 2012: https://newint.org/blog/2012/12/18/hunger-strike-palestinian-prisoners (accessed 2 June 2023). There have been many hunger-strikes by Palestinians held in the Israeli prison system. See, for example, Zena Tahhan, 'A timeline of Palestinian mass hunger strikes in Israel', *Al Jazeera*, 28 May 2017: https://www.aljazeera.com/news/2017/5/28/a-timeline-of-palestinian-mass-hunger-strikes-in-israel (accessed 2 June 2023).

29 Samidoun. Palestinian prisoner solidarity network, *Irish Republican prisoners' statement of solidarity with Palestinian political prisoners*, 15 May 2017: https://samidoun.net/2017/05/irish-republican-prisoners-statement-of-solidarity-with-palestinian-political-prisoners/ (accessed 2 June 2023).

30 Jewish Virtual Library, no date, *Marwan Barghouti*: https://www.jewishvirtuallibrary.org/marwan-barghouti (accessed 2 June 2023).

31 BBC News, *Profile: Marwan Barghouti*, 2 June 2011: https://www.bbc.co.uk/news/world-middle-east-13628771 (accessed 2 June 2023).

32 James Bennet, 'Jailed in Israel, Palestinian symbol eyes top post', *The New York Times*, 19 November 2004: https://www.nytimes.com/2004/11/19/world/middleeast/jailed-in-israel-palestinian-symbol-eyes-top-post.html (accessed 2 June 2023).

33 Abeer Baker, no date, *The Definition of Palestinian Prisoners in Israeli Prisons as 'Security Prisoners' – Security Semantics for Camouflaging Political Practice*, 65–78: https://www.adalah.org/uploads/oldfiles/Public/files/English/Publications/Review/5/Adalahs-Review-5-65-Baker-Definition-Security-Prisoners.pdf (accessed 2 June 2023). Baker is quoting from two sources, namely paragraph 1(A) of the Israeli Prison Service Commission directive of 4 May 2000 and paragraph 1(B) of the same organisation's directive of 3 February 2000. See also Hedi Viterbo, 'Security Prisoners', in O. Ben-Naftali, M. Sfard, and H. Viterbo (eds), *The ABC of the OPT: A Legal Lexicon of the Israeli Control over the Occupied Palestinian Territory* (Cambridge: Cambridge University Press, 2018), pp. 383–98.

34 *http://www.geocities.com/lawrenceofcyberia/palbios/pa06000.html* (accessed 2 June 2023).

35 MEMO, 'B'Tselem: Israel is committing war crimes in Gaza Strip', *Middle East Monitor*, 18 May 2021: *https://www.middleeastmonitor.com/20210518-btselem-israel-is-committing-war-crimes-in-gaza-strip/* (accessed 2 June 2023).

36 *https://www.idf.il/en/articles/defense-and-security/israel-under-fire/* (accessed 2 June 2023).

37 Nesma Seyam, 'Learning the enemy's language', *The Electronic Intifada*, 11 August 2016: *https://electronicintifada.net/content/learning-enemys-language/17661* (accessed 2 June 2023).

38 Aloysius Wong and Terence McKenna, 'Who is Yahya Sinwar, the Hamas political leader in Gaza?' *CBC News*, 1 December 2023: *https://www.cbc.ca/news/world/yahya-sinwar-hamas-leader-gaza-1.7042283* (accessed 8 February 2024). He has been leader of Hamas since August 2024, following the assassination of Ismail Haniyeh.

39 European Council on Foreign Relations, 'Yahya Sinwar', *Mapping Palestinian Politics* – *https://ecfr.eu/special/mapping_palestinian_politics/yahya_sinwar/* (accessed 8 February 2024).

40 The Editors of Encyclopedia Britannica, 'Yahya Sinwar', *Encyclopedia Britannica*, 8 February 2024: *https://www.britannica.com/biography/Yahya-Sinwar* (accessed 8 February 2024).

41 Ivana Kottasová and David Shortell, 'Who is Yahya Sinwar, the Hamas leader Israel has called a "dead man walking"', *CNN*, 8 December 2023: *https://edition.cnn.com/2023/12/07/middleeast/yahya-sinwar-profile-intl/index.html* (accessed 8 February 2024).

42 Frank Gardner, 'Yahya Sinwar: who is the Hamas leader in Gaza?' BBC News, 21 November 2023: *https://www.bbc.com/news/world-middle-east-67473719.amp* (accessed 8 February 2024).

43 Rasha Abou Jalal, 'Palestinians learning Hebrew for strategic advantage', *Al Monitor*, 22 September 2015: *https://www.al-monitor.com/originals/2015/09/gaza-hamas-teach-hebrew-israel-conflict.html* (accessed 2 June 2023).

44 Israel Ministry of Foreign Affairs, 2014, *The Kidnapper's Handbook by Hamas*: *https://mfa.gov.il/MFA/ForeignPolicy/Terrorism/Palestinian/Pages/The-Kidnapper-Handbook-by-Hamas.aspx* (accessed 2 June 2023).

45 Mark Landler, 'Trump recognizes Jerusalem as Israel's capital and orders U.S. Embassy to move', *The New York Times*, 6 December 2017: *https://www.nytimes.com/2017/12/06/world/middleeast/trump-jerusalem-israel-capital.html* (accessed 2 June 2023).

46 John Irish and Robin Emmott, 'Trump's Jerusalem plan revives tensions in EU diplomacy', *Reuters*, 8 December 2017: *https://www.reuters.com/article/*

us-usa-trump-israel-france/u-s-has-excluded-itself-from-middle-east-peace-process-france-idUSKBN1E2102 (accessed 2 June 2023).

47 Dan Williams and Nidal al-Mughrabi, 'Hamas calls for Palestinian uprising over Trump's Jerusalem plan', *Reuters*, 7 December 2017: https://www.reuters.com/article/us-usa-trump-israel/hamas-calls-for-palestinian-uprising-over-trumps-jerusalem-plan-idUSKBN1E11BR?feedType=RSS&feedName=topNews (accessed 2 June 2023).

48 Al Jazeera, 'Fatah, Hamas say deal reached on Palestinian elections', *Al Jazeera*, 24 September 2020: https://www.aljazeera.com/news/2020/9/24/fatah-hamas-say-deal-reached-on-palestinian-elections (accessed 2 June 2023).

49 He is more commonly known by Israelis and Palestinians alike as Abu Mazen, meaning 'the father of Mazen'. Mazen is the name of Abbas's first-born son. He died in 2001. See https://legacy.npr.org/programs/day/transcripts/2005/feb/050210.bowers.html (accessed 2 June 2023).

50 Al Jazeera, 'Abbas delays Palestinian parliamentary polls, blaming Israel', *Al Jazeera*, 30 April 2020: https://www.aljazeera.com/news/2021/4/30/palestinians-polls-hamas-plo (accessed 2 June 2023).

51 Wikipedia, *2021 Israel–Palestine Crisis*: https://en.wikipedia.org/wiki/2021_Israel%E2%80%93Palestine_crisis (accessed 2 June 2023).

52 BDS (the acronym for the movement known as Boycott, Divestment, Sanctions) self-describes its aim as 'to end international support for Israel's oppression of Palestinians and pressure Israel to comply with international law' arguing that '[i]n many countries, governments and corporations are deeply complicit with Israel's decades-old regime of military occupation, settler-colonialism and apartheid, just as they were complicit in the apartheid regime in South Africa': https://bdsmovement.net/ (accessed 2 June 2023).

53 This Bill, fully titled as the Control of Economic Activity (Occupied Territories) Bill 2018, reached the Third Stage in the Irish parliament before being stalled by the government in December 2020: https://www.oireachtas.ie/en/bills/bill/2018/6/ (accessed 2 June 2023).

54 Marie O'Halloran and Ellen O'Riordan, 'Ireland becomes first EU country to declare Israel is involved in "de facto annexation"', *The Irish Times*, 27 May 2021: https://www.irishtimes.com/news/politics/oireachtas/ireland-becomes-first-eu-country-to-declare-israel-is-involved-in-de-facto-annexation-1.4576250 (accessed 2 June 2023); Dáil Éireann debate – Tuesday, 25 May 2021. Vol. 1007 No. 5 Annexation of Palestine: Motion (Private Members): https://www.oireachtas.ie/en/debates/debate/dail/2021-05-25/9/?highlight%5B0%5D=annexation (accessed 2 June 2023) and Dáil Éireann debate – Wednesday, 26 May 2021. Vol. 1007 No. 6 Annexation of Palestine: Motion (Resumed) (Private Members): https://www.oireachtas.ie/en/debates/debate/dail/2021-05-26/17/?highlight%5B0%5D=annexation (accessed 2 June 2023).

55 Michael Hauser Tov, 'Israel election: Bennett backs unity with Lapid, inching closer to unseating Netanyahu', *Haaretz*, 30 May 2021: https://www.haaretz.com/israel-news/elections/.premium-bennett-backs-unity-with-lapid-inching-closer-to-unseating-netanyahu-1.9858937 (accessed 2 June 2023).

56 Human Rights Watch, *A Threshold Crossed: Israeli Authorities and the Crimes of Apartheid and Persecution*, 27 April 2021: https://www.hrw.org/report/2021/04/27/threshold-crossed/israeli-authorities-and-crimes-apartheid-and-persecution (accessed 2 June 2023).

57 Philip Weiss, '"Disgraceful" "anti-Semitic" "hatchet job" – HRW's "apartheid" report draws blood from Israel lobby', *Mondoweiss*, 28 April 2021: https://mondoweiss.net/2021/04/disgraceful-antisemitic-hatchet-job-hrws-apartheid-report-draws-blood-from-israel-lobby/ (accessed 2 June 2023). For a legalistic rebuttal of the HRW report, see Joshua Kern, 'Uncomfortable truths: how HRW errs in its definition of "Israeli apartheid", what is missing, and what are the implications?', *EJIL: Talk! Blog of the European Journal of International Law*, 7 July 2021: https://www.ejiltalk.org/uncomfortable-truths-how-hrw-errs-in-its-definition-of-israeli-apartheid-what-is-missing-and-what-are-the-implications/ (accessed 2 June 2023).

58 Clive Baldwin and Emile Max, 'Human Rights Watch responds: reflections on apartheid and persecution in international law', *EJIL: Talk! Blog of the European Journal of International Law*, 9 July 2021: https://www.ejiltalk.org/human-rights-watch-responds-reflections-on-apartheid-and-persecution-in-international-law/ (accessed 23 January 2024), p. 6.

59 John Dugard and John Reynolds, 'Apartheid, international law, and the Occupied Palestinian Territory', *European Journal of International Law*, 24/3 (August 2023), 867–913.

60 Dugard and Reynolds, 'Apartheid', p. 913.

61 The invocation of the term 'making the desert bloom' is replete with historical political meaning, implying that the transformation of this particular part of the Middle East into a prosperous country has been singularly and uniquely wrought by the Jewish people as they created the State of Israel. See, for example, Zina Rakhamilova, 'Israel made the desert bloom – this is fact, not racism', *The Jerusalem Post*, 2 May 2023: https://www.jpost.com/opinion/article-741801 (accessed 11 January 2024).

62 Reuters, 'Israeli minister repeats call for Palestinians to leave Gaza', *Reuters*, 31 December 2023: https://www.reuters.com/world/middle-east/israeli-minister-repeats-call-palestinians-leave-gaza-2023-12-31/ (accessed 11 January 2024) and Al Jazeera, 'Israeli minister reiterates calls for Palestinians to leave Gaza', 31 December 2023, *Al Jazeera*: https://www.aljazeera.com/news/2023/12/31/israeli-minister-reiterates-calls-for-palestinians-to-leave-gaza (accessed 10 January 2024).

63 Zeeshan Aleem, 'What Israel's plan to "encourage" migration out of Gaza is actually about', *MSNBC*, 7 January 2024: *https://www.msnbc.com/opinion/msnbc-opinion/israel-ethnic-cleansing-voluntary-migration-emigration-ben-gvir-rcna132378* (accessed 8 January 2024).

64 Amy Goodman, '"Utterly illegal": UN Special Rapporteur slams Netanyahu's "voluntary migration" plan for Gazans', *Democracy Now!*, 29 December 2023: *https://www.democracynow.org/2023/12/29/utterly_illegal_un_special_rapporteur_slams* (accessed 11 January 2024).

65 Ilan Pappé, *The Ethnic Cleansing of Palestine* (London: Oneworld Publications, 2006).

66 Lazar Berman, 'Netanyahu vows no Palestinian state, attacks Israeli media, denies blindsiding Gallant', *The Times of Israel*, 18 January 2024: *https://www.timesofisrael.com/netanyahu-vows-no-palestinian-state-attacks-israeli-media-denies-blindsiding-gallant/* (accessed 23 January 2024).

67 Emma Graham-Harrison and Toby Helm, 'Netanyahu defies Biden, insisting there's "no space" for Palestinian state', *The Guardian*, 20 January 2024: *https://www.theguardian.com/world/2024/jan/20/netanyahu-defies-biden-insisting-theres-no-space-for-palestinian-state* (accessed 23 January 2024).

68 Tal Schneider, Jacob Magid and Times of Israel Staff, 'Gallant's post-war Gaza plan: Palestinians to run civil affairs with global task force', *The Times of Israel*, 4 January 2024: *https://www.timesofisrael.com/gallants-post-war-gaza-plan-palestinians-to-run-civil-affairs-with-global-task-force/* (accessed 11 January 2024).

69 This road is, apparently, known by the codename Highway 749. It is also known as the Netzarim Corridor. See, for example, The New Arab staff, 'Israel's Netzarim Corridor to split Gaza in two with Ramadan deadline on Rafah assault', *The New Arab*, 19 February 2024: *https://www.newarab.com/news/israeli-corridor-set-split-gaza-two-amid-rafah-assault* (accessed 10 March 2024). See, also Abdirahim Saeed, Tom Spencer, Paul Brown and Richard Irvine-Brown, 'IDF completes road across width of Gaza, satellite images show', *BBC News*, 9 March 2024: *https://www.bbc.co.uk/news/world-middle-east-68514821* (accessed 10 March 2024). Netzarim was once a Jewish settlement, understood as illegal under international law. Its residents were the last to leave Gaza as a part of Israel's disengagement from Gaza in 2005. During Operation Cast Lead, in January 2009, the IDF temporarily re-occupied Netzarim.

70 For example, *Sky News*, 13 December 2023: *https://www.youtube.com/watch?v=FYOv_Jb8cA0* and *C4 News*, 13 November 2023: *https://www.youtube.com/watch?v=trm0IFwsz-o* (accessed 12 January 2024).

71 Robbins, 'Beyond the suffering subject', p. 455.

72 Robbins characterises this in terms of the philosophical concept of 'right action'. See, for example, Michael Slote, 'Right action', in T. Honderich

(ed.), *The Oxford Companion to Philosophy* (Oxford: Oxford University Press, 1995), pp. 774–6.
73 Middle East Eye, 'Ilan Pappe on Israel: "We are witnessing the beginning of the end"', *Middle East Eye*, 7 December 2024: https://www.youtube.com/watch?v=cB2_wgUd8Os (accessed 12 January 2024) and Makdisi Street, 'The beginning of the end of the Zionist project? With Ilan Pappé', *Makdisi Street*, 12 December 2023: https://player.fm/series/makdisi-street/the-beginning-of-the-end-of-the-zionist-project-w-ilan-pappe (accessed 12 January 2024).
74 Robbins, 'Beyond the suffering subject', p. 448.
75 Middle East Eye, '"I Am Personally Proud of the Ruins in Gaza," Says Israeli Minister May Golan', https://www.youtube.com/watch?v=Ya-dN9D4Y0E (accessed 5 March 2024). See also the discussion of this remark at the press briefing of the US Department of State on 21 February 2024: https://www.state.gov/briefings/department-press-briefing-february-21-2024/ (accessed 5 March 2024). A member of the press corps asked of the spokesperson for a response to the remark, noting with shock that 'this [May Golan] is not someone extremist. It's not Smotrich. It's not Ben-Gvir. This is in the Prime Minister's, Benjamin Netanyahu's party'.
76 Keenan, *An Evil Cradling*, p. ix.
77 Sebastian Faulks, 'Book review / An awful odyssey of the mind: An Evil Cradling – Brian Keenan: Hutchison', *The Independent*, 3 October 1992: https://www.independent.co.uk/arts-entertainment/book-review-an-awful-odyssey-of-the-mind-an-evil-cradling-brian-keenan-hutchinson-pounds-16-99-1555370.html (accessed 2 June 2023).
78 Faulks, 'Book review'.
79 See, for example, Elizabeth Mehren, 'The strength to survive', *The Los Angeles Times*, 14 October 1993: https://www.latimes.com/archives/la-xpm-1993-10-14-vw-45765-story.html (accessed 2 June 2023); Christopher Dickey, 'Too horrible to tell', *The Los Angeles Times*, 24 October 1993: https://www.latimes.com/archives/la-xpm-1993-10-24-bk-49000-story.html (accessed 2 June 2023); and Eugene Kennedy, 'Kidnapped in Beirut', *The New York Times*, 24 October 1993: https://www.nytimes.com/1993/10/24/books/kidnapped-in-beirut.html (accessed 2 June 2023).
80 Le Monde and AFP, 'Le corps de Michel Seurat enfin identifié', *Le Monde*, 1 February 2006: https://www.lemonde.fr/proche-orient/article/2006/02/01/le-corps-de-michel-seurat-enfin-identifie_736587_3218.html (accessed 2 June 2023) and Marie-Pierre Subtil, 'Marie Seurat, une histoire san fin', *Le Monde*, 19 January 2006: https://www.lemonde.fr/societe/article/2006/01/19/marie-seurat-une-histoire-sans-fin_732426_3224.html (accessed 2 June 2023).
81 Keenan, *An Evil Cradling*, p. xi.

82 The seminal paper is James W. Pennebaker and Sandra Klihr Beall, 'Confronting a traumatic event: towards an understanding of inhibition and disease', *Journal of Abnormal Psychology*, 95/3 (1986), 274–81.
83 Keenan, *An Evil Cradling*, pp. xi–xv.
84 See, for example, Ralph Riegel, 'State papers reveal the genesis of Northern peace process', *Independent*, 27 December 2020: https://www.independent.ie/irish-news/secret-state-papers-reveal-the-genesis-of-northern-peace-process-39902886.html (accessed 2 June 2023).
85 Sinn Féin, *Towards a Lasting Peace in Ireland* (1992): https://www.sinnfein.ie/contents/15212 (accessed 2 June 2023).
86 Sinn Féin, *John Hume/Gerry Adams Statement 23 April 1993*: https://www.sinnfein.ie/contents/15217 (accessed 2 June 2023).
87 *Joint Declaration on Peace: The Downing Street Declaration*, Wednesday 15 December 1993: https://cain.ulster.ac.uk/events/peace/docs/dsd151293.htm (accessed 2 June 2023).
88 Al Jazeera, 2009, *Did the PLO die in Lebanon?*, 28 July 2009: https://www.aljazeera.com/program/plo-history-of-a-revolution/2009/7/28/did-the-plo-die-in-lebanon (accessed 2 June 2023).
89 David Helmer, 'Hezbollah's employment of suicide bombing during the 1980s: the theological, political, and operational development of a new tactic', *Military Review*, July–August (2006), 71–82: https://www.armyupress.army.mil/Portals/7/military-review/Archives/English/MilitaryReview_20060831_art012.pdf (accessed 2 June 2023) and Michael C. Horowitz, 'The rise and spread of suicide bombing', *Annual Review of Political Science*, 18 (2015), 69–84.
90 Sixty-seven IDF soldiers, Israeli Border Police officers and secret service agents were killed as a result of this attack. Fifteen Lebanese and Palestinian prisoners being held in the building were also killed, according to Israeli government figures: https://www.shabak.gov.il/english/heritage/affairs/Pages/TheTyreHQBombing.aspx (accessed 2 June 2023).
91 Twenty-eight IDF soldiers, Israeli Border Police officers and secret service agents, along with thirty-one Lebanese prisoners, were killed as result of this attack, according to Israeli government figures: https://www.shabak.gov.il/english/heritage/affairs/Pages/TheTyreHQBombing.aspx (accessed 2 June 2023).
92 Not including the two suicide bombers, 299 American and French soldiers and six civilians died as a result of this attack.
93 Hillel Frisch, 'Motivation or capabilities? Israeli counterterrorism against Palestinian suicide bombings and violence', *Mideast Security and Policy Studies*, 70: https://besacenter.org/wp-content/uploads/2006/12/MSPS70.pdf (accessed 2 June 2023) and *Journal of Strategic Studies*, 29 (2006), 843–69.
94 Osi Rhys Osmond quoted in 'Powerful paintings in Oriel Q', *The Western Telegraph*, 9 June 2009: https://www.westerntelegraph.co.uk/leisure/

localentertainmentnews/4427945.powerful-paintings-in-oriel-q/ (accessed 2 June 2023).

95　Royal Commission on the Ancient and Historic Monuments of Wales (2021), *List of Historic Place Names. Recorded Name: Wharley Point*: https://historicplacenames.rcahmw.gov.uk/placenames/recordedname/3084cf42-6ce6-4f34-9b2c-fe365ed32206 (accessed 2 June 2023).

96　Clare Sturges, *My Brief Eternity. Ar Awyr Le* (2015): *https://claresturges.co.uk/my-brief-eternity-1* (accessed 2 June 2023). Literally translated, *ar awyr le* means 'at sky-place'.

97　Osmond quoted in Sturges, *My Brief Eternity*, 11 min., 37 sec.

98　Osi Rhys Osmond, *Machlud/Sunset* (2013): *https://osirhysosmond.wordpress.com/machlud/* (accessed 2 June 2023).

99　Osmond quoted in Sturges, *My Brief Eternity*, 3 min., 35 sec.

100　George Tremlett, *Laugharne Corporation. Founded AD 1290* (J. D. Lewis (Carmarthen) Ltd, 2007).

101　This is a nod not only to the peculiar continuity of some features of feudalism in shape of Laugharne Corporation but also to the strength of the protestant non-conformist tradition in this part of Wales, being an echo of Psalm 90: 4 (Authorised (King James) Version): 'For a thousand years in thy sight are but as yesterday when it is past, and as a watch in in the night.'

102　See *https://dyfedarchaeology.org.uk/HLC/EstuaryArea/area154.htm* (accessed 2 June 2023).

103　See *https://howardwilliamsblog.wordpress.com/2016/10/05/exploring-the-medieval-tombs-in-the-ruined-churchyard-of-st-michael-at-llanfihangel-abercowyn-carmarthenshire/* and also *https://coflein.gov.uk/en/site/102138/* (accessed 2 June 2023).

104　Cŵn Ebrill – 'fanciful name given to curlews, esp. when their cries are heard at night during spring' (lit. April dogs)', *Geiriadur Prifysgol Cymru. A Dictionary of the Welsh Language*: *https://welsh-dictionary.ac.uk/gpc/gpc.html?ci* (accessed 2 June 2023).

105　Dylan Thomas, 'Fern Hill' (1945): *https://poets.org/poem/fern-hill* (accessed 2 June 2023). The poem was first published in Horizon magazine in 1945, and subsequently published in the volume *Deaths and Entrances* (J. M. Dent) in 1946.

106　The 1954 BBC radio drama by Dylan Thomas, although it had its first reading in 1953, in the month of May, at the Poetry Center in New York, with Thomas himself playing the role of 'First Voice'. By the time the drama was broadcast by the BBC Thomas was dead, having passed away in Greenwich Village, New York in November 1953. Osmond directed a performance of the drama on the streets of Laugharne in 2006.

107 Nerys Williams, 'Where is war poetry? Part one', *Wales Arts Review* (2019): https://www.walesartsreview.org/where-is-war-poetry-part-one/ (accessed 2 June 2023).

108 Roberts is described in the blurb to the 2005 edition of the main collection of her poems, *Lynette Roberts: Collected Poems*, edited by Patrick McGuinness (Carcanet Press, Manchester), as 'principally a war poet'.

109 Alan Tucker, *Lynette Roberts: Collected Poems. Patrick McGuinness, Editor. Carcanet Press Ltd, Reviewed by Alan Tucker*, n.d.: https://www.flashpointmag.com/tucklyn.htm (accessed 2 June 2023).

110 Osi Rhys Osmond, *On Drawing* (unpublished fieldnote, c.2009/10).

111 Robert Graves (1895–1985), English 'poet, novelist, critic, mythographer, translator and editor': https://www.poetryfoundation.org/poets/robert-graves (accessed 2 June 2023).

112 Page 3 (online) in Charles Mundye, 'Outside the Imaginary Museum: mythology and representation in the poetry of Lynette Roberts and Keidrych Rhys', *Pn Review*, 40/2 (2013), 23–9: https://shura.shu.ac.uk/27908/1/Outside%20the%20Museum%20-%20Roberts%20and%20Rhys%202013%20%282%29.pdf (accessed 2 June 2023).

113 Mundye, 'Outside', p. 4.

114 Mundye, 'Outside'.

115 Zoë Skoulding, 'Lynette Roberts: Welsh poet who fused touch and sight into sound', *The Conversation*, 2 January 2019: https://theconversation.com/lynette-roberts-welsh-poet-who-fused-touch-and-sight-into-sound-105703 (accessed 2 June 2023).

116 'New exhibition opens at Oriel Q gallery', *Pembroke and Pembroke Dock Observer*, 29 May 2009: https://www.pembroke-today.co.uk/article.cfm?id=1968&headline=New%20exhibition%20opens%20at%20Oriel%20Q%20gallery&sectionIs=news&searchyear=2009 (accessed 2 June 2023).

117 'Wales, within Britain, is no longer a country for and says 'Hwyl Fawr' to an old artist called Osi Rhys Osmond', 13 March 2015: https://britainisnocountryforoldmen.blogspot.com/2015/03/wales-within-britain-is-no-longer.html (accessed 2 June 2023). See also https://www.bbc.co.uk/radio3/freethinking/2008/free-thought/osi-rhys-osmond.shtml (accessed 2 June 2023).

118 https://osirhysosmond.wordpress.com/exhibitions-events/ (accessed 2 June 2023).

119 The piece by Schwarz, from 1985, is a review article of Frank Kermode, *The Sense of An Ending: Studies in the Theory of Fiction* (Oxford: Oxford University Press, 1967).

120 Daniel R. Schwarz, 'The consolation of form: the theoretical and historical significance of Frank Kermode's "The Sense of an Ending"', *The Centennial Review*, 28/4–29/1 (Fall 1984–Winter 1985), 29–47, at 36.

121   Colum McCann, 'Two stories, so many stories', in M. Chabon and A. Waldman (eds), *Kingdom of Olives and Ash: Writers Confront the Occupation* (London: HarperCollins, 2017), pp. 389–404, at p. 390.
122   McCann, 'Two stories, so many stories', p. 404.
123   McCann, 'Two stories, so many stories', p. 404.
124   Narrative 4, 'Amblin nabs Israeli–Palestinian friendship novel "Apeirogon" (exclusive)', 2 November 2020, *Narrative 4*: *https://narrative4.com/spielbergs-amblin-partners-acquires-apeirogon-film-rights/* (accessed 2 June 2023).
125   McCann, 'Two stories, so many stories', p. 389.
126   The quotation is taken from the publisher's description of the volume on their website: *https://www.harpercollins.com/products/kingdom-of-olives-and-ash-michael-chabonayelet-waldman?variant=32207717433378* (accessed 2 June 2023).
127   Murphy, *A Month by the Sea*, p. xvi.
128   The title is a clear reference to the Palestinian nationalist slogan 'min al-nahr ila al-bahr – from the river to the sea'. For groups such as the PLO up until the Oslo Accords, and then Hamas after that point, the slogan was adopted because of its implication that the territory between the River Jordan and the Mediterranean Sea ought to comprise a single, indivisible Palestinian state. Some scholars indicate that the slogan is meant to stipulate also 'the obliteration of the Jewish state': see David Patterson, *A Genealogy of Evil: Anti-Semitism from Nazism to Islamic Jihad* (Cambridge: Cambridge University Press, 2011), p. 249. It also implies the imposition of 'the rule of Islam': see David Cook, *Contemporary Muslim Apocalyptic Literature* (Syracuse, NY: Syracuse University Press, 2005), p. 138. David Rich notes in 2010 that the slogan was 'ubiquitous in anti-Israel demonstrations' in the UK: see p. 124 in David Rich, 'The very model of a British Muslim Brotherhood', in B. Rubin (ed.), *The Muslim Brotherhood: The Organization and Policies of a Global Islamist Movement* (New York: Palgrave Macmillan, 2010), pp. 117–36. Other commentators argue to the contrary, and that the term implies the creation of an inclusive form of state in the region. See, for example, Maha Nassar, '"From the river to the sea": doesn't mean what you think it means', *Forward*, 3 December 2018: *https://forward.com/opinion/415250/from-the-river-to-the-sea-doesnt-mean-what-you-think-it-means/* (accessed 2 June 2023). In a rather surprising departure, perhaps, the former Israeli ambassador to South Africa, Tova Herzl, recently pointed out on the pages of *The Jerusalem Post* that the vision of the current government in Israel whereby 'the Jewish people' have an 'eternal, inalienable and exclusive right' to 'the Land of Israel' is, problematically, the mirror image of the claim made by Palestinian nationalists of the land 'between the river and the sea', noting that '[t]he Palestinian side's call for one entity between the river and the sea reads as though it was taken from the guidelines of our current government': Tova

Herzl, 'We have no right to criticize "From the River to the Sea" – opinion', *The Jerusalem Post*, 7 May 2024: *https://www.jpost.com/opinion/article-800150* (accessed 8 May 2024).

129   Dervla Murphy, *Between River and Sea: Encounters in Israel and Palestine* (London: Eland, 2015).

130   Dervla Murphy, *Full Tilt: Ireland to India with a Bicycle* (London: John Murray, 1965).

131   Ireland Palestine Solidarity Campaign, *From River to Sea: Encounters in Palestine and Israel – An Evening with Dervla Murphy*, 21 October 2015, Eden Quay, Dublin: *https://www.ipsc.ie/event/dublin-from-river-to-sea-encounters-in-palestine-israel-an-evening-with-dervla-murphy* (accessed 2 June 2023). The event was cancelled due to ill health.

132   Ireland Palestine Solidarity Campaign, *(Bantry) Film Screening: Tears of Gaza + Q&A with Dervla Murphy and Elaine Bradley (IPSC)*, 17 July 2015, Bantry, County Cork: *https://www.ipsc.ie/event/bantry-film-screening-tears-of-gaza-qa-with-dervla-murphy-elaine-bradleyipsc* (accessed 2 June 2023).

133   The Belfast Telegraph, 'Belfast boys: we profile ex-Beirut hostage Brian Keenan', *The Belfast Telegraph*, 21 August 2015: *https://www.belfasttelegraph.co.uk/life/features/belfast-boys-we-profile-ex-beirut-hostage-brian-keenan-31468636.html* (accessed 2 June 2023).

134   Siobhán Breatnach, 'Beirut hostage Brian Keenan: 30 years on from the Irishman's unimaginable kidnapping', *The Irish Post*, 12 April 2016: *https://www.irishpost.com/news/beirut-hostage-brian-keenan-30-years-irishmans-unimaginable-kidnapping-85914* (accessed 2 June 2023).

135   Joanna Moorhead, 'Life is sweet for Brian Keenan', *The Guardian*, 12 September 2009: *https://www.theguardian.com/lifeandstyle/2009/sep/12/brian-keenan-dublin-hostage* (accessed 2 June 2023).

136   Sam Wollaston, 'Last night's TV: Brian Keenan: Back to Beirut', *The Guardian*, 1 April 2008: *https://www.theguardian.com/culture/tvandradioblog/2008/apr/01/lastnightstvbriankeenanba#comment-1756102* (accessed 2 June 2023).

137   The Independent, 'Brian Keenan; "a man can take away my freedom, but he can't ever take my liberty"', *The Independent*, 7 November 2004: *https://www.independent.co.uk/news/people/profiles/brian-keenan-a-man-can-take-away-my-freedom-but-he-can-t-ever-take-my-liberty-18735.html* (accessed 2 June 2023).

138   Barry Roche, 'Decadent Theatre company to stage excerpts from hostage drama in Cork Prison', *The Irish Times*, 18 February 2018: *https://www.irishtimes.com/news/ireland/irish-news/decadent-theatre-company-to-stage-excerpts-from-hostage-drama-in-cork-prison-1.3396498* (accessed 2 June 2023).

CHAPTER 3

Making the Witness

In these times, we are all witnesses, as Bradford Vivian explains:

> The capacious logic of witnessing as we find it in modern and late modern public culture entrusts many different subjects with at least sufficient knowledge and authority to disseminate important social, political, and moral truths regarding historical atrocity and tragedy. Popular authors, politicians, citizens, tourists, and the like function as witnesses (in addition to those who directly experienced injustice or trauma) by adopting, or rhetorically inventing, commonplace idioms of witnessing.[1]

No longer is it a prerequisite of witnessing to have been there, to have suffered, or to have felt the suffering of others first hand. Rather, the witness is fashioned from materials other than immediate experience. For the creative artist it is made from their identity as an artist, an identity that is, in turn, only realised within a community of practice.[2] Much more than this, however, as Givoni implies,[3] the extent to which the metamorphosis of artist into witness succeeds depends upon the ability of the individual artist to bring new ethical and political subjectivities into being. It is upon this particular form of creativity, both aesthetic and moral, that the trust of public culture in the artist as witness is contingent.

Self

The creative artist may, with conviction, construct from their own imagination authentic witnesses of a fictional nature, as does the Irish author Sally Rooney in her novel from 2018 entitled *Normal People*:

> They went to a protest against the war in Gaza the other week with Connell and Niall. There were thousands of people there, carrying signs and megaphones and banners. Marianne wanted

her life to mean something then, she wanted to stop all violence committed by the strong against the weak, and she remembered a time several years ago when she had felt so intelligent and young and powerful that she almost could have achieved such a thing, and now she knew she wasn't at all powerful, and she would live and die in a world of extreme violence against the innocent, and at most she could help only a few people.[4]

But the contemporary style of witnessing seems to call for more than seeing and recounting in the abstract; it asks for engagement and activism also. In the case of Rooney, a novel of her making, namely *Beautiful World, Where Are You?* (2021), became a vehicle for pro-Palestinian activism when she prevented its translation into Hebrew by an Israeli company in an act of support for the BDS movement.[5] Much controversy followed.[6] It was also noted by several news outlets that Rooney had earlier in the year signed a public letter entitled *A Letter Against Apartheid* condemning Israel as a 'settler colonial' state that practices apartheid: 'there is no separation between the Israeli state and its military occupation: the two form a single apartheid system'.[7] Perhaps Rooney feels that the author as witness, the activist-artist, may help more than only a few people? Her authority and credibility as a witness, as presented in public discourse fora, are derived from her status as a successful writer. Thus, she is characterised as an 'Irish literary prodigy', a 'bestselling Irish author', and 'one of the premiere millennial authors' by RT, a brand of the Russian news agency TV-Novosti.[8] Similarly, she is identified as an 'award-winning Irish author' by *The Daily Mail*,[9] and as an 'acclaimed Irish author'[10] and 'star author'[11] by *The Forward*.

Colum McCann too had signed *A Letter Against Apartheid*. And McCann too is described as Rooney is: an 'award-winning',[12] bestselling author whose work of fiction, *Apeirogon*, has something 'to say to a seemingly endless real world battle'.[13] And while *Apeirogon* has been translated into 'several languages', amongst which is Arabic, there is no mention of a Hebrew translation.[14] As with Rooney again, McCann's profile as an activist derives from his identity as a novelist, as is made clear from his personal profile on the website of the NGO Narrative 4:

> Colum McCann is President and Co-Founder of Narrative 4, which he began to help shape in 2004. He is the author of

six novels and three collections of stories. Born and raised in Dublin, Ireland, he has been the recipient of many international honours, including the National Book Award, the International Dublin Impac Prize, a Chevalier des Arts et Lettres from the French government, election to the Irish Arts Academy, several European awards, the 2010 Best Foreign Novel Award in China, and an Oscar nomination. In 2017 he was elected to the American Academy of Arts. His work has been published in over 40 languages. His most recent novel, *Apeirogon*, was released in February 2020 and was a New York Times bestseller, and winner of several international prizes.[15]

As an NGO, Narrative 4 aims at 'creating narratives for peace, narratives for the environment, and narratives for social justice' through an approach it describes as 'radical empathy'.[16] *Apeirogon* may be read in that context.

In his interview with *Prospect Magazine* McCann self-describes as a middle-class Irish person, noting also that perhaps his being Irish has helped in the writing of the novel, implying an inherent Irish empathy for the case of Palestine. He wrote the novel, says McCann, out of a 'reckless inner need', an obsessive interest in the problem of the Israel–Palestine conflict. No mere object of distant obsession, McCann is at pains to emphasise that he has visited Palestine several times and has spent very considerable periods of time with each of his biographical subjects, Rami and Bassam, both in their homes in Israel and Palestine as well as at events in New York and elsewhere.[17] Moreover, McCann contends that given our own familiarity with Palestine and with the ancient city of Jerusalem in particular, none of us are innocent of the story of this conflict; rather we are all of us 'complicit' as 'all of us have visited there [Jerusalem] in one form or another'.[18]

Our complicity may be manifest in a number of ways. It may, perhaps, take the form of some of our political representatives sitting on their hands. For example, Claudio Francavilla of HRW, writing in February 2023, expresses alarm at the 'silence, inaction, and denialism' of the EU (Ireland remains a member state of the EU, of course) in response to the increasing numbers of killings by IDF in the West Bank along with the expansion of illegal Jewish settlements and the demolition of Palestinians' homes.[19] Francavilla's alarm is framed by the declaration by Prime Minister Benjamin Netanyahu of a guiding principle of his new government that 'all the territory between the Jordan River and Mediterranean Sea belongs to the Jewish people'[20] and them alone: 'These are the basic lines of the national government headed by me: The Jewish people have an exclusive and indisputable right to all areas of the Land of Israel. The government will promote and develop settlement in all parts of the Land of Israel – in the Galilee, the Negev, the Golan, Judea and Samaria'.[21] The complicity may be historical: Britain (of which Wales remains a constituent nation albeit with a devolved government) is the author of the Balfour Declaration, a document that is for many in the Arab world the root cause of the conflict in Palestine, tantamount to a 'gun to the head' of the Palestinian people.[22] However, by way of transcending our complicity, we may position ourselves so that we become a part of what Michael Ignatieff calls the 'internationalization of conscience'[23] and in our own witness, even as mere visitors with a tale to tell on our return home, we may even be drawn to consider what we might do to change the situation, as Gill Rye explains in her work on ethics, aesthetics and trauma fiction:

> Here, the ones who bear witness, the readers ..., are invited to take an active part in the ethical process of working through ... to interrogate our own responsibility in relation to the wars and atrocities that are still proliferating in our time, and to what is being done to fellow human beings in their name.[24]

In other words, the act of witnessing entails speaking out, advocacy, social activism.

Despite the unequivocal nature of *A Letter Against Apartheid* McCann also asserts that as an 'artist' who 'listens' it is not for him 'to judge' nor to tell people 'what to think' and that the 'most important thing' for him was 'not to be didactic' so that people 'can make up their own story about it'. He adds that there have been 'good reads' of *Aperiogon* from the 'various sides that are going on' in relation to the conflict in Palestine. Significantly, perhaps, he falls back upon Walt Whitman during the course of the interview, quoting the American poet on the inner multitudes and inherent contradictions of the self, drawing specifically from Section 51 of the poem *Song of Myself*:

> Do I contradict myself?
> Very well then I contradict myself,
> (I am large, I contain multitudes.)

In this sense it might be said that McCann is self-consciously adopting that which Susan Jarratt and Nedra Reynolds describe in relation to the analysis of rhetoric as 'split selves', or 'guises', something that allows him to adopt apparently multiple positions.[25] In other words, McCann presents differently to his various publics, as a novelist-activist facing a literature-reading public, on the one hand, and as an activist-novelist facing a politically engaged audience, on the other hand. Thus, McCann conforms with Johanna Schmertz's insight that 'ethos may be dislodged from identity' thereby allowing a rhetor to speak from multiple positions.[26] Or as Nedra Reynolds puts it, 'ethos, like postmodern subjectivity, shifts and changes over time, across texts, and around competing spaces'.[27] The self on its own is, however, inadequate in this context. McCann usefully describes the process of writing *Apeirogon* as a journey of personal education regarding the conflict in Palestine as well as presenting it as a type of rhetorical statement on the issue. In other words, to paraphrase Kate Ronald, *Apeirogon* is an exercise in both the persuasion of McCann and also of his audience. Thus, rhetoric here is conceived of as 'an internal way of knowing' as well as being a 'method of communication'.[28]

Additionally, the self is inadequate on its own in making ethos but instead it is made by the rhetor acting together with the audience. As Karen Burke LeFevre puts it, ethos 'appears in that socially created space, in the "between", the point of intersection between speaker or writer and listener or reader'.[29] Ethos thereby works in its appeal to the audience in terms of both ethics and character. The audience trusts the rhetor because of her character or due to the ethical manner in which she presents her argument. Ethical appeals therefore have two facets: (1) audience values and (2) authorial credibility and character. The rhetor in her argument invokes the sense of right held by the audience, in this case the injustices of Palestine, while the extent to which the argument has an impact upon the audience depends upon how the audience conceives of the credibility and character of the rhetor. In this manner the expertise of McCann as a novelist is essential to the extent to which his rhetoric carries weight. The qualities of his character are equally crucial. Observant, intelligent, measured, engaged, insightful: these are the qualities he projects in his interviews and public performances. Given the importance of character in the persuasion of others, it is crucial for the rhetor to know how this is comprehended by her audience.[30] Thus, while one might work upon one's own credibility and character as a rhetorician, ethos is in the gift of the audience, it is a communal construct.

Community

John Oddo's intertextual approach to rhetoric adroitly draws our attention to how a rhetor's ethos is made, or constituted, by the audiences or communities to which or via which the rhetor is making her appeal.[31] He also argues that ethos is made across the range of platforms, or texts, which the rhetor uses as her medium of communication. It is in this sense too that our rhetoricians, as witnesses, are situated in a distinctive genealogy of witnessing, a certain type of regime of witness, as creative practitioners that are a part of a community of practice that is comprised of not only their audience but also those other parties who are engaged in the production of their art, such as gallery owners, publishers, editors and curators, as well as their practitioner peers, their fellow artists. It is the case therefore that, even as their professional autonomy is bound to certain institutional platforms, the creative artists use their professional identity to insert themselves into the political field. In this context, therefore, the creative artists' ethea variously correspond to that of 'spokesperson of a public',[32] of 'defiant truth-tell(er)' as Michal Givoni puts it,[33] and of practitioner of non-governmental politics as critical practice as Judith Butler puts it.[34]

Evidence of such a community of practice is very salient indeed in relation to Osi Rhys Osmond in the form of an encomium entitled *Encounters with Osi* that was begun during the last months of his life but ultimately published posthumously:[35] Osmond had sight of the various contributions to the book in draft form before he passed. The different contributors to the volume reflect Osmond's engagement with bodies such as the Arts Council of Wales, the Welsh nationalist political party Plaid Cymru (also identified in the English language as the Party of Wales),[36] CND (the Campaign for Nuclear Disarmament),[37] Cymdeithas y Cymod (also identified in English as the Fellowship of Reconciliation in Wales),[38] the community of the village of Llansteffan,[39] the Eisteddfod (in English, the National Eisteddfod of Wales),[40] and Gorsedd Cymru (once known as the Gorsedd of the Bards of the Isle of Britain),[41] and the University of Wales Trinity St David (UWTSD), amongst others. Their texts can be easily read as testimonies to Osmond as a witness. For example, Dai Smith, who was Chair of the Arts Council of Wales when Osmond was one of its members, says this of him in the book:

> He has a European sensibility, set within comparative traditions and practices, observed and absorbed. Osi is a graphic historian. Osi is a visual intelligence operating in the mode of a public intellectual. Osi is, within himself, a palimpsest of his subject, scoured clean and scrubbed over, until it emerges transformed, and made translucent by his hand and through his mind.[42]

In his contribution, Iwan Bala places Osmond in a community of politically aware artists through comparing him directly to renowned 'art critic, essayist and novelist' John Berger.[43] Bala, like Osmond, is himself a practising artist based in south Wales, and, similarly, was once a lecturer in art at the local university, namely the UWTSD, and, of course, also like Osmond, has been a regular exhibitor at the Eisteddfod. And, as Osmond too once was, he is a member of the Arts Council of Wales. Bala says this of Osmond: 'He reminds me of John Berger ... an equally polymathic educator'.[44] Another contributor, Karl Francis, is a highly regarded film maker and television director, one time Head of Drama at BBC Wales. Notable, amongst other things, for his documentary programme entitled *Chekov in Derry* for C4 in 1983 on the staging of *The Three Sisters* by the Field Day Theatre Company,[45] Francis declares quite simply that Osmond possessed and articulated an 'intelligence' of the same nature as John Berger.[46]

It is surely significant that Osmond was reading *Hold Everything Dear* by Berger whilst he was working on *Ymateb/Response*. The Berger volume was a birthday gift to Osmond from an artist friend at that time precisely for the reason that it was known that he was doing something substantial on Palestine. Berger recounts in *Hold Everything Dear* making drawings whilst in Palestine in a manner that Osmond would, surely, have wholly identified with. First of all, take how he captures the desert and its sky:

If you contemplate this desert ('the Judean desert between Jerusalem and Jericho'), you quickly discover that it's a landscape whose gaze is totally directed towards the sky. A question of geology, not biblical history. It hangs there beneath the sky like a hammock. And when it's windy it twists like a winding sheet. As a result, the sky appears to be more substantial, more urgent, than the land.[47]

Then, read how Berger's notebook seems an emotional facsimile of Osmond's:

> I want to do a drawing for Abdelhamid Kharti ... I've chosen to draw the hills looking eastwards. I sit on a rock near a small blackish tent. I have only a notebook and this pen ... Suddenly frustrated by my lack of pigment, I pour water from the mug on to the dust at my feet, dip my finger into the mud and smear colour across the drawing of the animal's head. The sun is hot now. A mule brays. I turn the pages of the notebook to begin another and another. Nothing looks finished.[48]

And then, feel the disorientated sense of place Berger and Osmond both attune to:

> I have never seen such a light before. It comes down from the sky in a strangely regular way, for it makes no distinction between what is distant and what is close. The difference between far and near is one of scale, never of colour, texture or precision. And this affects the way you place yourself, it affects your sense of being here.[49]

Finally, hear the argument for the cause of Palestine that they share:

> And so I am here, a figure in a dream that some of my ancestors in Poland, Galicia and the Austro-Hungarian Empire must have nurtured and spoken about for at least two centuries. And here I unhesitatingly identify myself with the just cause and the pain of those whom the state of Israel (and cousins of mine) are afflicting to a degree that is tragically totalitarian.[50]

That the back cover to Berger's book carries on its cover extracts from positive reviews of it that had been published on the pages of *The Times*, *The Times Higher Educational Supplement*, *Metro* and *The Times Literary Supplement* lends weight and authority to it as a piece of persuasive writing in the eyes of both Berger and Osmond's community of practice.

The individual who gifted *Hold Everything Dear* to Osmond, Christine Kinsey, herself a practising artist, says this of him in *Encounters with Osi*:

> Osi has asked the question 'What is art for?' in an age of ubiquitous visual imagery. He answers the question through the wealth of visual imagery that he has created through painting which he says 'brings into physical form, painting and poetry, those thoughts, images and realisations for which no other means of being apprehended exists'.[51]

What is art for? It is for cultural activism. This is the conclusion drawn of Osmond by another contributor, namely the prominent Welsh language poet and language activist Menna Elfyn.[52] Significantly, as regards Osmond's immediate community of practice, Elfyn too has been a lecturer at UWTSD. She brings the artist and the activist in Osmond together, making them inseparable, when she says this of him: 'Contemplation and the need to be vocal and bear witness seem to me to be the two sides of Osi's personality, which have endeared him to all who know and admire him'.[53] Fellow activist with Cymdeithas y Cymod, the prominent Welsh language poet Mererid Hopwood casts Osmond in the same mould as Elfyn does when she says the following of him: 'From Wattsville, Sirhowy to the end of the world, all people are Osi's brothers and sisters'.[54] Note here too that Hopwood was also once a lecturer at UWTSD. Perhaps I should, in addition, make it clear here that I too was once a lecturer at UWTSD.

Osmond's sense of belonging to a broad sphere of Welsh language activism and cultural sensibility is reflected in a conversation between him and the presenter Beti George on the Welsh-language radio programme *Beti a'i Phobl* (English translation: Betty and Her People).[55] The programme is in the style of *Desert Island Discs* and for one of his records he chose a folk song by Gwenan Gibbard entitled 'Adar man y mynydd' (English translation: The small birds of the mountain),[56] explaining that he did so because he felt that birds relate especially to poetry, the most popular and highly regarded cultural form in Wales in Osmond's opinion. By way of evidence, he referred to the medieval poet Dafydd ap Gwilym and to the late R. S. Thomas (1913–2000). The latter is particularly apposite for Osmond to have specified given his active support of CND along with his expressions of sympathy for the radical Welsh-language organisation Meibion Glyndŵr and its struggle to secure the traditional Welsh-speaking heartlands of north and west Wales.[57]

Another from Osmond's community of practice, Lynne Crompton, once the curator of the art gallery named Oriel Q, in Narberth in west Wales, describes his exhibition *Ymateb/Response*, which she curated for Oriel Q, as something that 'stands out in my memory [as a] powerful response to the political situation in the Middle East'.[58] Similarly, Steve Wilson, a practising artist and former student of Osmond's, says that,

> it is his work on depicting the military presence in Wales and beyond that has left the deepest impression … to put this in context, a million people marched on London in 2003 to make it clear that war was not acceptable, I saw the coachloads of protesters leaving from west Wales, I was present at the local vigils. [His work] was the first time I saw Palestine in a contemporary rather than a Biblical context … Osi represents the views of many in his work; it resonates particularly with those who feel their voices are not heard.[59]

And Sam Vicary, curator, practising artist and former student of Osmond, echoes much of these sentiments when she says the following:

> The work (*Ymateb/Response*) was disturbing, uncomfortable, compelling and often very beautiful. It carried the harrowing message of war and the atrocities happening to the people of Gaza … The exhibition was a huge success, the conversation was interesting and people left feeling like they had connected with the artist and understood his visual language.[60]

This connection with his audience, some imagine, is replicated amongst the people he encountered and painted in Palestine. It is for this reason that Ali Anwar, the sponsor of *Encounters with Osi* and a native of the Middle East, says of Osmond that '[p]eople in these places call him "Rassam" which means painter in Arabic'.[61] Osmond exemplifies the creative artist becoming a witness as self and audience work upon one another in developing his ethos. But, according to Givoni, in turn borrowing from Foucault, a further step is required in this process of becoming, namely that of subjective transformation: the artist must 'become other than who they were'.[62]

Metamorphosis

One could say that Osmond became other than who he was. Indeed, it is clear from his final words, from an interview with Ann Oosthuizen just before his death, that this was something that he hoped he had succeeded in bringing about: 'I hope my painting has changed over the years, as I have changed'.[63] Osi Rhys Osmond, of course, was born Donald Malcolm Osmond in Bristol to Welsh parents. He was known as 'Don' by his siblings,[64] but became known as 'Ozi' to his wider community as an adult, and then became 'Osi'. Thus, says his son Luke, he was Ozi 'before he Welshified it',[65] or as it is put by John Barnie, the editor of the Welsh magazine *Planet*, 'the Cymricisation to "Osi" came later'.[66] And yet, even then, he was still, sometimes, Donald, and playfully so, as his adopted daughter Sara makes clear.[67] Rhys, most importantly, was adopted from his second wife, Hilary Rhys. For Osmond, his subjective remaking implicated every aspect of his life including language for it was after meeting Hilary and moving to live in Bristol House, Llansteffan, during the second half of the 1980s, just after his first visit to Palestine, that he set to it to learn 'o ddifrif' (English translation: seriously) the Welsh language and to master it as his own tongue.[68]

Becoming other than who they were, as Givoni says, is a process whereby the witness is understood to be 'a persona that individuals desire to be, need to become, and must work on themselves in order to craft'.[69] In other words, it is best that the witness is 'no longer construed as something that one *is*' but rather that the witness is 'something that one seeks to *become*'.[70] In so working on themselves, the individual thereby realises a new sense of self. As Givoni puts it, 'Acts of witnessing … are not concerned with the exposure and reaffirmation of a pre-existing identity but rather with the creation of ethical and political subjectivities that did not exist prior to them'.[71] And this new self is a moral and politically engaged actor in which 'witnessing and testimony

[are] polyvalent instruments of self-fulfillment, moral concern, and political indignation'.[72] Witnessing, as defined by Givoni, being the act and testimony being its discursive form.[73] This explains the phenomenon noted by Bradford Vivian at the outset of the chapter, namely the contemporary proliferation of the witness. Givoni puts it as follows:

> The reconfiguration of the witness as a daunting mode of being that has to be pro-actively assumed and the concomitant embracing of crises of witnessing as catalysts for the formation of new subjectivities are key ... to the impressive variety of contemporary forms of witnessing and, even more importantly, to its ethical transformation in the political sway.[74]

Moreover, argues Givoni, such subjective transformation is an inevitable feature of contemporary forms of witnessing. Thus: 'one of the decisive features of the "era of witness" has been the reframing of witnessing and testimony as gestures that, given the proper guidance and support, are bound to instigate a subjective transformation and not just produce empirical or metaphysical truths'.[75] This transformation has certain qualities, according to Givoni, and in particular that of the existential realisation of the moral self. She borrows this from Foucault's conception of ethics as 'care of the self', as follows: 'According to Foucault, ethics encompassed the cluster of discourses and practices that individuals adopted so as to style their own lives as meaningful and worthy endeavours'.[76]

This, in turn, has certain political and practical implications. As regards politics, the contemporary forms of witnessing are essential to what Givoni describes as non-governmental politics, which may be understood as the condition of being engaged in political activity, often related to the work of NGOs or civil society organisations or social movement groups, without holding as an end goal being a part of the task of governing. She concludes that, 'ethical witnessing has been to nongovernmental politics what discipline has been to the modern state: a procedure whose thrust is to bring into being the moral subjects that liberal citizenship – whether in its state or non-state version – requires and presupposes'.[77] Thus, to become a witness is to become a moral subject in which a sense of personal responsibility for the state of world is foregrounded, upon which ethically motivated intervention in the world is premised:

As I sought to show, the contemporary prominence of witnessing and testimony hinges on the new arenas of action they have fostered by allowing for the relations between truth and politics to be treated as a matter of personal responsibility, and by mobilizing truth in order to bring the care of the self and the commitment to others more closely together.[78]

One ought to be reminded here that, as with us all, Givoni is herself a witness too. More than this, she is, in her own terms, complicit in the Israeli occupation. In this regard she is no different to any other citizen of the State of Israel, as she points out:

Since the Israeli public is as much a part of the occupation regime as the occupation regime is a part of it – since in Israel there is both a soldier in every family and a potential witness in every house – critical detachment is a privilege that Israelis do not have, or at least, a desire that cannot be pursued in any purposeful manner.[79]

This complicity is a defining feature of the public sphere in Israel; it is 'sweeping'.[80] But, of course, let us be reminded too that McCann says that we are all complicit in the condition of Jerusalem.

Complicity and subjective transformation cohere in Brian Keenan as a witness to the agony of Palestine. Upon his release from captivity as a hostage in Beirut, Keenan confessed to being broken but confesses also to a sense of there being more of him at that moment than there had been of him before, somehow. He says it like this:

I feel like a cross between Humpty Dumpty and Rip Van Winkle – I have fallen off the wall and suddenly I find all the pieces of me, before me.// There are more parts than I began with.// All the King's horses, and all the King's men, cannot put Humpty together again.// Brian Keenan, Dutch Embassy, Damascus, 24th August 1990.[81]

Who puts Keenan together again? Keenan himself, along with a 'sea of faces and names':[82] a community of family, friends, fellow-writers and fellow-poets, editors and publishers, professional carers, the people of

Westport, and others from Dublin and from Belfast. Humpty Dumpty: the egg that must be broken. Perhaps Keenan too had in mind at that moment the cameo played by that egg in *Through the Looking-glass*. Humpty Dumpty: philosopher of language, scholar of semantics: "'When I use a word,' Humpty Dumpty said in rather a scornful tone, 'it means just what I choose it to mean – neither more nor less.' 'The question is,' said Alice, 'whether you can make words mean so many different things.' 'The question is,' said Humpty Dumpty, 'which is to be master – that's all.'" Keenan's complicity is that of a Belfast protestant, the oppressor caste in Northern Ireland. His complicity is that of being a child of the British Empire, the former imperial power in the region and architect of the Balfour Declaration and its poisonous legacy. There is more than an echo here of the purposeful self-implication that Vivian Gornick intuits in those personal narratives that eschew sentimental self-regard and thereby offer the depth of personal inquiry that moves them 'from essay and into memoir'.[83] Keenan's complicity is also that of being a westerner in the Middle East, a part of a new colonial adventurism, of increasingly forceful American intervention there. After all, he took up a post as a lecturer in English at the American University of Beirut. Perhaps he even knew at the time that some of the American faculty at the university availed themselves of Irish passports in order to remain there, given that the American government had banned US citizens from travelling to Lebanon due to the pervasive violence of the Lebanese Civil War.[84]

Keenan's subjective transformation is to do with claiming with confidence Irish nationality for himself, despite him being a protestant from NI, and also with his development as a serious writer. In regard to these two things, Keenan identifies himself with the figure of Suibhne mac Colmáin, king of Dál nAraidi in the north-eastern corner of Ulster, and his being driven to madness during the course of the battle of Moira, fought in the northern part of Ireland in the year AD 637, an event described by O'Keeffe in the definitive version of the text as being of 'great importance in Irish history'.[85] Keenan makes this explicit in the chapter entitled 'Music' in *An Evil Cradling*:

> Over the next few weeks I wrote about thirty poems. I can only remember that when I sat one evening in the candlelight trying to reread them I discovered with shock and amazement

that the madness of my diary was multiplied tenfold. For here was a body of poetry, some of it well crafted, other parts of it at least illuminating. A body of work which I could not believe was any part of me. It was as if I had seen my face again in the spoon and had failed to recognise it. This poetry, it seemed, was written by someone other than myself. It delighted me, yet I could hardly bear to see, not so much the words themselves, but the man who had put them there: Mad Sweeny hiding in his tree of words.[86]

The Mad Sweeny to whom Keenan refers here is, of course, Suibhne mac Colmáin, also known as Suibhne Geilt in Irish,[87] is the eponymous hero of the Irish language medieval prosimetrum *Buile Shuibhne* or *Buile Suibhne*, meaning the madness, or frenzy, of Sweeney.[88] The body of poems to which Keenan refers are the product of his decision, whilst held in his hostage cell, to write the 'memoir' of his captivity 'in the code of poetry'.[89] His subsequent discovery of these poems sometime later, whilst still held in his hostage cell, was accompanied by a sense that these poems of his had been written by another self, suggesting some intuition of ongoing subjective transformation, of the creation of a new Brian Keenan. Keenan came to Beirut as a national award-winning poet. He composed poetry during his captivity, but that work remained unpublished. Instead, he crafted *An Evil Cradling*, a work described by reviewers as 'beautifully and movingly written' and in which '[t]he poet is everywhere present'[90] and as 'beautiful and adroit' and in which the 'poet is omnipresent'.[91]

His choice of Mad Sweeny as the vehicle for articulating this reworking of the self is rich in meaning. After all, the poet laureate of Ireland's northern Troubles, Seamus Heaney, had recently published his own translation-cum-adaptation of *Buile Shuibhne*, entitled *Sweeney Astray*.[92] According to Stephen Regan, it is clear that Heaney identifies with Mad Sweeny, just as Keenan too does. Indeed, Regan reminds us that the poet remarked playfully in an interview at the time that, 'Sweeney is rhymed with Heaney autobiographically as well as phonetically'.[93] More specifically, Regan reminds us that the literary critic, poet, novelist, and fellow native of Derry, Seamus Deane, saw in *Buile Shuibhne* the 'story of a poet caught in the midst of atrocity and madness'.[94] Regan's own careful examination of Heaney's personal writings as he worked up the idea for his own version of the medieval prosimetrum reveals that Heaney saw further parallels between himself and Sweeney, including the fact that he found himself in exile from the north as Sweeney too had been exiled. Thus, he records, 'In a notebook that he used for draft translations of the eighty-seven verse and prose sections of *Buile Suibhne,* Heaney wrote at the top of a page: "Left Ulster myself/ allegory"'.[95] Moreover, that Sweeney is metamorphosed into a 'bird' or at the very least has 'bird-like' qualities,[96] and at the same time becomes transformed from warrior-king into poet-witness, is crucial to understanding the appeal to Heaney. That alternative subjectivities pertain to Sweeney has, for Heaney, enormous creative and aesthetic possibilities:

> As Neil Corcoran points out 'Sweeney' in 'Sweeney Redivivus' is the name for a personality, a different self, a congruence of impulses, a mask antithetical to much that the name 'Seamus Heaney' has meant in his previous books. One of those impulses is an obsessive revisiting and surveying of the poet's own early life and work, as if from the distant aerial perspective of a bird, combined with a new determination to fly beyond it.[97]

This is the witness-becoming process of the remaking of the self. Keenan and Heaney, therefore, respond to the same quality of metamorphosis in *Buile Shuibhne,* seeing in it the necessity of the creation of a new guise so that the poet may become a witness.

Regan, drawing upon Irish cultural critic Terence Brown, adds that one of the challenges confronting Heaney in the creation of *Sweeney Astray* was in 'balancing the aesthetic impulse with the ethical and social demands of the political crisis',[98] thereby drawing our attention to the imperative to bear witness, to comment upon the state of the world and how it ought to be. Keenan's version of subjective transformation entails identifying with an Irish, as opposed to British, sensibility. In other words, Keenan casts from him the ethno-sectarian labels of his upbringing and remakes his self as an Irish national. Regan feels that Sweeney calls to mind Terence MacSwiney, the Irish republican who died in Brixton prison following a hunger strike of seventy-four days. So famous was he that he was buried three times – in London, Dublin, and then in Cork.[99] By extension, Regan argues that Sweeney calls to mind also the Irish republican hunger strike of 1981 in which ten men died in the H-blocks of HMP the Maze.[100] Perhaps Keenan had the same intuition when he called Mad Sweeny to mind in his hostage cell: the significance of the hunger strike as a political tool to Irish republicanism was certainly on his mind. He refers to it in his description of his own, brief hunger strike whilst held in captivity.[101]

He lays claim to his Irish identity several times during the course of *An Evil Cradling*. For example, when first taken, Keenan declared to his 'Kalashnikov-toting' captors even as they bundled him into the back of a car that he was not English but instead Irish: 'At this point I sat up quite determined: "No … I am not English, I am Irish … Irlandais." They look shocked and puzzled'.[102] It would become an oft-repeated mantra, as if he too had to become used to the sound of the phrase. He took up the same refrain with his subsequent captors: 'He asked me "Are you English?" I noted that his English was an educated one. He spoke it well and I answered him. "No, I am not English … I am Irish"'.[103] And he did so again with a later set of captors, declaring to them, 'I am not American. I am not British. I am Irish'.[104]

A part of that Irishness is an engagement with Irish nationalism, including with the Irish republican prisoners that took part in the hunger strike of 1981. Keenan undertook a hunger strike of his own whilst held captive, understanding that '[h]unger-strike is a powerful weapon in the Irish psyche. It overcomes fear in its deepest sense. It removes and makes negligible the threat of punishment. It powerfully commits back into the hunger striker's own hands the full sanction of his own life and of his own will'.[105] At another point during his period of captivity Keenan refused to wear the clothes provided to him by his captors as to do so would be 'an act of submission … a capitulation'.[106] He explained this action to his fellow captive, John McCarthy, who was hesitant to join with Keenan in his act of protest, in terms of the experience of Irish republican prisoners in their refusal to wear prison uniforms:

> To calm myself, maybe to strengthen my resolve, I talked with John at some length about the 'dirty protest', in the prisons of the North of Ireland. They were an act of defiance and resistance, a means of holding yourself together against an absolute condemnation. It was a way of insisting more to oneself than to the world that one was innocent. I wanted to affirm that I was myself and would not allow my integrity to be taken from

me by a surrender to what another believed or would make me be ... Something in me – Irish stubbornness, the refusal to surrender no matter what the consequences – meant I could not take and wear these clothes.[107]

Of course, to say 'the North of Ireland', instead of NI, is to invoke an Irish republican worldview. In this regard, Keenan's transformation foreshadows the emergence of the Irish 'nationalist' northern protestant as a player in the peace process that culminated in the Belfast Agreement of 1998.[108] In some sense, therefore, Keenan's subjective transformation heralds a transformed NI. *An Evil Cradling* is a provocative title for his prosimetrum because a cradle is the place where something begins, a place of origin, the earliest period of life. What he is saying in the title is that Beirut was the cradle of new Keenan, wholly transformed.

Since the publication of *Venice* by Jan Morris (then James Morris) in 1960, one can say with some confidence that the genre of travel writing certainly offers, as Givoni puts it, 'a replicable trajectory of self-making':[109] the travelogue is a journey of self-reinvention as well as being a voyage to a place. Dervla Murphy is a case in point. Her transition from pro-Zionist, Irish nationalist to anti-Zionist internationalist is captured in her body of work as a celebrated travel writer. It is with something of a confessional tone that she writes in *Between River and Sea* that during her youth, prior to the creation of the State of Israel in 1948, she was 'a juvenile Irish nationalist with rabid tendencies' and that as such she 'admired the anti-British Zionist militias'[110] of the Haganah, Irgun and Lehi.[111] By the time she writes both *A Month by the Sea* (2013) and *Between River and Sea* (2015) she self-describes as 'being anti-political Zionism, and therefore anti-Israel as the state is at present constituted'.[112] Her journey on this matter, it could be said, is also the journey taken by Ireland in which initial sympathy for the anti-British, anti-imperialist Jew in Palestine is gradually eclipsed by affinity for the cause of the Palestinian Arabs.[113]

Intriguingly, Murphy was initially reluctant to pen her testimony as a witness to Palestine. She says, 'back home, I didn't want to talk to anyone about my impressions – much less write about them. Normally, at journey's end, I at once settle down to work – remaining mentally and emotionally in the place I'm writing about. But for weeks I shirked remaining with the Palestinians'.[114] Perhaps she was cowed by the failure of such testimonies to accumulate? After all, Murphy prefaces *A Month by the Sea* with a quotation from the psychoanalyst Martin Kemp[115] in which he laments 'the apparent inconsequentiality' of such acts of witnessing.[116] In commenting in particular on the despair of activists on the Israeli left-wing regarding their inability to influence the end of the occupation, Givoni writes that '[the] testimonies keep piling up and yet somehow refuse to accumulate',[117] indicating that the power of testimony is becoming 'illusive',[118] and in turn suggesting that, for some, 'testimony, unsettling though its contents may be, is as politically futile as it is morally tantalizing'.[119]

Murphy does not take this view. Rather, she was eventually persuaded to write when 'a few friends … devised a cunning therapy, reminding me that the Palestinians need people with access to the media to expose their sufferings and honour their quite extraordinary courage and resilience'.[120] In addition, these friends suggested to Murphy that 'a travel writer's book might reach a readership uninformed about the Middle East and disinclined to study political tangles'.[121] Thus, Murphy wrote *A Month by the Sea* (2013), followed by *Between River and Sea* (2015). In actual fact, upon her death in 2002, her publisher stated to Richard Sandomir of *The New York Times* that she had 'left behind an unpublished book … about her time in a Palestinian refugee camp in Jordan'[122] meaning therefore that there remained 'an unfinished trilogy on Palestinian territorial fragments – Gaza Strip, West Bank, Jordanian camps', as Veronica Horwell put it in *The Guardian*.[123] That it was never finished is due to Murphy herself, according to *The Irish Times*, destroying the material for the final volume out of fear that it being published would imperil the lives of some of those whom she encountered and lived amongst in those Jordanian camps.[124]

Be that as it may, Murphy's audience for her work, of course, is not the people of Palestine but instead she is writing to the consumers of travel writing in English, and in particular the people of Ireland. One could say also that in this context her writing has had an impact as her testimony has informed the activism[125] that has propelled the Occupied Territories Bill 2018, often described in the Israeli media as the BDS Bill,[126] to the brink of being legislated by the parliament of Ireland[127] and also moved the Irish parliament to declare that Israel is complicit in the 'de facto annexation' of Palestinian territories,[128] a move welcomed by the array of Irish NGOs supportive of the cause of Palestine.[129] Indeed, such has Murphy's impact been upon her audience that her death was marked by a public statement made by no less a citizen than the President of the Republic of Ireland. In that statement, a rare honour in and of itself, she is celebrated as Ireland's 'ethical visitor' to a troubled world. In this case at least, it appears, the testimonies yet accumulate.

Notes

1. Vivian, *Commonplace Witnessing*, p. 197.
2. Étienne Wenger, *Communities of Practice: Learning, Meaning and Identity* (Cambridge: Cambridge University Press, 1999).
3. Givoni, 'The ethics of witnessing', p. 139.
4. Sally Rooney, *Normal People* (London: Faber and Faber, 2018), p. 228.
5. Ben Sales, 'Sally Rooney won't let her new novel "Beautiful World, Where Are You?" be published by an Israeli press', *Jewish Telegraphic Agency*, 11 October 2021: https://www.jta.org/2021/10/11/culture/sally-rooney-wont-let-her-new-novel-beautiful-world-where-are-you-be-published-in-hebrew (accessed 5 June 2023).
6. BBC News, 'Irish author Sally Rooney in Israel boycott row', *BBC News*, 12 October 2021: https://www.bbc.co.uk/news/entertainment-arts-58886915 (accessed 5 June 2023).
7. *A Letter Against Apartheid*: https://www.againstapartheid.com/ (accessed 5 June 2023).
8. RT, 'Irish literary prodigy Sally Rooney, who supports the "BDS" boycott of Israel, is blasted for "refusing to publish book in Hebrew"', *RT*, 12 October 2021: https://www.rt.com/news/537223-irish-writer-book-israel/ (accessed 5 June 2023).
9. James Robinson, Bhvishya Patel and Jon Abiona, 'Normal People author Sally Rooney, 30, says she banned Israeli publisher translating her book into Hebrew on political grounds after critics accused her of anti-Semitism', *The Daily Mail*, 12 October 2021: https://www.dailymail.co.uk/news/article-10084491/Sally-Rooney-30-says-banned-Israeli-publisher-translating-book-political-grounds.html (accessed 5 June 2023).
10. Ben Sales and Louis Keene, 'Hebrew translation, where are you? Sally Rooney boycotting Israel with new novel', *The Forward*, 11 October 2021: https://forward.com/news/476556/sally-rooney-beautiful-world-hebrew-translation-boycott/ (accessed 5 June 2023).

11 P. J. Grisar, 'Sally Rooney clarifies; She's boycotting Israel, not the Hebrew language', *The Forward*, 12 October 2021: *https://forward.com/news/476556/sally-rooney-beautiful-world-hebrew-translation-boycott/* (accessed 5 June 2023).

12 Ranen Omer-Sherman, 'Apeirogon. Colum McCann', *The Jewish Book Council*, 21 May 2020: *https://www.jewishbookcouncil.org/book/apeirogon* (accessed 5 June 2023).

13 Prospect Team, 'The Prospect interview #124: Colum McCann on writing the Israel-Palestine conflict', *Prospect Magazine*, 8 April 2020: *https://www.prospectmagazine.co.uk/podcasts/the-prospect-interview-colum-mccann-apeirogon-israel-palestine-podcast-book-author-interview* (accessed 5 June 2023).

14 *http://colummccann.com/about-colum/* (accessed 5 June 2023).

15 Narrative 4, *Colum McCann*: *https://narrative4.com/colum-mccann/* (accessed 5 June 2023).

16 *http://colummccann.com/narrative-4-main-page/* (accessed 5 June 2023).

17 Prospect Team, *Prospect Magazine*.

18 Prospect Team, *Prospect Magazine*.

19 Claudio Francavilla, 'EU buries head deeper in sand over Israel's apartheid', *EU Observer*, 8 February 2023: *https://euobserver.com/opinion/156689* (accessed 24 January 2024).

20 Francavilla, 'EU buries head deeper'.

21 A post on X (formerly known as Twitter) by Benjamin Netanyahu on 28 December 2022 @*netanyahu* *https://twitter.com/netanyahu* (accessed 24 January 2024).

22 See, for example, Al Jazeera, 'More than a century on: the Balfour Declaration explained', *Al Jazeera*, 2 November 2018: *https://www.aljazeera.com/features/2018/11/2/more-than-a-century-on-the-balfour-declaration-explained* (accessed 31 January 2024); Al Jazeera, 'How Britain destroyed the Palestinian homeland', *Al Jazeera*, 10 April 2018: *https://www.aljazeera.com/features/2018/4/10/how-britain-destroyed-the-palestinian-homeland* (accessed 31 January 2024); Rashid Khalidi, *The Balfour Declaration from the Perspective of the Palestinian People*, Lecture at the UN 2 November 2017, p. 2: *https://www.un.org/unispal/wp-content/uploads/2017/10/Lecture-by-Prof.-Rashid-Khalidi-100-years-since-Balfour-Decl-UN-2Nov2017.pdf* (accessed 31 January 2024).

23 Michael Ignatieff, 'Is nothing sacred? The ethics of television', *Daedalus* (1985), 57–78.

24 Gill Rye, 'The ethics of aesthetics of trauma fiction: memory, guilt and responsibility in Louise L. Lambrichs's Journal d'Hannah', *Journal of Romance Studies*, 9/3 (Winter 2009), 48–59, at 55.

25 Susan Jarratt and Nedra Reynolds, 'The splitting image: contemporary feminisms and the ethics of ethos', in J. S. Baumlin and T. F. Baumlin

26 Johanna Schmertz, 'Constructing essences: ethos and the postmodern subject of feminism', *Rhetoric Review*, 18/1 (1999), 82–91.
27 Nedra Reynolds, 'Ethos as location: new sites for discursive authority', *Rhetoric Review*, 11/2 (1993), 325–38.
28 Kate Ronald, 'A re-examination of personal and public discourse in classical rhetoric', *Rhetoric Review*, 90/1 (1990), 36–48, at 39.
29 Karen Burke LeFevre, *Invention as a Social Act* (Carbondale, IL: Southern Illinois University Press, 1987), pp. 45 and 46.
30 See, for example, p. 10 in Daniel N. Robinson, 'Rhetoric and character in Aristotle', *The Review of Metaphysics*, 60/1 (2006), 3–15.
31 John Oddo, *Intertextuality and the 24-hours News Cycle: A Day in the Rhetorical Life of Colin Powell's UN Address* (East Lansing, MI: Michigan State University Press, 2014) and John Oddo, 'Variation and continuity in intertextual rhetoric: from the "war on terror" to the "struggle against violent extremism"', *Journal of Language and Politics*, 13/3 (2014), 513–38.
32 Givoni, 'The ethics of witnessing', p. 139.
33 Givoni, 'The ethics of witnessing', p. 128.
34 Butler, 'What is critique?'.
35 Iwan Bala and Hilary Rhys Osmond (eds), *Encounters with Osi* (Swansea: H'mm Foundation, 2015).
36 *https://www.partyof.wales/* (accessed 5 June 2023).
37 *https://cnduk.org/* (accessed 5 June 2023).
38 *https://www.cymdeithasycymod.cymru/en/home/* (accessed 5 June 2023).
39 *https://en-gb.facebook.com/groups/192209400831866/about* (accessed 5 June 2023).
40 *https://eisteddfod.cymru/eisteddfod-genedlaethol-cymru* (accessed 5 June 2023).
41 *http://www.gorsedd.cymru/* (accessed 5 June 2023).
42 Dai Smith, 'Osi: a palimpsest in persona', in Bala and Osmond, *Encounters with Osi*, pp. 61–5, at p. 64.
43 Michael McNay, 'John Berger obituary', *The Guardian*, 2 January 2017: *https://www.theguardian.com/books/2017/jan/02/john-berger-obituary* (accessed 5 June 2023).
44 Iwan Bala, 'Worker of the word and the image', in Bala and Osmond, *Encounters with Osi*, pp. 9–18, at p. 9.
45 Karl Francis, *Chekov in Derry* (Channel 4, 1983 – uploaded 2020): *https://vimeo.com/474143989* (accessed 5 June 2023).
46 Karl Francis, 'Notes, prose and poetry. An essay of sorts', in Bala and Osmond, *Encounters with Osi*, pp. 68–79, at p. 74.

47 John Berger, *Hold Everything Dear: Dispatches on Survival and Resistance*, (London: Verso, 2007), p. 17.
48 Berger, *Hold Everything Dear*, pp. 62–3.
49 Berger, *Hold Everything Dear*, p. 68.
50 Berger, *Hold Everything Dear*, p. 69.
51 Christine Kinsey, 'On painting', in Bala and Osmond, *Encounters with Osi*, pp. 57–60, at p. 60.
52 For a measure of her contribution to cultural activism in Wales, see the chapter 'Menna Elfyn: *Tro'r haul arno* (1982) and *Cell angel* (1996)', in Mac Giolla Chríost, *Welsh Writing, Political Action and Incarceration: Branwen's Starling*, pp. 127–47.
53 Menna Elfyn, 'Auspicious', in Bala and Osmond, *Encounters with Osi*, pp. 192–3, at p. 192.
54 Mererid Hopwood, 'Mewn heddwch', in Bala and Osmond, *Encounters with Osi*, pp. 200–3, at p. 200.
55 Beti a'i Phobl – Osi Rhys Osmond, *BBC Radio Cymru* (published 20 April 2015; originally broadcast 10 May 2007): *http://www.listenersguide.org.uk/bbc/podcast/episode/?p=b007rkcw&e=p02s01x5* (accessed 5 June 2023).
56 Gwenan Gibbard, *Adar Man y Mynydd* (2006): *https://open.spotify.com/track/6MZ2ddUvjuHAzde2lQcmDL* (accessed 5 June 2023).
57 Darren Devine, 'Celebrations mark 100 years since birth of Welsh great RS Thomas', *Walesonline*, 8 March 2013, updated 1 April 2013: *https://www.walesonline.co.uk/news/wales-news/celebrations-mark-100-years-birth-2493890* (accessed 5 June 2023).
58 Lynne Crompton, 'Fragments from our past', in Bala and Osmond, *Encounters with Osi*, pp. 153–55, at p. 154.
59 Steve Wilson, 'Cheese on toast', in Bala and Osmond, *Encounters with Osi*, pp. 119–20.
60 Sam Vicary, 'Knowing Osi', in Bala and Osmond, *Encounters with Osi*, pp. 126–7.
61 Ali Anwar, 'Foreword. To Osi: the colourful internationalist druid', in Bala and Osmond, *Encounters with Osi*, pp. 2–5, at p. 4.
62 Givoni, 'The ethics of witnessing', p. 127.
63 Ann Oosthuizen, 'Osi Rhys Osmond: educator, creator, thinker, friend. An interview with Ann Oosthuizen', in Bala and Osmond, *Encounters with Osi*, pp. 206–29, at p. 218.
64 Lesley Davies, 'My brother', in Bala and Osmond, *Encounters with Osi*, pp. 180–1, at p. 180.
65 Luke Osmond, 'Encounters with Osi', in Bala and Osmond, *Encounters with Osi*, pp. 146–7, at p. 146.

66 John Barnie, 'Planet essays', in Bala and Osmond, *Encounters with Osi*, pp. 188–91, at p. 188.
67 Sara Rhys-Martin, 'Osi, not just my mother's husband', in Bala and Osmond, *Encounters with Osi*, pp. 142–3, at p. 142.
68 Beti a'i Phobl – Osi Rhys Osmond, *BBC Radio Cymru*.
69 Givoni, 'The ethics of witnessing', p. 124.
70 Givoni, 'The ethics of witnessing', p. 128.
71 Givoni, 'The ethics of witnessing', p. 139.
72 Givoni, 'The ethics of witnessing', p. 125.
73 Givoni, 'The ethics of witnessing', p. 124.
74 Givoni, 'The ethics of witnessing', p. 125.
75 Givoni, 'The ethics of witnessing', p. 126.
76 Givoni, 'The ethics of witnessing', p. 126.
77 Givoni, 'The ethics of witnessing', p. 128.
78 Givoni, 'The ethics of witnessing', p. 138.
79 Givoni, 'Indifference and repetition', p. 620.
80 Givoni, 'Indifference and repetition', p. 622.
81 Keenan, *An Evil Cradling*, p. ix.
82 Keenan, *An Evil Cradling*, p. vii.
83 Gornick, *The Situation and the Story*, p. 85. See also, Bell Gale Chevigny, 'The uses of solitude. The situation and the story: the art of personal narrative by Vivian Gornick', *The Women's Review of Books*, XIX/4 January (2002), 6–7.
84 Marvine Howe, 'The American University of Beirut: a year of tragedy and hope', *Washington Report On Middle East Affairs*, December (2005), 42–3: *https://www.wrmea.org/005-december/special-report-the-american-university-of-beirut-a-year-of-tragedy-and-hope.html* (accessed 5 June 2023).
85 James George O'Keeffe (ed.), *Buile Suibhne* (Dublin: Dublin Institute for Advanced Studies, 1975), p. v.
86 Keenan, *An Evil Cradling*, p. 81.
87 The Irish term 'geilt' is defined as 'madman' in the authoritative version of the text, namely O'Keeffe, *Buile Suibhne*. O'Keeffe says (at p. 102) that the term 'seems to have been applied specially to a crazy person living in woods; also endowed with the power of flying'.
88 *Buile Suibhne*, CELT: The Corpus of Electronic Texts: *https://celt.ucc.ie/published/T302018/index.html* (accessed 2 June 2023).
89 Keenan, *An Evil Cradling*, p. 81.
90 Eugene Kennedy, 'Kidnapped in Beirut', *The New York Times*, 24 October 1993: *https://www.nytimes.com/1993/10/24/books/kidnapped-in-beirut.html* (accessed 5 June 2023).

91 The New York Times, 'Notable books of the year 1993', *The New York Times*, 5 December 1993: *https://www.nytimes.com/1993/12/05/books/notable-books-of-the-year-1993.html* (accessed 5 June 2023).

92 Seamus Heaney, *Sweeney Astray: A Version from the Irish* (Derry and Dublin: Field Day Publications, 1983).

93 Stephen Regan, 'Seamus Heaney and the making of "Sweeney Astray"', *Hungarian Journal of English and American Studies*, Fall 21/2 (2015), 317–39, at 318.

94 Regan, 'Seamus Heaney and the making of "Sweeney Astray"', p. 332.

95 Regan, 'Seamus Heaney and the making of "Sweeney Astray"', p. 317.

96 Susan Shaw Sailer, 'Leaps, curses and flight: Suibne Geilt and the roots of early Irish culture', *Études Celtiques*, 33 (1997), 191–208, at 192.

97 Regan, 'Seamus Heaney and the making of "Sweeney Astray"', p. 337.

98 Regan, 'Seamus Heaney and the making of "Sweeney Astray"', p. 333.

99 Maggie Scull, 'The three funerals of Terence MacSwiney', *The Irish Times*, 24 October 2020: *https://www.irishtimes.com/culture/heritage/the-three-funerals-of-terence-macswiney-1.4387267* (accessed 5 June 2023).

100 Regan, 'Seamus Heaney and the making of "Sweeney Astray"', p. 334.

101 Keenan, *An Evil Cradling*, pp. 55–8.

102 Keenan, *An Evil Cradling*, p. 27.

103 Keenan, *An Evil Cradling*, p. 33.

104 Keenan, *An Evil Cradling*, p. 58.

105 Keenan, *An Evil Cradling*, p. 55.

106 Keenan, *An Evil Cradling*, p. 109.

107 Keenan, *An Evil Cradling*, pp. 109 and 110.

108 Northern Ireland Office, *The Belfast Agreement* (London: The Stationery Office, 1998): *https://www.gov.uk/government/publications/the-belfast-agreement* (accessed 5 June 2023).

109 Givoni, 'The ethics of witnessing', p. 134.

110 Murphy, *Between River and Sea*, 'Foreword'.

111 See, for example, J. Bowyer Bell, *Terror out of Zion: The Fight for Israeli Independence 1929–1949: Irgun Zvia Leumi, Lehi, and the Palestine Underground* (Dublin: Academy Press, 1979).

112 Bowyer Bell, *Terror out of Zion*.

113 See, in particular, Marie-Violaine Louvet, *Civil Society, Post-colonialism and Transnational Solidarity: The Irish and the Middle East Conflict* (Basingstoke: Palgrave Macmillan, 2016) and also, Rory Miller, *Ireland and the Palestine Question: 1948–2004* (Dublin: Irish Academic Press, 2005). For a popular summary, see Rory Miller, 'Why the Irish support Palestine. Once upon a time, Ireland was a huge supporter of Jewish aspirations in the Promised

114 Land. What happened?', *Foreign Policy*, 23 June 2010: https://foreignpolicy.com/2010/06/23/why-the-irish-support-palestine-2/ (accessed 5 June 2023).
114 Murphy, *Between River and Sea*, p. 410.
115 Kemp is the author of the journal article, quoted often by Murphy, entitled 'The psychoanalytic encounter with settler colonialism in Palestine/Israel', *International Journal of Applied Psychoanalytic Studies*, 17/2 June (2020), 93–125.
116 Murphy, *A Month by the Sea*, p. xx.
117 Givoni, 'Indifference and repetition', p. 602.
118 Givoni, 'Indifference and repetition', p. 612.
119 Givoni, 'Indifference and repetition', p. 624.
120 Murphy, *Between River and Sea*, p. 410.
121 Murphy, *Between River and Sea*.
122 Richard Sandomir, 'Dervla Murphy, travel writer who preferred her bike, dies at 90', *The New York Times*, 27 May 2022 and updated 30 May: https://www.nytimes.com/2022/05/27/books/dervla-murphy-dead.html (accessed 5 June 2023).
123 Veronica Horwell, 'Dervla Murphy obituary', *The Guardian*, 26 May 2022: https://www.theguardian.com/travel/2022/may/26/dervla-murphy-obituary (accessed 5 June 2023).
124 The Irish Times, 'Dervla Murphy obituary: a ground-breaking and fearless travel writer,' *The Irish Times*, 23 May 2022: https://www.irishtimes.com/life-and-style/people/dervla-murphy-obituary-a-ground-breaking-and-fearless-travel-writer-1.4886092 (accessed 5 June 2023).
125 Such as here, for example: https://www.ipsc.ie/past-events (accessed 2 June 2023).
126 Arutz Sheva staff, 'BDS Bill excluded from Irish coalition government program', *Arutz Sheva. Israel National News*, 16 June 2020: https://www.israelnationalnews.com/News/News.aspx/281947 (accessed 5 June 2023).
127 As of 9 December 2020, the bill was 'currently before Dáil Éireann (the Irish Parliament), Third Stage': https://www.oireachtas.ie/en/bills/bill/2018/6/ (accessed 5 June 2023).
128 Marie O'Halloran and Ellen O'Riordan, 'Ireland becomes the first EU country to declare Israel is involved in "de facto annexation"', *The Irish Times*, 26 May 2021: https://www.irishtimes.com/news/politics/oireachtas/ireland-becomes-first-eu-country-to-declare-israel-is-involved-in-de-facto-annexation-1.4576250 (accessed 5 June 2023).
129 For example, Caoimh de Barra, 'Ireland passes historic motion on Israeli annexation of Palestinian land – what does this mean and where do we go from here?', *Trócaire*, 27 May 2021: https://www.trocaire.org/news/ireland-passes-historic-motion-on-israeli-annexation-of-palestinian-land-what-does-this-mean/ (accessed 5 June 2023).

CHAPTER 4

Taking up Form

I called to mind a question posed by Caroline Levine as I crossed the threshold to their apartment in Ramallah: 'What happens, then, when a man enters a home?'[1] I am conscious of how my form might appear in that bounded space: male, white, western European. 'Our experience,' Levine says, 'our day-to day lives [are] organized and disorganized by multiple, overlapping forms working at different scales and with different coercive and productive power … forms, both aesthetic and social, cross paths, making and remaking life as they move'.[2] The door closes behind me. The street is disappeared. The encounter between different forms can have 'strange and unpredictable consequences', she continues;[3] it may generate 'instabilities',[4] and in doing so upset the particular 'ordering of bodies and spaces, hierarchies and narratives, containments and exclusions [that] are the stuff of injustice'.[5] The once-upon-a-time suicide bomber stands before me in the vestibule. Therefore also, Levine says, such encounters between forms may provide a means of imagining 'how we might make our world more just',[6] and of then making it so.

Whole numbers

Comprised of 1,001 'bursts',[7] or 'sections',[8] or 'passages',[9] 'fragments'[10] or 'fragmentary chapters',[11] 'mosaic-like segments'[12] or 'incantatory factual segments',[13] or 'facets',[14] or 'cantos',[15] *Apeirogon* is a novel. We know that it is from its given, full title: *Apeirogon: A Novel*. In her review of *Apeirogon*, Claire Lowdon asks, purposefully, 'Why do some novels feel the need to self-identify?'[16] She provides her own answer, saying, '"A novel" can be a way of preparing readers for a work that pushes formal boundaries. Or it can function as a disclaimer when a book contains a lot of non-fictional material … Apeirogon ticks both boxes'. Writing in *New Statesman* on this specific matter, Johanna Thomas-Corr suggests that the author's intention is to provoke his readers into questioning the very form of his text. She puts it as follows: 'McCann adds the provocative subtitle "a novel" because he wants us to question that claim. *Apeirogon* occupies the unsettled, disputed territory between fact and fiction'.[17] The book's reviewers are divided on its identity as a novel. Thus, Julie Orringer declares that it is 'indisputably a novel'[18] while Lowdon, in contrast, asserts, simply, that 'it is not a novel'.[19] Ellen Atkins is satisfied that it is a novel but that it takes the form of a 'narrative pastiche'.[20] Ben East likens it to a 'fragmentary collage';[21] Donna Steadman to an 'associative collage'.[22] Ian Sansom, noting its 'curious arrangement of parts', says that the work is 'odd' and eludes 'easy categorisation',[23] while Charles Finch finds that *Apeirogon* 'resists the narrative model'.[24] Similarly, Marion Winik likens the work to a 'long braided essay'.[25] Ben Libman notes that the book has an 'unconventional form' comprised of 'an arrangement of 1,001 narrative sections' and that it may, perhaps, best be thought of as a 'spectacle-like … magazine profile'.[26]

Adrian Salmon, however, goes as far as claiming that it is best described as an 'anti-novel, or even an exploded novel', adding that it is a form that is 'uniquely appropriate to the stories of its protagonists, and the appalling circumstances from which their stories have arisen'.[27] The term 'exploded novel' is derived, no doubt, from the concept of the exploded view, namely a depiction of an object, usually, but not always, a complicated mechanism, that shows the individual parts or components of the object separately, suspended in space at a short distance from each other and indicating their relative positions. The impression is of the object having been exploded from its centre, causing the component parts to be separated at an equal distance away from their original locations. The form is often used in instructional material. Certainly, other reviewers find the work to be broken apart in some sense, at least. Some, for example, find the work 'splintered'[28] or 'chopped … up'.[29] McCann himself refers to the novel's 'fractured form',[30] a term shared with Jerome Boyd Maunsell in his review of the work; thus: '[a] jagged, fractured, teeming novel'.[31] Elizabeth Toohey too describes it as fractured, but yet 'novelistic'.[32] More specifically, it is, according to its author, 'a hybrid novel';[33] it is a hybrid novel 'with invention at its core, a work of storytelling which, like all storytelling, weaves together elements of speculation, memory, fact and imagination'.[34]

Levine might argue that sense may be made of *Apeirogon* by viewing it as an encounter between multiple forms. Thus, one might say that it is hybrid in that it draws together certain bounded wholes, to borrow again terminology from Levine: 'To speak of *the* form of a work of art is to gesture to its unifying power, its capacity to hold together disparate parts.'[35] After all, as McCann puts it, 'apeirogon means … every story is a world' and it means also 'to put a whole world in there'.[36] And, *Apeirogon* is to 'tell a story'; it is 'an all-embracing form'.[37] Form thereby as wholeness:

95
Apeirogon: a shape with a countably infinite number of sides.
…
93
As a whole, an apeirogon approaches to the shape of a circle, but a magnified view of a small piece appears to be a straight line. One can finally arrive at any point within the whole … At the same time, one can arrive anywhere within an apeirogon and the entirety of the shape is complicit in the journey, even that which has not yet been imagined.[38]

An apeirogon is therefore 'a bounded, enclosed space'.[39] In extending this analysis of the form of *Apeirogon* further, or perhaps it would be better to say its forms, I bear in mind certain other insights of Levine. *Apeirogon* seems to exemplify how 'aesthetic and political forms may be nested inside one another' while also illustrating how, in this nesting, 'each is capable of disturbing the other's organizing power'.[40] One of the key affordances of *Apeirogon* is that it allows for the encounter, overlap and collision between different forms whether aesthetic, literary, social or political. Bear in mind too that Levine conceives of form in terms much more expansive and inclusive than those of 'its ordinary usage' in literary criticism;[41] that form pertains as much to the 'sociopolitical world [as it does to that] of art'.[42] Moreover, in this reading of *Apeirogon*, the following question by Caroline Levine and her own response to it, together, are particularly apposite, 'How should we understand the relationship between literary and political forms? Moving beyond the practice of reading aesthetic forms as indexes of social life, I consider ways in which literary and social forms come into contact and affect one another, without presuming that one is the ground or cause of the other'.[43] In this way, therefore, I see the politics, rhetorics and aesthetics of *Apeirogon* in collision, with none neither to the fore nor backgrounded. It could be said that this position echoes that put forward by Tariq Jazeel and Nayanika Mookherjee in their overview of the connections between aesthetics and violent political conflict in the field of ethnography, in which they stated, quite simply, that 'politics and conflict are always entwined with aesthetics'.[44] In reading *Apeirogon* as a novel with persuasive qualities or affordances, I take it that Levine would enjoin one not ask 'what artists intend or even what forms do' but rather to consider 'what potentialities lie latent'[45] in the given aesthetic and social forms.

Under this approach to its reading, *Apeirogon* is restrained from becoming a 'harmfully totalizing'[46] whole because it is not a single, whole story but rather a 'constellation'[47] of stories, of other bounded wholes, overlapping and in contention. As Erica Wagner puts it, 'this remarkable book rises to embody within the geometric form, folding an uncountable number of stories within itself, the lives of Palestinians and Israelis, stretching back into the past and off into the future'.[48] Again, yet, it is a story told of an event on a single day (another whole) in 2016, opening at the beginning of the book as follows: 'The hills of Jerusalem are a bath of fog';[49] closing thus at the end of the book: 'The hills of Jericho are a bath of dark.'[50] But this story is also told in its completeness, timelessly and placelessly, at the very centre of the book in the section numbered 1,001 (a number that is tetradic, strobogrammatic and palindromic in its wholeness): 'Once upon a time, and not so long ago, and not so far away …'.[51] And during the course of that day two complete biographical histories are recounted as a single story in 'bloody biographical symmetry'.[52] *Apeirogon* juxtaposes these two biographies, allowing them to frame section 1,001: each of these stories is numbered 500; that of Rami Elhanan precedes section 1,001 and that of Bassam Aramin antecedes the same. While these two stories inform the whole, they are also set apart: 'The transcripts of both men in the centre section of the book are pulled together from a series of interviews in Jerusalem, New York, Jericho and Beit Jala, but elsewhere in this book Bassam and Rami have allowed me to shape and reshape their words and worlds'.[53] Indeed, the peculiar dispositio of *Apeirogon* communicates the violence that McCann is keen to see resolved: 'their first-person accounts … nestle, like the core of a bomb, in the central section of *Apeirogon*'.[54]

However, if not harmfully totalising, opinion amongst the network of reviewers is divided as to whether *Apeirogon* causes damage because of its salient duality. After all, it is a book of two halves, counting sections from one to 500 and then from 500 to one; the two halves sandwiching section 1,001 in perfect symmetry; the book's two blank sections, one for each half of the book, are both numbered 284. This is no mere absence of language, or even of its failure because blank pages are, according to Theo van Leeuwen, 'rhetorical connotators' or 'signs' that 'trigger "myths", those complexes of "commonsense" ideas that constitute ideologies, rather than explicitly formulating them'.[55] It is a book of two biographies: Rami Elhanan and Bassam Aramin. It is a book of two places: the State of Israel and the Occupied Palestinian Territories. And it is in Section 222 in which is laid out the resolution to the conflict – 'harmonic integration'.[56] And if the West Bank is a lung suffering under the constriction of occupation, as McCann says repeatedly,[57] then it follows that the other part of that paired organ is the lung of the unfettered State of Israel. The lungs also suffer together.[58]

Susan Abulhawa, perhaps the most prominent of Palestinian critics of *Apeirogon*, accuses McCann of mystifying the conflict.[59] The very same accusation was laid before Seamus Heaney by fellow northern poet Ciarán Carson in his review of the former's 1975 collection entitled *North*: '[I]n employing the modernist literary strategem of mythic interrogation, [Heaney] inadvertently became "a laureate of violence – a mythmaker, an anthropologist of ritual killing, an apologist for 'the situation', in the last resort, a mystifier"'.[60] Moreover, as Kevin Murphy further notes, Carson possessed unusual authority in making his criticism: 'As a Catholic raised in an Irish-speaking household on the Falls Road and as a poet who [unlike Heaney] stayed in Belfast throughout the violence, Carson possessed unassailable qualifications'.[61] Susan Abulhawa is similarly qualified: her parents, born in Jerusalem, became refugees of the Six Day War of 1967. Itinerant in the years following, Susan Abulhawa was born to them in Kuwait in 1970. She is a novelist,[62] a poet,[63] and an activist for Palestine.[64] Her qualifications elevate her in the hierarchy of reviews of *Apeirogon* for hers is the only one that has been described as 'famous'.[65]

Her case is that McCann posits the biographies of Rami Elhanan and Bassam Aramin as equivalent, and that he reduces the condition of Palestine to a 'complicated' conflict of 'thousands of years' of duration between 'two equal sides'.[66] He presents the violence of these two sides as if they are equal, as if they correspond: 'There is an implicit parity, you see? All fear is the same, all violence is the same, all insecurity is the same'.[67] For her, *Apeirogon* is analogous to the draining of the Hula wetlands by the State of Israel: 'An ambitious project to "heal", conceived by foreigners, ignorant of the local terrain, its history and ecology; eager to solve, civilise, and lay claim; well-intended; sure of their own glory; but in reality, profoundly harmful – irreparably so for the most vulnerable lives'.[68] There is no equivalence between the coloniser and the colonised, she says, and nor can there be; and to say otherwise is to normalise the occupation. In his own defence, McCann says that while '[t]here is an occupier and an occupied' he says also that 'it's wrong to keep referring to "both sides" here. There are more than two sides. It is polygonal. Hamas does not necessarily speak for Palestinians. And Netanyahu doesn't speak for Israelis'.[69] Indeed: Benjamin Netanyahu, then the democratically elected Prime Minster of Israel, and Hamas, the winners of 2006 elections to the Palestinian Legislative Council, the last democratic election held in Palestine. All voices count, but not all voices count in the same way.

Yellow books

Inside the apartment in Ramallah, her face is uncovered, like a book opened. It is only to the outside world that she is presented masked. As we greet each other, I wonder what my own face reveals. Is a face a piece of 'persuasive design'?[70] What is the meaning of a book's cover? Everything, perhaps. *Celtic Palestine* has its face. Osi Rhys Osmond's *Gwystl Glas*, literally translated as *Blue Hostage*, gazes eyelessly at the reader. The hostage is called blue in English, but the Welsh word means many other things too:[71] 'glas', a Welsh language adjective – azure, blue, bright, cold, fresh, green, grey, new, livid, pale, pallid, raw, transparent, silver, verdant, young; a Welsh language noun – stream. And for the Celtic reader the Irish language cognate is equally diverse in its potential senses:[72] 'glas', an Irish language adjective – blue, bright, green, grey, pale, raw, unseasoned, young; an Irish language noun – stream, lock; an Irish language prefix – locked, tight, secure, *faoi ghlas* – imprisoned. It is also symbolic of death; it is the colour of martyrdom. But perhaps Osmond himself would have expressed a preference for Kevin Murray's conception of glas: 'the colour of sky in water'.[73]

Judge a book by its cover, exhorts Ellie Violet Bramley: 'Last week's big literary event was not the publication of a new book, the million-pound signing of a celebrity author or the announcement of a prestigious prize. Instead, it was the unveiling of a cover: the jacket of the forthcoming novel by Sally Rooney'.[74] Jacket covers, adds Bramley, quoting a designer at the publishing house of Faber, serve to, 'advertise the aspirations of the book and the person who reads it'.[75] Writing in the same vein, Michael John Goodman asserts that the jacket cover of a book relates to 'the very material substance of the book itself'.[76] Thus, the jacket cover, together with its book, is part of a multimodal strategy of visual persuasion, to paraphrase both Caroline van Eck[77] and Theo van Leeuwen.[78]

In addition, Goodman reminds us that the phenomenon of the significant jacket cover is not new; it is not the product of Instagram, despite the reach and indeed popularity of #bookstagram[79] – at the time of writing, over sixty-seven million posts have been made using this tag. In actual fact, says Goodman, there is a long history of judging books by their covers, going back to *The Yellow Book* literary magazine that was published from 1894 to 1897.[80] The journal's distinctive yellow cover signalled, at least in part, an engagement with a culture of shock and scandal through association with other yellow-clad publications, 'for yellow was not only the décor of the notorious and dandified pre-Victorian Regency, but also of the wicked and decadent French novel'.[81] Since then, a book's cover has been taken to carry some significance. Or to put it another way, all books since *The Yellow Book* are clad in yellow. Or, applying Levine once more, here we have an encounter between forms, between cover and book, image and text. What are the consequences of that encounter? Some of such consequences will have been intended by our creative rhetoricians while others will be aleatory and disruptive.

The encounters between each of *An Evil Cradling*, *A Month by the Sea* and *Apeirogon* and their jacket covers have their consequences. For example, the original jacket cover of *An Evil Cradling*, in which an untitled painting by the Belfast-born visual artist Dermot Seymour is embedded in what would appear to be pages from a Celtic-style manuscript and from an Arabic-style document, both typical of the medieval period, and which is partly framed by strands of barbed wire, generates a variety of possibilities in its encounter with Brian Keenan's text. The painting is characteristic of Seymour's work on the subject of the conflict in NI. It depicts a cow perched on a tiny island, every side of which is a precipice. Behind the cow sits a telegraph pole set at a sharp angle, absent wires. Ahead of the cow stands a naked, white man, his hands bound behind his back, his eyes bound by white cloth. The backdrop to this scene is a glaringly bright and repellent sky. This is Seymour's 'imagery of disintegration';[82] it is the landscape of 'anxiety, bewilderment and absurdity';[83] it is an Ireland of 'sulphrous skies, dazed and bewildered animals and unstable landscapes'.[84] Here, as Aidan Dunne puts it, 'lurid, ominous and displaced borderlands are marked with bizarre juxtapositions. Nothing seems to be what it is. If the Ulster problem is about territory, then it is about insecurities'.[85] The cow looks out from the painting in silent witness, as Seymour's animals 'always' do.[86] Its isolation on a barren sea stack too is usual for Seymour; the creature is 'stranded … with no way to escape',[87] signalling a 'dislocated world of imminent collapse and moral breakdown'.[88] His work, which he describes as magical realist rather than surreal, is not political but rather is about a violently politicised society, as he implies here in interview with Noel Kelly:

> I mean obviously I don't like to be referred to as the 'political artist'. I grew up in Belfast in Northern Ireland at a time when it was just 'madness at large'. I didn't know it was mad at the time; it's just when you leave the country and live somewhere else and you realise that your vernacular is insane and the world you live in is abnormal, but you don't know that. So when you use all that imagery, it's just what's around you, it's your landscape. You just play with that. That's all you do with it. It's not political in the sense that you are taking a partisan position on anything. The hardest thing growing up here was actually walking the middle; you know a lot of people talk about somebody sitting on the fence, in Ireland and the North that was such a skill.[89]

It seems that in order to gain a proper perspective on the state of NI as it was at that time it was necessary to develop a sense of detachment, and indeed to make that detachment physically real. He puts this detachment to Noel Kelly in terms of both departing the city of Belfast and there being nobody left there, neither family nor friends:

Noel Kelly: Last night we were talking about you coming back to Belfast and asking what would you like to do this time, would you like to go see where you were brought up, etc. What is the relationship you have now with Belfast?

Dermot Seymour: Oh it's strange because there's nobody left here. All my family are either dead or have moved to other places. I have no real connection with the city anymore. All the places I went to during The Troubles … there's no way I could ever go back into those places. But that's the thing about the North nothing was what it seems.[90]

He puts this detachment to Tina O'Sullivan somewhat differently, as an emotional response and an ethical choice necessary to the practice of his art:

Everything I took for normality was absolutely abnormal, but you're only aware of that when you leave the place and realise that all the things you take for granted, as part of day-to-day life, are anything but. It's totally abnormal and absurd. That's where the imagery comes out of. If you found a dead body, you can't really sit down with an easel to paint, and be painterly about it. You have to detach yourself from it, and it's that detachment from the circumstances you're in that gives a kind of horror and absurdity, and an unreality based in complete and utter total reality. The way I work evolves, it's a way of detaching myself from what was all around me and that becomes the way I look and see things. I carried that way of working all through my life, where I always tried to detach myself from the obvious, to make the obvious more obvious.[91]

Without detachment, the horror is overwhelming: one is hostage to it.

Keenan, it could be said, also partakes in the detachment from NI as illustrated by Seymour. After all, he deliberately departed for Beirut because he felt the necessity of experiencing for himself that sense of distance, of separation, for his own emotional and psychological wellbeing:

I have been asked so many times 'Why did you go? What took you to that place?' In answering, I can at last find my beginning ... I am a product of my city and of this awful period in its history. Before I left Belfast, I had been torn with a desperate kind of love and distaste for my place and my people and even after coming back these scars of anger and of desire still mark me ... When I think of my choice to leave Ireland, I constantly ask myself was it a wearisome walking away? Was it time to find another set of values, breathe another kind of air? ... I remember talking to a friend before I made my decision to go. I said to him 'There comes a time when you get so utterly empty that you've got to move somewhere else ...'.[92]

And yet, it is his engagement that transforms Keenan, the hostage: his engagement not only with his fellow hostages, and John McCarthy in particular, but also with his captors. He communicates with them in pidgin English and French despite the initial shock of 'the babble' of 'fearfully incomprehensible' Arabic;[93] he personalises them by bestowing nicknames upon them – the Grim Reaper, the Shuffling Acolyte,[94] Jeeves,[95] Joker;[96] he develops a relationship with them; and he became a new self as a result of his 'strange sojourn in the Lebanon'.[97] Indeed, he becomes several things he could not have become so readily were he to have stayed all the while in Belfast, as we see in Chapter 3, 'Making the Witness'. For Keenan, fulfilling himself as a serious writer comes from a new, Irish self. We see this when Keenan identifies with the Irish language medieval prosimetrum *Buile Shuibhne*, or *Mad Sweeny* in English, as well as with its eponymous hero, when he determines to write the 'memoir' of his captivity 'in the code of poetry'.[98] Hence, *An Evil Cradling* could never have been simply an autobiography. Rather, it was imperative that it also be a prosimetrum. Of the guises of *An Evil Cradling*, it is its essential form.

Kept rhythms

It is the work of a female artist that adorns the jacket cover of *A Month by the Sea*, an image from a series by Laila Shawa from 1994 entitled *Walls of Gaza I* and *II*.[99] Shawa is a native of Gaza, having been born there in 1940 into a 'wealthy and politically influential family'[100] when

Gaza was governed by the UK as a part of Mandatory Palestine. After the 1948 Arab–Israeli War, when Gaza was governed by Egypt, Shawa was educated at the Leonardo da Vinci Institute in Cairo, a school of Italian origins for the children of Egyptian society's elite, in Rome at the Accademia di Belle Arti and the Accademia San Giacomo, and at the School of Seeing[101] in Salzburg, Austria. She returned briefly to Gaza for a period between 1965 and 1967, teaching art classes in the Palestinian refugee camps there under the auspices of UNESCO and UNRWA. In 1967 she moved to Beirut, Lebanon, at the same time as the PLO established itself there following the Six Day War, where she remained as a practising artist for almost a decade. She returned to Gaza at the outbreak of the Lebanese Civil War in 1975 in order to contribute to the construction of the Rashad Shawa Cultural Centre, named after her father who was appointed mayor of Gaza by Israel in 1971,[102] a position he held until dismissed by Israel in 1982. He was dismissed from the post by Israel previously, in 1973, before being restored to the position by Israel in 1975.[103] Gaza was, during this period, under the control of Israel. Laila Shawa moved to London in 1987, where she currently lives and works.[104] 'Hybrid between east and west ... the relationship between the female body, society and politics' runs 'like a thread' through the work of Shawa.[105] Thus, Shawa says:

> In 1990 I had breast cancer. While undergoing radiotherapy, I watched on television the precision bombing of Baghdad by US airplanes, forever linking the two events in my mind and in my art. The body woman and the body land amalgamate; the invasion of one is equated with the invasion of the other and the implicit fact that both leave scars.[106]

And she gazes at the world from her publicity photographs – full face on view, smiling, bare-headed, smoking, cross-legged, limbs exposed. Little wonder then that one learns that she 'resent[s] the degraded status of women in the Muslim world today', that being 'contrary to the heart of Islam', and that it is one of her goals as an artist to 'speak out and criticise, and reach the minds and hearts of Muslims' and to bring about 'change' to that status.[107] Indeed, in explaining her 2012 exhibition *The Other Side of Paradise*, an exploration of the phenomenon of the shahida, the female suicide bomber – 'a troubling confusion of eroticization and weaponization'[108] – Shawa claims that 'after the First Intifada suddenly women became much more targeted by their menfolk, to suppress them ... because they became too powerful',[109] they had to be put in their place. While recognising that female suicide bombers may have many motivations, Mia Bloom presents evidence that underscores Shawa's assertion, noting that 'the first four female Palestinian suicide bombers were in situations where the act of martyrdom was seen as their sole chance to reclaim the "family honor" that had been lost by their own actions or the actions of other family members', while adding that in other parts of the world too 'sexual violence against women – and the ensuing social stigma associated with rape in patriarchal societies – appears to be a common motivating factor for [female] suicide attackers'.[110]

That the jacket cover artist for *A Month by the Sea* is a Gazan woman is not incidental. Gender is central to the work. After all, the inside folds of the jacket cover carry, in postcard-brevity style,[111] Dervla Murphy's headline message to her readers:

> Time and time again she meets men who have returned to the Strip as an act of presence. Yet the mosque is often their only daily activity, as difficulties obtaining supplies mean few opportunities for creative work. This acts as a recruiting sergeant for the Islamist Qassam brigades and a pressure cooker for the creation of domestic tyrants. In this situation, Dervla becomes a shameless supporter of women's rights – acting as agony aunt and feminist mentor by turn.[112]

Murphy's name along with the title of the volume are etched in earthy-red ink on the image made by Shawa, *12th Century AD, Walls of Gaza II*. The etched writing, personal name and book title, takes the form of graffiti. Appropriately so, given that the *Walls of Gaza* series emerged from a set of photographs taken by Shawa of graffiti daubed on the walls of Gazan houses during the First Intifada, 1987–93. Clearly, the First Intifada is her point of inflection for the status of women in Gaza. This graffiti is different to graffiti found elsewhere, according to Shawa, in that it was not merely a means for locals to communicate with each other under the circumstances of the media blackout imposed by Israel during this period[113] but also constituted at that time a 'mode of engagement between occupiers and occupied'.¹¹⁴ Shawa's Gazan wall encloses Murphy's text as a jacket cover. That wall carries the graffiti of Murphy's name and the title of her book, thereby situating *A Month by the Sea* in the same place as Shawa's original, autochthonous graffiti.

There is extensive empirical evidence that the 'pressure cooker' alluded to by Dervla Murphy, comprising the occupation and blockade of Gaza along with the reality of Gaza's patriarchal society, has had a direct and disproportionate effect on women. For example, in her report for the European Parliament in 2011, Sophie Richter-Devroe notes the 'struggle for women's rights in Palestine' is 'complex and difficult', adding that 'more conservative voices … gaining ground particularly in Gaza'¹¹⁵ and that 'women activists need to continue and be supported in their struggle against dual oppression from Israeli occupation and patriarchal control, if women's rights and gender equality are to be secured in Palestine'.¹¹⁶ She further explains that '[w]ithout ending the political and economic repression and de-development exercised by Israeli occupation and settler colonial policies, Palestinian women's rights and gender equality will most probably continue to be restricted', arguing in addition the following:

> [T]he PA should guarantee equal rights for women in all domains … Public awareness-raising campaigns should be intensified, providing information about family planning, but also about taboo subjects such as domestic violence, inheritance, and women's rights more broadly. Such efforts, if placed carefully and in a culturally-sensitive way, can be a first step towards changing cultural norms that reinforce patriarchal structures and a subordinate position of women in society, and thus towards constructing alternative gender models in Palestine.¹¹⁷

Writing over a decade later, on 16 August 2023, the organisation UN Women reports that little, if any, progress has been made in the interim: 'Decades of occupation and conflict have jeopardized women's economic security, protection, and access to services in Palestine … ending GBV (gender-based violence) is difficult in a patriarchal community, especially one that is also under military occupation'.¹¹⁸ The status of women in Gaza has been widely used by Israel for the purposes of anti-Hamas propaganda.[119] However, there are one or two nuances to the relationship between the entrenchment of patriarchal norms and Hamas being the dominant political faction in Gaza throughout this period. Islah Jad argues, for example, that Hamas' 'gender ideology … is contradictory and in continuous flux',[120] while research by Minna Cowper-Coles shows that in the OPT more women than men support Hamas, adding that there are many, complicated reasons for this.[121]

And as I write now, the consequences of the Israel–Hamas War for women have already been disastrous and they worsen as the war continues. In a press release by UN Women on 20 October 2023 it is noted in angrily measured tones that the war was having a 'differentiated impact' upon 'women and girls',[122] noting also the 'unique and urgent needs and vulnerabilities' of women and girls in Gaza, explaining that '[t]hese vulnerabilities are rooted in structural gender discrimination, including laws in Palestine that assume women to be under the protection and guardianship of men. This legal framework increases the risks women face, including gender-based violence and food insecurity, making them more likely than men to live in substandard temporary shelters when displaced, and less likely to access financial assets or documentation'.[123]

On 20 November 2023, as the war spirals with increasingly brutal, intense and often indiscriminate violence,[124] Reem Alsalem, the UN Special Rapporteur on Violence against Women and Girls, notes with harsh clarity in her press release that 'women are bearing the brunt', adding by way of clear-eyed and horrifying exemplification that 'more than 180 women a day [are] being forced to give birth in inhumane, degrading and dangerous conditions'.[125] Then, on 4 March 2024, Pramila Patten, the UN Special Representative of the Secretary-General on Sexual Violence in Conflict, reports that there is 'clear and convincing information' of 'incidents and patterns' of CRSV (conflict-related sexual violence) largely against women[126] both during the 7 October 2023 attack and in its aftermath. Patten ascribes to Hamas and 'other armed groups, including reportedly Palestinian Islamic Jihad, Popular Resistance Committees'[127] violence that includes 'rape, sexualized torture and sexualized cruel, inhuman and degrading treatment'.[128] She notes also the increasing occurrence of types of CRSV by 'Israeli security forces' in the West Bank since 7 October 2023, comprising 'cruel, inhuman and degrading treatment … including the increased use of various forms of sexual violence, namely invasive body searches;

threats of rape; and prolonged forced nudity'.[129] Patten very sadly confesses that 'the true prevalence of sexual violence during the 7 October attacks and their aftermath may take months or years to emerge and may never fully be known, given that sexual violence remains a chronically underreported crime in every conflict-affected setting, due *inter alia* to trauma, stigma and fear faced by survivors'.[130]

Back to Dervla Murphy: as an unaccompanied woman, and as a western European feminist, Murphy is often a transgressive presence in Gaza. Cultural and literary historian Dúnlaith Bird says of the travelling style of Dervla Murphy that the authorities in such like places are of the view that 'the solitary woman traveller generates trouble that threatens to spread'.[131] But for Murphy, says Bird, 'solitary travel facilitates a less unequal meeting of cultures' and that as a result of this 'Murphy negotiates her own path through imperialism'.[132] Bird thus reads Murphy's work as a type of writing in the style of 'vagabondage' and that it is 'not an account of women's resistance against a monolithic official repression, but a deliberate negotiation within changing scenes of constraint'.[133] Here, Bird consciously borrows from Judith Butler's conception of 'improvisation within a scene of constraint'.[134] As she travels, Murphy is self-aware as well as being aware of the tension of which she is a cause. She enters Gaza as a 'brazen lone woman',[135] much to the obvious irritation of the passport control officials at the Rafah Crossing Point. Her solitary presence is the subject of several contentious exchanges. For example, in asking the following questions of one of her female hosts, named Nita, Murphy alludes to one confrontation on this subject while initiating another:

> Invariably, people voiced anxiety about my walking alone in the dark; I had regular arguments with *serveeces* reluctant to put me down not directly outside my destination – because of my gender, not my hostage potential. I mentioned this to my companions, and wondered, 'When these sex-related fears are cultivated, what does it do to a society? When girls are taught to regard all non-related men as possibly "bad", poised to rape given a chance?'[136]

At the home of Yara, another such female contact, Murphy is treated with disdain by her host's father for the same reason: 'Her father appeared then, returning from the mosque; tall and heavily built, he avoided my eye and greeted me gruffly while passing through the salon. "He doesn't like independent women," observed his daughter'.[137] Transgressive females unaccompanied by males are especially vulnerable, whether they travel alone or in company. When visiting the home of an Islamic Jihad martyr, Murphy's female guide to reaching their destination, Nita, is made nervous by the male youths loitering in the vicinity. First of all, on arrival:

> From the junction we walked between a long line of blank grey 'purdah' walls and a cultivated space around where several men, tending a guava crop, paused to stare at us. Around a corner, youths kicking a football also paused to stare at us and shouted something hostile. Nita looked uneasy. 'It's because you're uncovered,' she muttered ... 'I shouldn't have brought you here without a hijab.'[138]

And then, upon the point of departing the home, Nita says, '"We can't walk past those heroes outside – I'll ring a taxi." ... Nita insisted on a taxi: until then, I hadn't realised how much she feared the Salafist influence'.[139] Advice given to Murphy at the beginning of her stay in Gaza to 'buy a sunhat' is presented by her to us as if in passing, as if it were a casual suggestion made in the spirit of protecting oneself against the sun. It was in fact a warning, not at first understood by Murphy, misread by her western sensibilities. The female head is to be kept hidden. Murphy is told as much, in no uncertain terms, by a female host at UNRWA, named Aida: '[W]hen we were on our own Aida immediately reprimanded me for being "naked". "The Holy Koran," she sternly asserted, "orders every woman to keep every one of her hairs covered".'[140]

Murphy complies on at least some occasions. For example, on visiting the Islamic University of Gaza she paused on the pavement outside in order to conceal her 'white locks' underneath a hijab loaned to her by one of the security guards.[141] Once, she tells us, with something of a confessional tone, that 'it soon became apparent that as an improperly dressed woman, walking alone, I was hated by Gaza's fanatics, men quite capable of killing a non-conforming relative. Extreme disapproval may be disguised but hatred is unmistakable and looks so loaded [as to] have the force of something physical'.¹⁴² At another point, Murphy asks of Nita why it is the case that the female face is best hidden from view:

> I asked about the *niqb* [full face veil] and Nita explained some women (on the Strip an increasing number) choose it because it's more respectful to Allah. A visible woman's face can make her seem more attractive to men – especially 'bad men'. Also, it may tempt her to communicate with people outside the family … 'She could smile at people she shouldn't communicate with, in the market of the street.' … it's wrong … we [women] shouldn't do it! But of course most of us do, unless we feel we're being watched by some jihadists.¹⁴³

What Murphy says of Hamas must hold true of Gaza also: 'as a European woman Hamas is not where I belong'.¹⁴⁴ Neither is it where Shawa belongs. In Gaza the rhythms of female lives are to be kept by men for men. They are kept through the violence of segregation. Thus, the female body is sequestered on the street, in the café, on the beach, in the swimming pool, at university, in the government office, in the mosque.¹⁴⁵ And the goal for women is motherhood as martyrdom; and in the home each male a martinet.¹⁴⁶ Against Israel and Zionism, and against patriarchy, Murphy makes her case for Gaza.

The general 'kindness'¹⁴⁷ with which Murphy was welcomed during her visit to Gaza, the circumstances of her entrance to and exit from Gaza notwithstanding, is tempered by the obvious hostility that was directed towards her by some she encountered there, both male and female. In their view, Murphy was offensively 'naked', being unaccompanied and inappropriately clothed. I reflect that my twin, my own parallel life, could not have entered that apartment in Ramallah as I did. It is an enclosed space, and male controlled. I consider too that I was made complicit in the construction of that space as I interacted with the daughter of the home in full compliance with house rules. My twin's welcome would have been much different to the one I experienced: she would have had to have been masked, to have worn modestly coloured clothes, to have been accompanied by me. It is for a reason that she is a visual artist who does not choose to depict the political. Together we are Janus-like, for she cannot look, while I cannot look away. I am fatally flawed. I am as if I stare at the sun, eyes wide open. Unseen, the ultraviolet waves flood my eyes. Unfelt, the light burns my retina. The damage is disabling. In my staring, I turn the sun into a scorching orb, like the eye of Balor,[148] a photochemical bomb. In our own ways, she and I both are products of the 'gendered constitution of political violence' that is the Troubles of NI.[149]

Of course, none of the gendered effects of political violence are fixed but rather they are, according to the anthropologist Begoña Aretxaga, 'constantly shifting, depending on the contingencies of history, social class, and ethnic identity';[150] and, as the very substantial body of research on gender and the Troubles amply demonstrates, women are therefore as likely to be activists engaged in political struggle, as they might be activists for peace, or perpetrators of violence, or indeed amongst its victims.[151] Whatever our differences, we find common ground in the Troubles novels of Anna Burns (*No Bones*, 2001, *Little Constructions*, 2007, and *Milkman*, 2018) wherein she deploys 'absurdity, carnivalesque and fantastical imagery to explore the unknowability at the centre of trauma'.[152] Burns's aim in her writing, according to Anthea E. Cordner, is 'to defamiliarise the reader and enable the trauma of the violence to be understood in ways that other forms of writing would be unable to access'.[153] Burns, Cordner, notes, does not share much of her personal biography, even when being interviewed. Cordner suggests that perhaps this particular reticence 'is a way of preventing the closing down of interpretations of her novel into autobiographical interpretations and therefore allowing it to speak as a representation, not only of the Northern Troubles but of more universal themes concerning the impact of violence and trauma'.[154] Perhaps so: there may be much common ground between Palestine and Ireland on that front. And one of its defining characteristics is, surely, the omnipresence of PTSD and the fracturing of self and past.[155] Certainly, that which Cordner says of *No Bones* (2001) and *Little Constructions* (2007), is true also of *Milkman* (2018):

> In both of Burns' novels dysfunctional family life mirrors the dysfunctional violence of the surrounding community to show how invasive and insidious political violence can be on the supposedly private world of the family, and ultimately on the

individual. Burns explores gender by creating fragmented character, unreliable narration, disjointed plotlines and innovative stylistics.[156]

Indeed, this could have been written for my twin, about my twin, by my twin. This could have been her personal narrative, her memoir, her autoethnography.

Not unreasonably, criticism is made of the maleness of *Apeirogon*, noting McCann's 'apparent lack of interest in the novel's female characters' whereby 'the dead daughters are voiceless: the wives are passive, shadowy figures' and noting also his preference for 'lofty ruminations on male genius'.[157] I might draw attention in addition to the wholly male environment of *An Evil Cradling* but then note that the campaign to secure Keenan's release from captivity was 'spearheaded' very publicly by his sisters Brenda Gillham and Elaine Spence. Their story has been told by the journalist Anne Maguire in the book *For Brian's Sake*.[158] Maguire was an outstanding contemporary of mine at the Queen's University Belfast, being the president of the students' union there between 1986 and 1987. She died at the age of twenty-eight in a fatal car crash in County Tyrone on 30 June 1992.[159] *For Brian's Sake* had been published barely two months previously, on 1 May 1992. Stories within stories. When aesthetic, rhetorical and social forms meet, overlap, or even collide, the conditions are created for a kind of social epistemology, defined as 'an enterprise concerned with how people can best pursue the truth (whichever truth is in question) *with the help* of, or *in the face* of, others'.[160] According to Lorraine Code, the interaction of rhetoric and social epistemology allows for the development of non-ideal 'truth' that is constructed from 'testimony' from 'somewhere in particular'.[161] This in turn enables the 'affective engagement with the subject matter'.[162] In other words, it is to do with 'attempting to know responsibly and well in a real, diversely configured, and multiply populated world'.[163] She argues that epistemology is not rhetorically neutral, rather, 'When place and epistemic subjectivity claim a constitute part in hitherto dislocated inquiry (i.e. idealised theorisation), rhetorical strategies claim a new legitimacy'.[164] Thus, the forms at hand here are all rhetorical statements also, whether autobiography, biography, prosimetrum, novel, travelogue or painting.

Equally, the reviews of these aesthetic or creative works too are rhetorical statements. Taken together, these constitute an epistemic community and create a dialogue of moral social epistemology in the shape of an ongoing argument as exemplified by Abulhawa's antagonistic review of *Apeirogon*, in which she articulates in particular her hostility to the fact that Steven Spielberg has acquired the film rights to *Apeirogon*, referring to his stated willingness to, if necessary, 'die for Israel'.[165] The shape of this argument is exemplified too by Bright's criticism of *A Month by the Sea* as a 'flawed, partisan portrait' and 'not a travel book at all', contending instead that '[t]his is a travelogue entirely without a journey'.[166] If this collision of forms is a moral disagreement as to what Palestine ought to be, then it serves to bring into focus a number of problems: to the extent that Palestine is a moral disagreement, are the fault lines that define this issue symptomatic of differences in moral sensibilities rather than being to do with differences over substantive matters of fact? Alternatively, if moral knowledge about Palestine may be said to be attainable, is it the case that the moral facts of the case are relative to the epistemic community at hand here, and that there are no universal moral truths to be known and held about Palestine? The conflict in Palestine may appear to be wholly intractable,[167] but we ought not despair because moral progress is possible,[168] even with the most recondite of issues.

Notes

1. Caroline Levine, 'Forms, literary and social', *Dibur Literary Journal*, 2/Spring (2016), 75–9, at 76.
2. Levine, 'Forms, literary and social', p. 79.
3. Levine, 'Forms, literary and social', p. 76.
4. Caroline Levine, *Forms: Whole, Rhythm, Hierarchy, Network* (Princeton, NJ: Princeton University Press, 2015), p. xiii.
5. Levine, *Forms: Whole, Rhythm, Hierarchy, Network*, p. xii.
6. Levine, *Forms: Whole, Rhythm, Hierarchy, Network*, p. xii.
7. Carolyn Kellogg, 'Colum McCann journeys to Israel and Palestine', *Kirkus*, 30 March 2020: https://www.kirkusreviews.com/news-and-features/articles/colum-mccann-apeirogon-interview/ (accessed 6 June 2023).
8. Lisa Morgan and Marion Winik, 'Around the world: new novels from Christine Baker Kline and Colum McCann', *WYPR – 88.1 FM Baltimore*, 1 September 2020: https://www.wypr.org/wypr-features/2020-09-01/around-the-world-new-novels-from-christine-baker-kline-and-colum-mccann (accessed 6 June 2023).

9   Donna Seaman, 'Apeirogon by Colum McCann', *Booklist*, 1 December 2019: https://www.booklistonline.com/Apeirogon-Colum-McCann/pid=9726923 (accessed 6 June 2023).

10 Charles Finch, 'Colum McCann's "Apeirogon" takes an elliptical approach to the unending Middle East conflict', *The Washington Post*, 10 March 2020: https://www.washingtonpost.com/entertainment/books/colum-mccanns-apeirogon-takes-an-elliptical-approach-to-the-unending-middle-east-conflict/2020/03/10/5670fd48-62db-11ea-acca-80c22bbee96f_story.html (accessed 6 June 2023).

11 Julie Orringer, 'Apeirogon by Colum McCann', *The New York Times*, 24 February 2020: https://www.nytimes.com/2020/02/24/books/review/colum-mccann-apeirogon.html (accessed 6 June 2023).

12 Ben Libman, 'Also about birds: the Israeli–Palestinian conflict in Colum McCann's "Aperiogon"', *The Los Angeles Review of Books*, 28 February 2020: https://lareviewofbooks.org/article/also-about-birds-the-israeli-palestinian-conflict-in-colum-mccanns-apeirogon/ (accessed 6 June 2023).

13 Desmond Traynor, 'Apeirogon: a brave high-wire act piecing together loss', *The Irish Times*, 3 March 2020.

14 Sarah Murdoch, 'Puzzling over Colum McCann and Catherine Steadman's hotly anticipated new books', *The Toronto Star*, 26 February 2020: https://www.thestar.com/entertainment/books/2020/02/26/were-colum-mccann-and-catherine-steadmans-hotly-anticipated-new-books-worth-the-wait.html (accessed 6 June 2023).

15 New York State Writers Institute, *Colum McCann on His Latest Novel Apeirogon*, 18 September 2020: https://www.youtube.com/watch?v=e2lQSmiKayw (accessed 6 June 2023).

16 Claire Lowdon, 'Apeirogon, a novel by Colum McCann review – on fiction's front line', *The Sunday Times*, 23 February 2020: https://www.thetimes.co.uk/article/apeirogon-a-novel-by-colum-mccann-review-on-fictions-front-line-tkxc9zdbk (accessed 6 June 2023).

17 Johanna Thomas-Corr, 'Colum McCann's Apeirogon: an ambitious work of "documentary fiction"', *New Statesman*, 19 February 2020: https://www.newstatesman.com/column-mcann-apeirogon-review (accessed 6 June 2023).

18 Orringer, *The New York Times*: https://www.nytimes.com/2020/02/24/books/review/colum-mccann-apeirogon.html (accessed 6 June 2023).

19 Lowdon, *The Sunday Times*: https://www.thetimes.co.uk/article/apeirogon-a-novel-by-colum-mccann-review-on-fictions-front-line-tkxc9zdbk (accessed 6 June 2023).

20 Ellen Atkins, '"Apeirogon" by Colum McCann', *The Star Tribune*, 25 February 2020: https://www.startribune.com/review-apeirogon-by-colum-mccann/568074272/ (accessed 6 June 2023).

21 Ben East, '"Apeirogon": why Colum McCann felt compelled to tell a story of the Palestinian–Israeli conflict', *The National News*, 2 April 2020: https://www.

      thenationalnews.com/arts-culture/books/apeirogon-why-colum-mccann-felt-compelled-to-tell-a-story-of-the-palestinian-israeli-conflict-1.998244?gclid=EAIaIQobChMI1N Ch1djs8gIVR-vtCh1pQwUnEAMYASAAEgIUi_D_BwE (accessed 6 June 2023).

22 Donna Steadman, 'Apeirogon', *Booklist*, 1 December 2019: *https://www.booklistonline.com/Apeirogon-Colum-McCann/pid=9726923* (accessed 6 June 2023).

23 Ian Sansom, 'Apeirogon by Colum McCann review – new perspectives on Palestine', *The Guardian*, 12 March 2020: *https://www.theguardian.com/books/2020/mar/12/apeirogon-by-colum-mccann-review* (accessed 6 June 2023).

24 Finch, *The Washington Post*: *https://www.washingtonpost.com/entertainment/books/colum-mccanns-apeirogon-takes-an-elliptical-approach-to-the-unending-middle-east-conflict/2020/03/10/5670fd48-62db-11ea-acca-80c22bbee96f_story.html* (accessed 6 June 2023).

25 Morgan and Winik, *WYPR – 88.1 FM Baltimore*: *https://www.wypr.org/wypr-features/2020-09-01/around-the-world-new-novels-from-christine-baker-kline-and-colum-mccann* (accessed 6 June 2023).

26 Libman, *The Los Angeles Review of Books*: *https://lareviewofbooks.org/article/also-about-birds-the-israeli-palestinian-conflict-in-colum-mccanns-apeirogon/* (accessed 6 June 2023).

27 Adrian Salmon, '"Apeirogon" Colum McCann', *The Blue Nib Literary Magazine*: *https://thebluenib.com/adrian-salmon-reviews-colum-mccanns-apeirogon/* (accessed 6 June 2023).

28 Kirkus, 'Apeirogon by Colum McCann', *Kirkus Reviews*, 28 October 2019: *https://www.kirkusreviews.com/book-reviews/colum-mccann/apeirogon/* (accessed 6 June 2023).

29 Rosemary Sorensen, 'Colum McCann's Apeirogon review: a courageously ambitious novel of our time', *Daily Review*, 3 April 2020: *https://dailyreview.com.au/colum-mccanns-apeirogon-review-a-courageously-ambitious-novel-of-our-time/* (accessed 6 June 2023).

30 McCann, *Colum McCann on his latest novel Apeirogon*: *https://www.youtube.com/watch?v=e2lQSmiKayw* (accessed 6 June 2023).

31 Jerome Boyd Maunsell, 'Taking sides: Tales of fracture and repair by Ronit Matalon, Zeruta Shalev and Colum McCann', *The Times Literary Supplement*, 13 March 2020: *https://www.the-tls.co.uk/articles/pain-shalev-apeirogon-mccann-matalon-maunsell/* (accessed 6 June 2023).

32 Elizabeth Toohey, 'Two fathers' broken hearts guide them toward heroic empathy', *The Christian Science Monitor*, 5 March 2020: *https://www.csmonitor.com/Books/Book-Reviews/2020/0305/Two-fathers-broken-hearts-guide-them-toward-heroic-empathy* (accessed 6 June 2023).

33 McCann, *Apeirogon*, p. 461.

34 McCann, *Apeirogon*, p. 461.

35 Levine, *Forms: Whole, Rhythm, Hierarchy, Network*, p. 24.
36 Waterstones, *Colum McCann: The Waterstones Interview*, 25 February 2020: https://www.youtube.com/watch?v=D2iBL-I_FiY&t=596s (accessed 6 June 2023).
37 East, *The National News*: https://www.thenationalnews.com/arts-culture/books/apeirogon-why-colum-mccann-felt-compelled-to-tell-a-story-of-the-palestinian-israeli-conflict-1.998244?gclid=EAIaIQobChMI1NCh1djs8gIVR-vtCh1pQwUn-EAMYASAAEgIUi_D_BwE (accessed 6 June 2023).
38 McCann, *Apeirogon*, p. 417.
39 Levine, *Forms: Whole, Rhythm, Hierarchy, Network*, p. 48.
40 Levine, *Forms: Whole, Rhythm, Hierarchy, Network*, pp. 16–17.
41 Levine, 'Forms, literary and social', p. 75: https://arcade.stanford.edu/sites/default/files/article_pdfs/Dibur-v02i01-article07-Levine.pdf (accessed 1 June 2023).
42 Levine, 'Forms, literary and social', p. 75.
43 Levine, *Forms: Whole, Rhythm, Hierarchy, Network*, p. 22.
44 Tariq Jazeel and Nayanika Mookherjee, 'Aesthetics, politics, conflict', *Journal of Material Culture*, 20/4 December (2015), 353–9, at 356.
45 Levine, *Forms: Whole, Rhythm, Hierarchy, Network*, pp. 6–7.
46 Levine, *Forms: Whole, Rhythm, Hierarchy, Network*, p. 46.
47 Libman, *The Los Angeles Review of Books*: https://lareviewofbooks.org/article/also-about-birds-the-israeli-palestinian-conflict-in-colum-mccanns-apeirogon/ (accessed 6 June 2023).
48 Erica Wagner, 'Apeirogon – a daring, humane story of reconciliation Colum McCann's novel is based on a real-life Israeli–Palestinian friendship', *The Financial Times*, 21 February 2020: https://www.ft.com/content/0efe30b6-4e59-11ea-95a0-43d18ec715f5 (accessed 6 June 2023).
49 McCann, *Apeirogon*, p. 3.
50 McCann, *Apeirogon*, p. 457.
51 McCann, *Apeirogon*, p. 229.
52 Stephan Phelan, 'Review: Apeirogon by Colum McCann', *The Herald*, 22 February 2020: https://www.heraldscotland.com/life_style/arts_ents/18241497.review-apeirogon-colum-mccann/ (accessed 6 June 2023).
53 McCann, *Apeirogon*, Author's Note.
54 Maunsell, *The Times Literary Supplement*: https://www.the-tls.co.uk/articles/pain-shalev-apeirogon-mccann-matalon-maunsell/ (accessed 6 June 2023).
55 Theo van Leeuwen, 'Rhetoric and semiotics', in M. J. MacDonald (ed.), *The Oxford Handbook of Rhetorical Studies* (Oxford: Oxford University Press, 2014), p. 2.
56 McCann, *Apeirogon*, p. 98.
57 McCann, *Apeirogon*, pp. 13, 83, 115, for example.
58 McCann, *Apeirogon*, p. 296.

59 Susan Abulhawa, 'Apeirogon: another colonialist misstep in commercial publishing', *Al Jazeera*, 11 March 2020: *https://www.aljazeera.com/opinions/2020/3/11/apeirogon-another-colonialist-misstep-in-commercial-publishing* (accessed 6 June 2023).

60 Kevin Murphy, 'Reinvention and rejuvenation', *Irish Literary Supplement*, 20/2 (1 September 2001), 12–13, at 12. The quotation by Carson is from p. 186 in Ciarán Carson, 'Escaped from the massacre?', *Honest Ulsterman*, 50 (Winter 1975), 183–6.

61 Murphy, *Irish Literary Supplement*, p. 12.

62 *Mornings in Jenin* (2006), *The Blue Between Sky and Water* (2015), *Against the Loveless World* (2020).

63 *My Voice Sought the Wind* (2013).

64 BDS: *https://bdsmovement.net/* (accessed 2 June 2023); Al-Awda, the Palestine Right to Return Coalition: *https://al-awda.org/* (accessed 6 June 2023); Playgrounds for Palestine: *https://playgroundsforpalestine.org/* (accessed 6 June 2023).

65 Philip Weiss, 'Abulhawa on her Palestinian epic: "My exile has defined my life and I don't need to account for the sensitivities of the people who did that to me"', *Mondoweiss*, 3 December 2020: *https://mondoweiss.net/2020/12/abulhawa-on-her-palestinian-epic-its-really-important-to-me-for-palestinian-characters-and-literature-to-speak-their-truth-without-apology/* (accessed 6 June 2023).

66 Abulhawa, *Al Jazeera*: *https://www.aljazeera.com/opinions/2020/3/11/apeirogon-another-colonialist-misstep-in-commercial-publishing* (accessed 6 June 2023).

67 Abulhawa, *Al Jazeera*.

68 Abulhawa, *Al Jazeera*.

69 V. Mahesh, '"The Israeli Occupation is fundamentally and undeniably unjust": Colum McCann', *The Hindu*, 29 May 2021: *https://www.thehindu.com/books/books-authors/the-occupation-is-fundamentally-and-undeniably-unjust-colum-mccann/article34664100.ece* (accessed 6 June 2023).

70 I borrow the term here from Caroline van Eck, 'Rhetoric and the visual arts', in MacDonald, *The Oxford Handbook of Rhetorical Studies*, pp. 461–74, at p. 461.

71 See, for example, Jessica Hemming, 'Pale horses and green dawns: elusive colour terms in early Welsh heroic poetry', *North American Journal of Celtic Studies*, 1/2 (November 2017), 189–223.

72 See, for example, p. 227, footnote 40 in John Carey, 'The three sails, the twelve winds, and the question of Early Irish colour theory', *Journal of the Warburg and Courtauld Institutes*, 72 (2009), 221–32.

73 The definition is ascribed to Murray on p. 31 in Alfred K. Siewers, 'The bluest-greyest-greenest eye: colours of martyrdom and colours of the winds

as iconographic landscape', *Cambrian Medieval Celtic Studies*, 50 (Winter 2005), 31–66.

74   Ellie Violet Bramley, 'In the Instagram age, you actually can judge a book by its cover', *The Guardian*, 18 April 2021: *https://www.theguardian.com/books/2021/apr/18/in-the-instagram-age-you-actually-can-judge-a-book-by-its-cover* (accessed 6 June 2023).

75   Bramley, *The Guardian*: *https://www.theguardian.com/books/2021/apr/18/in-the-instagram-age-you-actually-can-judge-a-book-by-its-cover* (accessed 6 June 2023).

76   Michael John Goodman, 'Yes, you really can judge a book by its cover', *The Conversation*, 29 September 2016: *https://theconversation.com/yes-you-really-can-judge-a-book-by-its-cover-65768* (accessed 6 June 2023).

77   Van Eck, 'Rhetoric and the visual arts'.

78   Van Leeuwen, 'Rhetoric and semiotics'.

79   *https://www.instagram.com/explore/tags/bookstagram/?hl=en* (accessed 6 June 2023).

80   *Yellow Nineties 2.0*: *https://1890s.ca/yellow-book-volumes/* (accessed 6 June 2023).

81   Stanley Weintraub, 'The Yellow Book: a reappraisal', *The Journal of General Education*, 16/2 (July 1964), 136–52, at 137.

82   Culture Northern Ireland, *A Profile of Dermot Seymour*, 5 January 2006: *https://www.culturenorthernireland.org/article/486/a-profile-of-dermot-seymour* (accessed 6 June 2023).

83   Arts Council of Northern Ireland, *Artist of the Month February 2019 – Dermot Seymour*, 1 February 2019: *http://artscouncil-ni.org/advocacy/article/northern-ireland/artist-of-the-month-february-2019-dermot-seymour* (accessed 6 June 2023).

84   Jim Smyth, 'Dermot Seymour. A load of old Boellix', in J. Hurley et al (eds), *Contemporary Art from Ireland, 19 May 2005–12 August 2005* (Frankfurt am Main: European Central Bank, 2005), pp. 62–3, at p. 62.

85   Aidan Dunne, 'Art in focus: Hiberno god by Dermot Seymour', *The Irish Times*, 23 November 2019: *https://www.irishtimes.com/culture/art-and-design/visual-art/art-in-focus-hiberno-god-by-dermot-seymour-1.4088223* (accessed 6 June 2023).

86   Slash/Paris, *Dermot Seymour – Des bêtes et des homes* (2012): *https://slash-paris.com/en/evenements/dermot-seymour-des-betes-et-des-hommes* (accessed 6 June 2023) and Dunne, *The Irish Times*: *https://www.irishtimes.com/culture/art-and-design/visual-art/art-in-focus-hiberno-god-by-dermot-seymour-1.4088223* (accessed 6 June 2023).

87   Arts Council of Northern Ireland. Troubles archive, *On the Balcony of a Nation by Dermot Seymour* (2014): *http://www.troublesarchive.com/artforms/visual-art/piece/on-the-balcony-of-a-nation* (accessed 6 June 2023).

88   Culture Northern Ireland, *A Profile of Dermot Seymour*: *https://www.culturenorthernireland.org/article/486/a-profile-of-dermot-seymour* (accessed 6 June 2023).

89 Noel Kelly, 'In conversation with Dermot Seymour', *The Painting Imperative. International Contemporary Painting Magazine*, 15 December 2011: https://thepaintingimperative.wordpress.com/archive/issue-2/in-conversation-with-dermot-seymour/ (accessed 6 June 2023).

90 Kelly, *The Painting Imperative. International Contemporary Painting Magazine*: https://thepaintingimperative.wordpress.com/archive/issue-2/in-conversation-with-dermot-seymour/ (accessed 6 June 2023).

91 Tina O'Sullivan, 'Northern exposure: an artist in the Troubles', *Irish Examiner*, 30 August 2012: https://www.irishexaminer.com/lifestyle/arid-20205726.html (accessed 6 June 2023).

92 Keenan, *An Evil Cradling*, pp. 1 and 2.

93 Keenan, *An Evil Cradling*, p. 34.

94 Keenan, *An Evil Cradling*, p. 41.

95 Keenan, *An Evil Cradling*, p. 97.

96 Keenan, *An Evil Cradling*, p. 100.

97 Keenan, *An Evil Cradling*, p. 1.

98 Keenan, *An Evil Cradling*, p. 81.

99 Walls of Gaza (1 of 12): https://www.barjeelartfoundation.org/collection/laila-shawa-walls-of-gaza-1/ (accessed 6 June 2023).

100 The Recessionists, *Laila Shawa*: http://www.therecessionists.co.uk/middle-eastern/laila-shawa (accessed 6 June 2023).

101 https://www.p-art-icipate.net/salzburgs-school-of-seeing-the-salzburg-international-summer-academy-of-fine-arts/ (accessed 6 June 2023).

102 Some sources say 1972.

103 See, for example, David K. Shipler, 'Palestinian mayor of Gaza is dismissed by the Israelis', *The New York Times*, 10 July 1982: https://www.nytimes.com/1982/07/10/world/palestinian-mayor-of-gaza-is-dismissed-by-the-israelis.html (accessed 6 June 2023) and The Los Angeles Times, 'Rashad Shawwa: Palestinian leader in Gaza Strip', *The Los Angeles Times*, 28 September 1988: https://www.latimes.com/archives/la-xpm-1988-09-28-mn-2622-story.html (accessed 6 June 2023).

104 https://artsandculture.google.com/exhibit/the-walls-of-gaza-ii-contemporary-art-platform-kuwait/3wLyhN7aSWVkIw?hl=en (accessed 6 June 2023).

105 http://www.therecessionists.co.uk/middle-eastern/laila-shawa (accessed 6 June 2023).

106 http://www.therecessionists.co.uk/middle-eastern/laila-shawa (accessed 6 June 2023).

107 Amira Nagy, 'Women and the veil: the art of Laila Shawa. In conversation with Amira Nagy', *Women in Islam Journal*, 7 November 2018, online publication date: https://www.womeninislamjournal.com/articles/2018/10/30/women-and-the-veil-the-art-of-laila-shawa (accessed 6 June 2023).

108 Laila Shawa, 'Laila Shawa. Artistic statement', *Signs: Journal of Women in Culture and Society* (2012): *http://signsjournal.org/laila-shawa/* (accessed 6 June 2023).
109 Laila Shawa, *YouTube*, 17 September 2014: *https://www.youtube.com/watch?v=4rMGAIsfMK0* (accessed 6 June 2023).
110 Mia Bloom, 'Mother. Daughter. Sister. Bomber', *Bulletin of the Atomic Scientists*, November/December (2005), 54–62, at p. 59.
111 One reviewer describes the title *A Month by the Sea* as having the effect of ironically disguising the work as a 'picture-postcard account' – Tom Adair, 'Book review: A month by the sea: encounters in Gaza', *The Scotsman*, 16 March 2013: *https://www.scotsman.com/arts-and-culture/book-review-month-sea-encounters-gaza-1585260* (accessed 6 June 2023).
112 Murphy, *A Month by the Sea*, jacket cover.
113 *https://artsandculture.google.com/exhibit/the-walls-of-gaza-ii-contemporary-art-platform-kuwait/3wLyhN7aSWVkIw?hl=en* (accessed 6 June 2023).
114 *https://artsandculture.google.com/exhibit/the-walls-of-gaza-ii-contemporary-art-platform-kuwait/3wLyhN7aSWVkIw?hl=en* (accessed 6 June 2023).
115 Sophie Richter-Devroe, *Gender Equality and Women's Rights in Palestinian Territories* (Brussels: European Parliament Directorate-General for Internal policies. Policy Department C. Citizens' Rights and Constitutional Affairs, 2011), p. 15.
116 Richter-Devroe, *Gender Equality and Women's Rights in Palestinian Territories*, p. 1.
117 Richter-Devroe, *Gender Equality and Women's Rights in Palestinian Territories*, p. 16.
118 UN Women, *Giving a Voice to Gender-based Violence Survivors in Palestine*, Feature, 16 August 2023: *https://www.unwomen.org/en/news-stories/feature-story/2023/08/giving-a-voice-to-gender-based-violence-survivors-in-palestine* (accessed 21 February 2024).
119 IDF, *The Status of Women in Gaza*, 25 January 2018: *https://www.idf.il/en/mini-sites/the-hamas-terrorist-organization/the-status-of-women-in-gaza/* (accessed 2 February 2024).
120 Islah Jad, 'Islamist women of Hamas: between feminism and nationalism', *Inter-Asia Cultural Studies*, 12/2 (2011), 176–201, at p. 184.
121 Minna Cowper-Coles, *Gender and Political Support: Women and Hamas in the Occupied Palestinian Territories* (London: Routledge, 2022).
122 UN Women, *UN Women Report Reveals Devastating Impact of the Crisis in Gaza on Women and Girls*, Press Release, 20 October 2023: *https://www.unwomen.org/en/news-stories/press-release/2023/10/press-release-un-women-report-reveals-devastating-impact-of-the-crisis-in-gaza-on-women-and-girls* and p. 1 in UN Women, *UN Women rapid assessment and humanitarian response in the Occupied Palestinian Territory*, 20 October 2023: *https://www.unwomen.org/sites/default/*

123 UN Committee on the Exercise of the Inalienable Rights of the Palestinian People, *UN Women Report Reveals Devastating Impact of the Crisis in Gaza on Women and Girls*, Press Release, 20 October 2023: https://www.un.org/unispal/document/un-women-report-reveals-devastating-impact-of-the-crisis-in-gaza-on-women-and-girls/ (accessed 22 February 2024).

files/2023-10/un-women-rapid-assessment-and-humanitarian-response-in-the-occupied-palestinian-territory-en.pdf (accessed 21 February 2024).

124 See, for example, Global Centre for the Responsibility to Protect, *Atrocities Present, Past and Future – Escalating Crimes and Consequences in Israel and Occupied Palestine*, Commentary, 27 October 2023: https://www.globalr2p.org/publications/atrocities-present-past-and-future-escalating-crimes-and-consequences-in-israel-and-occupied-palestine/ (accessed 22 February 2024).

125 UN, Office of the High Commissioner for Human Rights, *Women Bearing the Brunt of Israel-Gaza Conflict: UN Expert*, Press Release, 20 November 2023: https://www.ohchr.org/en/press-releases/2023/11/women-bearing-brunt-israel-gaza-conflict-un-expert (accessed 21 February 2024).

126 UN News, *'Clear and Convincing Information' that Hostages Held in Gaza Subjected to Sexual Violence, says UN Special Representative*, 4 March 2024: https://news.un.org/en/story/2024/03/1147217 (accessed 5 March 2024). See also, Office of the Special Representative of the Secretary-General on Sexual Violence in Conflict, *Mission Report. Official Visit of the Office of the SRSG-SVC to Israel and the Occupied West Bank 29 January–14 February 2024*: https://news.un.org/en/sites/news.un.org.en/files/atoms/files/Mission_report_of_SRSG_SVC_to_Israel-oWB_29Jan_14_feb_2024.pdf (accessed 5 March 2024).

127 Office of the Special Representative of the Secretary-General on Sexual Violence in Conflict, *Mission Report*, p. 11, and see also p. 19.

128 Office of the Special Representative of the Secretary-General on Sexual Violence in Conflict, *Mission Report*, pp. 4–5.

129 Office of the Special Representative of the Secretary-General on Sexual Violence in Conflict, *Mission Report*, pp. 5–6.

130 Office of the Special Representative of the Secretary-General on Sexual Violence in Conflict, *Mission Report*, p. 15.

131 Dúnlaith Bird, *Travelling in Different Skins: Gender Identity in European Women's Oriental Travelogues, 1850–1950* (Oxford: Oxford University Press, 2012), p. 240.

132 Bird, *Travelling in Different Skins*, p. 238.

133 Bird, *Travelling in Different Skins*, p. 240.

134 Bird, *Travelling in Different Skins*, p. 1.

135 Murphy, *A Month by the Sea*, p. 11.

136 Murphy, *A Month by the Sea*, p. 182.

137 Murphy, *A Month by the Sea*, p. 175.

138 Murphy, *A Month by the Sea*, p. 104.
139 Murphy, *A Month by the Sea*, p. 105.
140 Murphy, *A Month by the Sea*, pp. 202–3.
141 Murphy, *A Month by the Sea*, p. 156.
142 Murphy, *A Month by the Sea*, p. 57.
143 Murphy, *A Month by the Sea*, pp. 181–2.
144 Murphy, *A Month by the Sea*, p. 85.
145 Murphy, *A Month by the Sea*, pp. 22–4, 33–5, 46–7, 154–60, 187–9, 202–3, 226.
146 Murphy, *A Month by the Sea*, pp. 22–4, 42–3, 50–1, 60, 76–7, 172–4, 178–9, 180, 203–8, 210–13.
147 Adair, *The Scotsman*.
148 Dáithí Ó hÓgáin, *Myth, Legend and Romance: An Encyclopedia of the Irish Folk Tradition* (London: Prentice Hall, 1991), pp. 43–5.
149 Begoña Aretxaga, *Shattering Silence: Women, Nationalism, and Political Subjectivity in Northern Ireland* (Princeton, NJ: Princeton University Press, 1997).
150 Aretxaga, *Shattering Silence*.
151 The literature on this is very extensive, but see, for example, the following: Begoña Aretxaga, 'The sexual games of the body politic: Fantasy and state violence in Northern Ireland', *Culture, Medicine and Psychiatry*, 25/1 (2001), 1–27; Begoña Aretxaga, 'Dirty Protest: Symbolic Overdetermination and Gender in Northern Ireland Ethnic Violence', *Ethos*, 23/2 (1995), 123–48; Hannah Piecuch, 'Feminism during the Troubles in Northern Ireland', *The Onyx Review: The Interdisciplinary Research Journal*, 3/1 (2017), 37–4 ; Aisling Swaine, 'Resurfacing gender: a typology of conflict-related violence against women for the Northern Ireland Troubles', *Violence Against Women*, 29/6–7 (2023), 1391–418; Mary S. Corcoran, *Out of Order: The Political Imprisonment of Women in Northern Ireland 1972–1998*, (London: Routledge, 2006); Monica McWilliams, 'Struggling for peace and justice: reflections on women's activism in Northern Ireland', *Journal of Women's History*, 7/1 (1995), 13–39; Joyce P. Kaufman, 'Women and political violence in Northern Ireland: newspaper imagery during the troubles', *Women's History Review*, 30/7 (2021), 1141–61; Valerie Morgan, *Peacemakers? Peacekeepers? Women in Northern Ireland 1969–1995. A Professorial Lecture given at the University of Ulster on Wednesday 25 October 1995*: https://cain.ulster.ac.uk/issues/women/paper3.htm (accessed 21 February 2024); Theresa O'Keefe, 'Policing unruly women: the State and sexual violence during the northern Irish Troubles', *Women's Studies International Forum*, 62 (2017), 69–77.
152 Anthea E. Cordner, 'Writing the Troubles: gender and trauma in Northern Ireland' (unpublished PhD thesis, Newcastle University, 2014). Available at: *https://theses.ncl.ac.uk/jspui/handle/10443/3437*

153 Cordner, 'Writing the Troubles', p. 198.
154 Cordner, 'Writing the Troubles', p. 197.
155 Cordner, 'Writing the Troubles', pp. 203–211.
156 Cordner, 'Writing the Troubles', p. 201.
157 Thomas-Corr, *New Statesman*.
158 Anne Maguire, *For Brian's Sake: The Story of the Keenan Sisters* (Belfast: Blackstaff Press Ltd, 1992).
159 Emily Moulton, 'Bleak history of the Ballygawley Road', *The Belfast Telegraph*, 2 June 2008: https://www.belfasttelegraph.co.uk/news/bleak-history-of-the-ballygawley-road-28397826.html (accessed 6 June 2023).
160 Stanford Encyclopedia of Philosophy, *Social Epistemology* (2001, revised edition 2019): https://plato.stanford.edu/entries/epistemology-social/ (accessed 6 June 2023).
161 Lorraine Code, 'Rhetoric and social epistemology', in MacDonald, *The Oxford Handbook of Rhetorical Studies*, pp. 721–32, at p. 724.
162 Code, 'Rhetoric and social epistemology', p. 722.
163 Code, 'Rhetoric and social epistemology', p. 724.
164 Code, 'Rhetoric and social epistemology', p. 721.
165 The statement comes from an interview Spielberg gave to *Spiegel* magazine as part of the publicity round for his film *Munich* on the topic of the Olympic massacre of 1972, during which the Palestinian group Black September killed eleven members of the Israeli Olympic team: Spiegel, 'Spiegel interview with Steven Spielberg "I would die for Israel"', *Spiegel International*, 26 January 2006: https://www.spiegel.de/international/spiegel/spiegel-interview-with-steven-spielberg-i-would-die-for-israel-a-397378.html (accessed 6 June 2023).
166 Martin Bright, 'Book of the week: A month by the sea: encounters in Gaza, by Dervla Murphy', *The Independent*, 22 March 2013: https://www.independent.co.uk/arts-entertainment/books/reviews/book-of-the-week-a-month-by-the-sea-encounters-in-gaza-by-dervla-murphy-8546386.html (accessed 6 June 2023).
167 This conflict is, for many, the very definition of intractable. See, for example, the chapter entitled 'An intractable conflict and an irreconcilable past: contesting the "other" through commemoration in Israel/Palestine', in Sara McDowell and Máire Braniff, *Commemoration as Conflict: Space, Memory and Identity in Peace Processes* (Basingstoke: Palgrave Macmillan, 2014), pp. 102–24; Amnon Aran, *The Middle East: Intractable Conflict?: The Israeli-Palestinian Impasse: Will This Time be Different?* (LSE IDEAS, London School of Economics and Political Science, London UK, 2009): http://eprints.lse.ac.uk/43643/1/The%20Middle%20East_the%20Israeli-Palestinian%20impasse(lsero).pdf and Clotilde de Swarte, 'Explaining the intractability of the Israeli-Palestinian conflict', *Fair Observer*, 23 November 2014: https://www.fairobserver.com/region/middle_east_north_africa/explaining-the-intractability-of-the-israeli-palestinian-conflict-17124/

(accessed 6 June 2023); Nathan J. Brown, 'The old Israeli-Palestinian conflict is dead – long live the emerging Israeli-Palestinian conflict', *Carnegie Endowment for International Peace*, 5 May 2021: *https://carnegieendowment.org/2021/05/05/old-israeli-palestinian-conflict-is-dead-long-live-emerging-israeli-palestinian-conflict-pub-84457* (accessed 6 June 2023); Jacob Bercovitch and S. Ayse Kadayifci, 'Conflict management and Israeli-Palestinian conflict: the importance of capturing the "right moment"', *Asia-Pacific Review*, 9/2 (2002), 113–29; Josef Olmert, 'A half century of occupation: Israel, Palestine, and the world's most intractable conflict by Gershon Shafir (Oakland, CA: University of California Press, 2017), reviewed by Josef Olmert', *Israel Journal of Foreign Affairs*, 12/1 (2018), 113–15; Philippe Assouline and Robert Trager, 'Concessions for concession's sake: injustice, indignation, and the construction of intractable conflict in Israel–Palestine', *Journal of Conflict Resolution*, 65/9 (2021), 1489–520; United Nations, *Question of Palestine Remains Most Intractable Conflict Situation in United Nations History*. Press Release GA/9250. GA/PAL/761, 10 June 1997: *https://www.un.org/press/en/1997/19970610.ga9250.html* (accessed 6 June 2023).

168 Allen Buchanan and Russell Powell, *The Evolution of Moral Progress: A Biocultural Theory* (New York: Oxford University Press, 2018).

CHAPTER 5

The Seeing Places

What might it mean to say, 'There, that is where it happened', and to say that it was once called home? Any poet of the dispossessed would put it like this, surely: 'My address:/ An unarmed village – forgotten –/ Whose streets are nameless,/ And all its men are in the field and quarry./ Are you angry?'[1] The poet would have been no more than seven years of age when his family were uprooted from the village of al-Birwa[2] in Galilee during the 1948 Arab–Israeli War. He wrote the poem as a young adult, sixteen years later. By then, al-Birwa was no more, neither people nor place. In its vicinity, the kibbutz[3] of Yas'ur and the moshav[4] of Ahihud had been built, as if in its stead. By then too, many of the villagers of al-Birwa had found shelter in the Lebanese refugee camp of Ain al-Hiweh.[5] And by now, the Lebanese government has built a wall, complete with watchtowers, all around Ain al-Hiweh.[6]

Shore

One of my gatekeepers in Palestine told me once the story of how he took his family to Jaffa to see the Mediterranean Sea. It is called the White Middle Sea: al-Baḥr al-Abyad al-Muttawasit البحر الأبيض المتوسط. It has many names. Some call it the Sea of Philistines, did I know? Others call it the Syrian Sea.[7] It was a very difficult journey from east Jerusalem. It should only take forty minutes. It is only sixty kilometres. But it took all day. Imagine that, for a trip to the sea. His wife's voice. Full of humour. The car, an ancient Volkswagen Golf, was the reason. Then, his voice. Perhaps it was indeed overpriced. But it was a good car. From Europe. And they had to do it. It was a political act. Because of al-Nakba,[8] he had to take them to the sea. The Catastrophe. To remember. You see? I reflected on this later in my fieldnotes. He did not remember. None of them did. Indeed, none of them could for they were each born at least twenty years after the events of 1948. To memorialise, was what he meant. And if the memory is involved at all in this procedure it is not that of individual psychology but rather of collective culture.[9]

It is not obvious from *An Evil Cradling* that Brian Keenan ever noticed the seafront of Beirut, but he certainly remembered it. Thus, when he returned to the city for a BBC television documentary[10] about his period of captivity there, one of the places he was determined to visit, bringing his wife and two young sons with him, was the beach. This was part of an effort on his part to ensure that they 'see the country as something other than a land of imprisonment and hate' and 'to see the country I never got to see'.[11] Indeed, the beach holds a special place for Keenan in the making of this new life for he proposed to his wife on 'an absolutely deserted beach in the west of Ireland'.[12] Moreover, while not the actual subject of his writing, the beach is a point of reference in the process of writing for Keenan. For example, when first attempting to pen *An Evil Cradling* Keenan says the following:

> With 'Evil Cradling' I drove around for weeks and weeks thinking how I am going to write this? There was a long time when nothing happened and everything happened. I drove to an empty beach, an ancient graveyard and a beautiful hilltop looking out over the sea. I sat for ages writing metaphors and other stuff, thoughts on eternity, emptiness and death – anything that came into my head. And then I went home, tore all the pages out, laid them out on the bed and switched the tape recorder on. I didn't look at the notes once but it all just came pouring out. The next morning I listened back to the tapes and I sat there, in my cottage with the tears rolling down my face because that was me back in Lebanon talking to me now.[13]

This typically western world notion of the beach and the place it conjures – pleasure destination, contrastive escape from the city, site of staged authenticity, part carnivalesque, part sexualised[14] – is something our other rhetoricians, McCann, Murphy and Osmond, manipulate in their presentation of the Palestinian shore to their intended audience.

At the structural heart of *Apeirogon*, in terms of its internal arrangement or dispositio, McCann uses the beach to contrast the parallel lives of Rami Elhanan and Bassam Aramin. This part of the text is also the physical centre of the book. Here, in two separate chapters, adjacent to one another but both numbered '500', the two senses of place held each by Rami and Bassam are drawn in relation to access to the beach. Thus, Rami's world is as follows: 'It may sound strange but in Israel we don't really know what the Occupation actually is … Our lives are good … The beach is open'.[15] And from McCann's portrait of Bassam, voice is given to the alternative in this manner: 'You see, the Occupation exists in every aspect of your life, an exhaustion and a bitterness that nobody outside it really understands. It deprives you of tomorrow … It stops you from going to the market, to the hospital, to the beach, to the sea'.[16] In anticipation of this, McCann imagines Bassam's daughter, Abir, longing for a trip to the shores of the sea. She has seen it from afar but knows that it will always be beyond reach for as long as 'the Occupation' remains: 'In art class, at school in Anata, Abir sketched out a picture of the blue Mediterranean that she had only ever seen from the tops of tower blocks'.[17] Abir is in prison as much as her father once was. And there, Bassam and his fellow prisoners, says McCann, would draw succour from incanting the poetry of Mahmoud Darwish: 'A sea for us, a sea against us'.[18] The line is from the poem entitled 'We journey towards a home'.[19] The 'vivid'[20] and unsettling sea; desirable and unattainable; connecting us and dividing us.

In addition, physical images of the sea adorn *Apeirogon* in several places.[21] McCann tells us what that means here:

> On the clearest of days, from the highest vantage points of Beit Jala,[22] you can see all the way to the Mediterranean in one direction and to the Dead Sea in the other./ The eye cannot rest. Down below, in the valley, an orchard, a watchtower, a terraced field, the roof of a synagogue, a minaret, a military gate, a series of mist nets among the remaining trees./ Stay here long enough, looking down into the valley, and you will notice the settlements emerging in a pattern around Jerusalem: red tile, red tile, red tile./ Coming together, a perfect ring: the rim of a tightening lung.[23]

Framed by sea, the 'tightening lung' is that of 'the Occupation'. And yet, here too are revealed certain limitations to *Apeirogon* arising out of the tension between the text as a work of serious literary fiction, and in particular as a novel, and the text as a rhetorical disquisition or commentary. While the 'rim of a tightening lung', oft-repeated in the book, may be valued by McCann as a rhetorical device, it is 'an overdone image' according to literary critic Claire Lowdon.[24] That said, McCann's horizon, where the earth of Palestine meets the seas, here evokes a place beyond 'the Occupation': liminal space, where it is possible to be in two places at once; the shore, where the world is two things at once; *Aperiogon*, an infinite polygon, where Rami and Bassam are one and the same.

Dervla Murphy does not see a multiplicity of sides; she does not see two sides; she sees one side, and makes of that a virtue. 'Of all the countries that I visited, that is the only one where I felt it was my actual *duty* as a writer *not* to be neutral ... We must *only* look at the fact that the Palestinians are treated utterly outrageously' (the italics are in the original text), she said in an interview subsequent to the publication of *Between River and Sea*.[25] Similarly, elsewhere, she is quoted extensively by Rosemary Behan during the course of an interview upon the publication of *A Month by the Sea*:

> One of the big differences between Ireland and Israel is that I never had any problem looking at the two sides in Ireland./ That is, not only looking at but seeing both sides. And actually, even in South Africa among the Boers and Afrikaaner farmers in the Transvaal I could feel a certain sympathy for their cause, horrendous though the basis for apartheid was. None of this can I see in Israel ... I think it's wrong to say, 'I'm going to be neutral about the Palestine thing ... I'm going to be objective and balanced.' The situation is so appalling that I think it would be immoral to be fair, neutral and balanced.[26]

The blockade of Gaza is 'the situation', of course, and Murphy's choice of title and subtitle for her book draws attention to it by juxtaposing a cliché from western world tourism, the notion of a month by the sea as an idyllic retreat to a sun-kissed shore, with the grim reality of the Gaza Strip. The following excerpt from Tom Adair's review of *A Month by the Sea* captures the effect of this:

> Her humour is tersely understated, injected with irony. You sample it here in the title, A Month by the Sea, which disguises

a far from picture-postcard account of the writer's latest foray into risk, with nothing remotely resembling a deck-chair to be seen – although admittedly there are beaches (one long string of beach, to be accurate) pocked and rubble strewn, beneath an astringent sky, which has weathered more than its fair share of rocket-propelled explosives, fired with intent in both directions, but mostly from Israel into Gaza./ The book's subtitle sets us straight. "Encounters in Gaza" perfectly summarises what follows ... The boundaries of the Strip are everywhere evident – from the guard towers sealing the border, under the gaze of suspicious Israelis, to the perimeter of beach, 23 miles long, blockaded intensively round the clock.[27]

For Murphy, the abnormality of Gaza's beach, in particular the lack of urban development that mars the western Mediterranean littoral in the west, is deceptively alluring. But this is only at first glance for further enquiry reveals the unpleasant truth of the matter:

> Back on the coast road – the sea dancing brightly a few yards away, the sandy roadside vegetable fields densely green – I marvelled at the absence of any building. That evening Nabil explained: an acute shortage of fresh food made it essential to protect this fertile stretch where native Gazans maintain an ancient tradition of using morning dew to supplement an ever-dwindling water supply. Those few miles reminded us that Gaza, when normally populated, had its own sort of tranquil beauty.[28]

And if Nabil is guilty of harnessing nostalgia in explaining this peculiar consequence of the blockade of Gaza in terms of an almost forgotten practice of gathering the morning dew to replenish water supplies, Murphy also sees value in the same when contrasting the present lifelessness of Gaza's beach with its former vibrancy: 'Under Egyptian rule ... [there was] dancing on the beach ... tax-free shopping, safe swimming off a smooth, 20-mile-long beach and seafood restaurants with snob-value'.[29] Nostalgia for Egyptian rule? The blockade of Gaza is not Israel's alone, of course, for Egypt is a partner in that. Their joint blockade was imposed after Hamas ejected Fatah from the Gaza Strip by force as the endgame of the Battle of Gaza in June 2007: a bloody and brutal[30] internecine affair, involving the murky involvement of MI6 in its prelude[31] as well as the CIA and others in its execution.[32] Egypt's motivations, different to those of Israel, are founded in a fear of the increasing influence of Iran in Gaza through Hamas.[33] While the blockade has been sporadically eased since June 2010, it remains in place.

In other parts, the reality of the beach is failed development and damaged lives. Murphy lays this out almost from her first day in Gaza:

> On Day Two I walked indirectly to the beach ... The pavements were ankle-deep in fine golden sand, many of the office blocks, engineering works, stores and restaurants looked either partially used or abandoned ... Here I gave thanks for the relief of a frisky breeze off the Mediterranean. Below me children played on a poisonously littered shore – untreated sewage flowing into the sea, domestic garbage heaped around chunks of people's bombed homes.[34]

Not all of the emotional damage is caused by the actions of external others such as Israel: Murphy's beach is also a site of gendered, internal oppression:

> During the summer holidays Saleh often took them all to Gaza's most beautiful beach, near Khan Younis and previously reserved for settlers ... [T]he three girls – aged thirteen, fourteen and sixteen – couldn't go to the beach (or anywhere else) without an adult male relative ... Nita caught my eye and made a soothing gesture. She could guess what I was thinking – "How outrageous that a girl old enough to be married can't take her younger siblings to the beach!"[35]

Murphy notes too how the UNRWA was threatened with bullets in the post for having organised beach camps for girls[36] and how it seemed that the beach was under perpetual surveillance by certain 'soberly dressed youths',[37] the watchmen foot soldiers of some militia group. It was on this beach too that Murphy was 'kidnapped'[38] by a family and taken to their home in Shatti refugee camp: 'Not for many years have I visited a crowded place as tourist-free as Gaza beach, where I was seen

The Seeing Places

as an object of interest, a stranger to be offered help and hospitality'.[39] Thus, Murphy presents this place, this dangerous and abnormal beach, to her audience as the portal to the world of the dispossessed of the Palestinian shore.

This is the Gaza beach that Osmond sees (Illustration 1), even as he casts his local gaze over the beach in his own Llansteffan: a horrific aberration;[40] this is the beach of Operation Cast Lead. The sun sits askew in the sky, bruised red and raw, dizzied by the violence. Yet, neither does Osmond's own shore at home survive this onslaught, for only a short year or so later he comes to see that also much differently. Sensitised, perhaps, by the trauma of Gaza, he sees that place too as a site of militarised violence. Announcing his *Hawk and Helicopter* exhibition of 2011, Mission Gallery in Swansea describes how this work, which is Osmond's 'account by drawing, painting and text'[41] of the shoreline around Llansteffan and the neighbouring village of Laugharne, an area that is a government sanctioned wildlife conservation site but also a military practice zone and testing ground. Thus, '[t]he innocence of coastal land suddenly becomes something else. This is the hawk's home

Illustration 1 *Operation Cast Lead by Osi Rhys Osmond, 2009*

and he kills to live. The helicopter comes to rehearse killing for strategic reasons, the land, sea and air lose their virtue, beauty becomes conflated with terror'.[42]

Street

A contact escorted me through Qalandiya[43] refugee camp. We walked its streets and alleyways (Photograph 2). Established in 1949 and currently home to around 10,000 souls, it is situated between Jerusalem and Ramallah. Importantly for how things are run there, it has been designated as being in Area C[44] under the Oslo II Accord[45] and therefore under Israeli control in terms of civil administration and security control, for the time being. But, in practice, the activity of any agent of the State of Israel there is much contested, and it could be said that Israeli control is not much more than nominal in a number of regards. Qalandiya is in reality subject to the claims of sovereignty of various actors, as is the case, indeed, with Palestinian refugee camps in many locations.[46] When the camp was first established, the UNRWA and Fatah were indisputably the dominant actors. But by now the power and influence of the UNRWA has been undermined by the Oslo II Accord because the expectation is that the body will become redundant when responsibility for the camp is transferred to the PNA. As regards Fatah, its position as the dominant political faction has been eroded by Hamas since the death of Yasser Arafat in 2004 along with the bloody fall-out from the Palestinian legislative election of 2006, which was won by Hamas, and the subsequent Palestinian Civil War, 2006–7. Criminal gangs with various, loose political affiliations exercise some power too in Qalandiya, specifically because PNA security forces are legally not allowed to enter the camp. And when they do so they are un-uniformed as a matter of necessity, apparently: 'the [Palestinian security] forces typically arrive dressed as civilians and … pluck people off the streets by pulling them into vehicles, and quickly heading off towards Ramallah'.[47] As a result, Qalandiya has been described as 'no man's land' and as a 'chaotic base for terror'.[48] According to the UNRWA,[49] the security forces of Israel 'conduct frequent operations' in the Qalandiya.[50] During one such incursion in 2014 two residents were killed, one of whom was a member of staff of the UNRWA. Such violence is an ongoing feature of daily life there as attested by the following report from November 2020:

The Seeing Places

Two Palestinian young men were shot and injured by rubber-coated steel bullets in clashes that broke out during an Israeli military raid into Qalandia refugee camp, north of occupied Jerusalem, according to local sources./ Eye-witnesses told WAFA news agency that Israeli forces raided Qalandia refugee camp and took over the rooftops of several buildings, including a Fatah movement headquarters, and turned them into military outposts, leading to clashes./ Forces fired rubber-coated steel bullets, stun grenades, and a barrage of tear gas canisters at residents, shooting and injuring two youth, including one in his eye. Dozens of Palestinians reportedly suffocated due to heavy tear gas inhalation.[51]

As we walked, Qalandiya closed around us, the gloomy architecture the signature of the deliberate underdevelopment of this quasi-temporary urban slum. I hesitate to use the word ghetto. My contact does not. The lack of development is deliberate in so far as the resident refugees are resistant to the site feeling permanent in any sense.[52] Yet, if not

Photograph 2 *Figures on an unnamed street in Qalandiya refugee camp, April 2017*

permanent, it is much more than temporary: it is a 'protracted encampment'.[53] This condition of permanent temporariness is not exceptional, unfortunately, for the refugees of today's world. Dorota Woroniecka-Krzyzanowska notes that as of 2015 'nearly half of the world's refugees lived in protracted situations that, on average, lasted for over twenty-five years'.[54] A fourth generation is now being born there in Qalandiya.[55] By when does such displacement change meaning and the transient identity of the refugee become something else? What do the streets say?

> The semi-public alleys that constitute the camp spaces can momentarily be transformed into 'private' refuge for those who are persecuted by different political structures. While usually these alleys have specific functions constrained by social considerations of privacy, at certain moments the alleys can acquire other functions, reinvented as strategic escape and supply routes when it comes to supporting the resistance movements in the camp. During the second intifada, the Israeli army demolished large swathes of the Jenin refugee camp in an attempt to undo the spatial order of the alleys.[56]

Similar such things have been said about the redevelopment undertaken during the 1980s in relation to the streets of 'Free Derry', a large section of the western part of the city that had declared autonomy and resisted incursions by the British Army and the RUC between 1969 and 1972.[57] But I could see at the time, even with my own young eyes, the newness of the Rossville Flats[58] in the Bogside area of Free Derry; after all, this multi-storey block of flats, where our elderly baby-sitter lived, had been completed only in 1966. These are the streets of dislocation and alienation, the alleyways of al-Nakba.

McCann has Bassam walking Palestine amongst the streets of the Holylands in Belfast. He is there for an academic conference. There is a sense that he is beguiled, almost, by the symmetry: 'Bassam was taken by the names of the streets: Palestine, Cairo, Jerusalem, Damascus .../ Palestine Street was a row of red-brick houses, dark gates, tiny gardens. Jerusalem Street ran into a cul-de-sac. There had, he heard, been many shootings here, late into the night. Short streets, long memories'.[59] If the analogy drawn between Palestine and NI is Bassam's by origin, McCann soon owns it as well. Thus, the 'slalom' of NI acronyms, 'DUP, UVF,

IRA, UFF, RIHA, ABD, RSF, UDA, INLA', is 'another smashed jigsaw' in Palestine, 'PLO, JDL, DFLP, LEHI, PFLP, ALA, PIJ, CPT, IWPS, ICAHD, AIC, AATW, EIJ, JTJ, ISM, AEI, NIF, ACRI, RHR, BDS, PACBI, BNC', and both places equate to a shape comprised of '[a] countably infinite number of sides',[60] namely the apeirogon. For Keenan too the streets of Belfast become those of another city: 'We arrived, eventually at The Mayflower Hotel in the Hamra area of Beirut. There was a curious comfort in this. Apart from the reassurance of light and convivial surroundings, the name itself was welcoming. My home in Belfast was in Mayflower St. "Home from home?" I thought and then again: "Frying pan to fire? Another Belfast?"'[61] I see the same thing too. It could be that Belfast was at one time nothing more than Beirut in the rain[62] and that Hebron and Derry are of one. Someone has written it on the wall in Irish – Tiocfaidh ár lá / Our day will come (Photograph 3): the idiom of Irish republicanism.[63] It is the rhetoric that makes it real.

What do the streets feel? I revisit Duke Street in Derry on 5 October 1968 via YouTube.[64] I hope to see my father again, full of life. It is the occasion of the Civil Rights March. I watch for his face. Other faces and

Photograph 3 *Irish language political graffito on the West Bank separation barrier, Abu Dis, April 2017*

voices speak out. History will remember them. It's official.⁶⁵ Professor Paul Arthur of the University of Ulster calls the events of Duke Street, where the RUC cudgelled the peaceful demonstrators to the ground, from the street, 'the game changer'. I gaze into the old television footage like a medieval alchemist scrying into an obsidian mirror. He is there. Elsewhere, Martin McGuinness, of Sinn Féin and Deputy First Minister of NI, says that the participation of his own father in the march on Duke Street on that day had 'a massive impact' on him, especially so given that his father was the 'mildest' of men, non-political and very religious.⁶⁶ So, our fathers shared Duke Street.

I thought that I shared another Derry street once with Martin McGuinness. On my way home from school, having stayed late, and the light was fading. Perhaps it was autumn, and the Irish republican hunger strike was in its seventh month. Those who would die had already died. Ten men dead.⁶⁷ Waiting for the bus on John Street, it was late, delayed by some unknowable event, and the city was quiet. I waited, and as I waited some part of the city unquietened. The sound rose gradually, as if soft, as if gentle, as if soothing. I could hear it upon the river as it was carried on an ebb tide from the heart of the city and out into the darkness of the ocean of the north Atlantic. I could hear their feet falling upon the streets now and their voices calling in rhythm. Then I could see them at the top of the street, and those leading them could see me too. I thought that I saw Martin McGuinness there, to the fore. They called out their support for the dead Irish hunger strikers, and for those who would yet live. My school uniform, sectarian maroon, marked me out as not one of them and so they fell silent as they approached me alone on the street. That colour, how it was hated, and how I had been assaulted for its wearing many times already, in the city, on its streets. I had thought, for a moment, to run, but to where? They came towards me. I did not move. One of their voices, solitary, authoritative, owning the street, called out to me. I said nothing. Whatever you say, say nothing.⁶⁸ After all, these were his people, and not mine, the Irish republicans of Free Derry.⁶⁹ I said nothing, and they passed me by, in their hundreds, in silence. I thought of them one day on Sarei Yisrael Street in Jerusalem where I found myself amongst a Haredi throng of several hundred (Photograph 4). They filled the street and those around it with their darkly costumed figures. Those too young to venture into the street viewed the demonstration from the safety of the surrounding

The Seeing Places

Photograph 4 *Haredi demonstration, Sarei Yisrael Street, Jerusalem, July 2019*

rooftops. They were resisting the conscription of one of their people to the IDF; and not for the first time;[70] and they have sometimes asserted their resistance with violence.[71] This time they danced and they sang. How they filled the early evening air with their exhortations. They felt the streets tremble.[72]

'Short streets, long memories', McCann says of Bassam in the Holylands.[73] Lower Main Street, Strabane, 15 June 1982. The death of Hugh Cummings, UDR footsoldier. In *Lost Lives* he is entry number 2,436.[74] Our family and his own knew him as Lexie. We shopped often upon that street. We visited the dentist there. Killed, allegedly, by William Gerard McMonagle, IRA footsoldier, according to reports and rumours of reports.[75] McMonagle's family know him as Gerry. By some accounts it was a drive by shooting. Lexie was shot in his Mini car by a gunman seated in a Ford Cortina. He was on his lunch break from work. It was a menswear shop. Though arrested and charged with the shooting, the court case against Gerry McMonagle collapsed due to bureaucratic incompetence. He eventually escaped across the border to Donegal in the Republic of Ireland. As a part of the peace process of the late 1990s and early 2000s he was given an OTR (On The Run) letter[76] by the UK Government of Prime Minister Tony Blair, an amnesty, a get-out-of-jail-free card. Given a second life, he built something of a political career in Donegal as a leading member of Sinn Féin, becoming Mayor of Letterkenny, Chair of Donegal Council, and Mayor of Donegal. This is the politics of peace: (former) gunmen in government. In the meantime, the case of the killing of Lexie Cummings was reviewed by the Historical Enquiries Team (HET), a unit established in 2005 within the Police Service of Northern Ireland (PSNI) charged with examining hitherto unsolved political killings in the period between 1968 and 1998,[77] but it was found that the PSNI concluded that 'nothing further could be done with the case'.[78]

I remember it too for being in the middle of the 1982 football world cup tournament then being hosted by Spain. Another troubled place, and other troubled peoples, despite the fact that the fascist dictator Franco had died a few years previously, in 1975. Even on his deathbed he authorised the execution of ETA[79] activists. ETA was not sated by the dictator's death. In 1975 ETA laid claim to twenty deaths; in 1980 it was fivefold that number.[80] NI's football team, a mixture of Catholics and Protestants, won a most famous victory over host nation Spain just a few days after he had been gunned down on Lower Main Street. Had he been witness to the game, Lexie would have loved that. He was a football man, a Spurs fan to boot. I should add too that although he was a member also of the Orange Order,[81] the Apprentice Boys of Derry,[82] and the Royal Black Preceptory,[83] the usual suspects to some, I'm sure, he had been born a 'Roman Catholic' and been 'saved' by his adoptive family. Even the dogs in the streets[84] of Strabane knew that. Such conversions were much prized in some quarters, as was for others the serving of retribution against them for their transgression.

The desire for closure is the defining affective quality of the seeing places. The seeing places are shaped by the architecture of closure – the checkpoint, the barrier, the wall, the closed gates. And yet, the principal feature of closure in these places is its unattainability. This is the sensibility of the careful witness. Closure for some means protection against the Other; and for some again it means exclusion as the Other. And perhaps it is the same for every such place. McCann shows us how the Interface Barriers of Belfast[85] are become the Separation Wall of the West Bank, for example:

> For five years it was the best-paying construction job in the area: the workers called it the Shekel Wall ... A plastic bag animated itself above the walls: it popped in the wind and sounded momentarily like a rifle shot. Nobody flinched. The Peace Walls were still up in Belfast even years after the Good Friday Agreement.[86]

And how many names this closure has! McCann lists them:

1) the Administration Wall,
2) the Annexation Wall,
3) the Apartheid Wall,
4) the Cage,
5) the Colonisation Wall,
6) the Coop,
7) the Curse Wall,
8) the Demographic Wall,
9) the Fear Wall,
10) the Infiltrator Wall,
11) the Isolation Wall,
12) the Noose,
13) the Noose Wall,
14) the Obstacle Wall,
15) the Peace Wall,
16) the Pen,
17) the Protector,
18) the Racist Wall,
19) the Reconciliation Wall,
20) the Sanctuary Wall,
21) the Security Wall / Barrier / Fence,
22) the Separation Wall / Barrier / Fence,
23) the Shame Wall,
24) the West Bank Wall,
25) the Saboteurs' Wall,

26) the Seam-Zone Wall,
27) the Territories Wall,
28) the Terrorist Wall,
29) the Trap,
30) the Unification Wall.[87]

Murphy transits the agony of unattainable closure twice. The first time is upon entering Gaza; the second is upon departure. Both times it is through Rafah Gate. Initially, there is keen anticipation: 'Half an hour after el-Arish, Rafah Gate's formidable superstructure rose above the desert's bleached flatness ... [I]t suddenly seemed incredible that I was about to enter Gaza'.[88] There's also an encouraging encounter with a native of Gaza in the vestibule: 'Welcome to Gaza! You are from where? From Ireland – then more welcomes to Gaza! In Ireland is Gerry Adams and many, many good friends for Palestine!'[89] But the first police officer she presents her papers to simply says, 'Today is problems'.[90] She had arrived Rafah Gate at 11.45 in the morning[91] but would not pass through it until sometime after 4.40[92] in the afternoon, five hours later, and seven pages of detailed and increasingly angry frustration. Departure began a month later, at 7.50 in the morning[93] in the vestibule of Rafah Gate. First it turned 10.40.[94] Then it turned 12.25.[95] Then 1.40.[96] And then 4.20.[97] It was 6.40 in the evening[98] as she left, around eleven hours and fourteen pages of exhausting text later. Even then she still feels compelled to return for her journey is incomplete.[99]

The completed, incomplete journey. For Abir, shot by school gates, the delay at the checkpoint was, perhaps, fatal. The decision to move her from the Palestinian hospital in the West Bank to the Hadassah Hospital in Jerusalem, the 'Israeli hospital', was repeated several times by McCann.[100] Rhetorical repetition underscores the polemic, the relative poverty of healthcare in the West Bank. The twenty-minute drive to Hadassah Hospital took much longer than it ought to have done. Two hours later the ambulance was still waiting at the checkpoint to cross into Jerusalem.[101] Hadassah, at Ein Kerem, 'an ancient Palestinian village, once'.[102] Hadassah, at Ein Kerem, a prism made by the painted windows of Marc Chagall (Photograph 5). Neither Bassam nor McCann, nor even Rami, spoke of this wonder. 'We have ... no Chagall', lamented Edward W. Said once of the impoverishment of the Palestinians.[103] There are no windows in such seeing places. And yet

Photograph 5 *Chagall windows – Asher, Naphtali, Joseph and Benjamin, Abbell Synagogue, Hadassah Hospital, Ein Kerem, July 2019*

there they are. Osmond, the artist, knew of them, and he told another to tell me to see them there for myself. Perhaps, as a synagogue, it felt a forbidden space to Bassam, beyond his places. Just as Free Derry was a forbidden city to some.

Osmond, in Palestine in July and August 1986, approached Nablus with the trepidation of a place that had 'the menace of the forbidden city'[104] but found for himself that the sentiment was largely in the mind of his Jewish friends. For them, of course, Nablus had been under the direct administration of the IDF since 1982 and would remain so until January of 1986. Two months after that the mayor whom the Israelis had installed on their departure was assassinated by gunmen of the Popular Front for the Liberation of Palestine, part of the PLO. Then, during the First and Second Intifada Nablus earned an empirically real reputation as a major hub for the origination of suicide bombers.[105] In contrast, Osmond found there 'his best day yet' for 'Palestinian people and landscape' and that it felt 'something like S. Wales'.[106] Both things are true. Seeing these places too, I thought how they are made and unmade. They could be made for me in the Prisoners' Section of Nablus Municipality Library[107] or in the Educational Bookshop on Salah ad-Din Street in east Jerusalem. These are the places for engaged internationals, for 'journalists, aid workers, activists and intellectuals'.[108]

Even while I am there I recall, however, the fate of the radical bookshop known as the Bookworm in Derry as it moved to from its original location on Orchard Street to Bishop Street in the city centre. Radicalism became commodified and mainstreamed,[109] presented up for consumerism and for John Urry's tourist gaze.[110] While I could conjure it so – Look! See the children playing happily on the street! (Photograph 6), optimism is not an obvious quality of Palestine's seeing places. See the male space that is the Haredi demonstration, and

Photograph 6 *Children, the Old City, Jerusalem, July 2019*

see too the common space of Qalandiya that is common only to those of the male persuasion, for as Alaqra admits 'women's access to the camp's common space is limited by implicit and explicit social norms'.[111] Murphy asks rhetorically, in feminist mode, 'are these the laws for which the Palestinian Street is waiting?' She hopes not.[112] And see too the end of history in the Palestine Papers in which it is recorded for posterity that the Palestinian negotiators were ready to give up the right of return of the refugees of al-Nakba. Such a thing would be 'illogical',[113] agreeing that only '10,000 refugees and their families' out of a population of five million should have the right to return.[114] What does this mean in Gaza? There, refugees constitute the overwhelming majority of the population, 1.4 million out of a total of 1.9 million;[115] it is a society of refugees. Whither home the children of al-Nakba?

Notes

1 Mahmoud Darwish, 1942–2008: *https://www.poetryfoundation.org/poets/mahmoud-darwish* and Salman Hilmy, 'ID Card by Mahmoud Darwish – a translation and commentary', *Washington Report on Middle East Affairs*, November/December 2017: *https://www.wrmea.org/017-november-december/id-card-by-mahmoud-darwish-a-translation-and-commentary.html* (accessed 7 June 2023).

2 *https://m.facebook.com/www.berwa/posts/barwa-palestinian-village-displaced-subsidiary-of-acre-district-located-105-km-k/140925049412780/* and *https://www.palestineremembered.com/Acre/al-Birwa/* (accessed 7 June 2023).

3 A Jewish community settlement based upon collectivist principles: *http://archive.jewishagency.org/first-home-homeland/program/16766* (accessed 7 June 2023).

4 A Jewish community settlement based upon cooperative, as opposed to collectivist, principles: *https://mfa.gov.il/MFA/AboutIsrael/Maps/Pages/Kibbutz-and-Moshav.aspx* (accessed 7 June 2023).

5 *https://www.unrwa.org/where-we-work/lebanon/ein-el-hilweh-camp* (accessed 7 June 2023).

6 Ghinwa Obeid, 'Ain al-Hilweh wall nearly completed', *The Daily Star. Lebanon*, 23 February 2017.

7 As Nur Masalha amply demonstrates in *Palestine: A Four Thousand Year History* (London: I. B. Tauris, 2018, new edition 2022), the naming and renaming of places is inherently political and is very often a feature of conquest and colonisation.

8   This refers to the displacement of around 750,000 Palestinian Arabs as a result of the Arab–Israeli War of 1948. For many of these refugees, along with their descendants, this displacement has become permanent as they have been granted no right of return by the State of Israel, notwithstanding UN General Assembly Resolution 194 (III) of 11 December 1948: *https://unispal.un.org/DPA/DPR/unispal.nsf/0/ C758572B78D1CD0085256BCF0077E51A*. As I write, in excess of 5.6 million Palestinians are registered by the UNRWA as refugees: *https:// www.unrwa.org/sites/default/files/about_unrwa_two_pager_english_2020.pdf* (accessed 7 June 2023).

9   The collective memory refers to 'both the shared frameworks that shape and filter ostensibly "individual" or "personal" memories *and* representations of the past sui generis', according to Christina Simko, 'Collective memory', *Oxford Bibliographies* (Oxford: Oxford University Press, 27 February 2019): *https://www.oxfordbibliographies.com/view/document/obo-9780199756384/obo-9780199756384-0215.xml* (accessed 7 June 2023).

10 BBC, 'Brian Keenan: back to Beirut', *BBC Two*, Monday 31 March 2008.

11 Antonia Hoyle, '18 years on, Beirut hostage Brian Keenan returns to the city that left him a "living corpse"', *The Daily Mail*, 16 March 2008: *https:// www.dailymail.co.uk/news/article-535370/18-years-Beirut-hostage-Brian-Keenan-returns-city-left-living-corpse.html* (accessed 7 June 2023).

12 The Irish Independent, 'How Brian Keenan found love and learned to live again', *The Irish Independent*, 25 August 1999: *https://www.independent.ie/ irish-news/how-brian-keenan-found-love-and-learned-to-live-again-26142070.html* (accessed 7 June 2023).

13 Brian Keenan quoted by BBC News, 'Brian Keenan on spirituality, faith, writing and fear', *BBC News*, 9 February 2011: *https://www.bbc.co.uk/news/ world-europe-isle-of-man-12409595* (accessed 7 June 2023).

14 See John Urry and Jonas Larsen, *The Tourist Gaze 3.0* (London: Sage, 2011, third edition), pp. 46–7, 68, 190–1 and 195. See also Lena Lencek and Gideon Bosler, *The Beach: The History of Paradise on Earth* (London: Secker and Warburg, 1998).

15 McCann, *Apeirogon*, p. 225.

16 McCann, *Apeirogon*, p. 236.

17 McCann, *Apeirogon*, p. 62.

18 McCann, *Apeirogon*, p. 88.

19 Published in translation in the volume edited by Mahmoud Darwish, Munir Akash, Carolyn Forché, Sinan Antoon, Amira El-Zein and Fady Joudah, *Unfortunately, It Was Paradise: Selected Poems* (Berkeley, CA: University of California Press, 2013), p. 10: *http://www.jstor.org/stable/10.1525/j. ctt2855v1.13* (accessed 7 June 2023).

20 I borrow this description from p. 64 in Khaled M. S. Masood, 'Manifestations of nature and politics in Mahmoud Darwish's metaphors', *Journal of Literature, Languages and Linguistics*, 66 (2020), 53–66.
21 McCann, *Apeirogon*, pp. 215, 244 and 459.
22 Beit Jala is a small Palestinian Christian town situated in the Bethlehem Governate in the West Bank: *http://vprofile.arij.org/bethlehem/pdfs/VP/Beit%20 Jala_cp_en.pdf* (accessed 7 June 2023).
23 McCann, *Apeirogon*, p. 83.
24 Claire Lowdon, 'Apeirogon, a Novel by Colum McCann review – on fiction's front line. A novelisation of the Israeli–Palestinian conflict told through two grieving fathers', *The Sunday Times*, 23 February 2020: *https://www.thetimes.co.uk/edition/culture/apeirogon-a-novel-by-colum-mccann-review-on-fictions-front-line-tkxc9zdbk* (accessed 7 June 2023).
25 MK, 'In Israel and Palestine, I felt it was my duty as a writer not to be neutral', *Deskbound Traveller. Writing That Takes You Away* (2015): *https://deskboundtraveller.com/travel-books/in-israel-and-palestine-i-felt-it-was-my-duty-as-a-writer-not-to-be-neutral/* (accessed 7 June 2023).
26 Rosemary Behan, 'Fighting words', *The National News. Arts & Culture*, 17 October 2013: *https://www.thenationalnews.com/arts-culture/books/fighting-words-1.302413* (accessed 7 June 2023).
27 Tom Adair, 'Book review: A Month by the Sea: Encounters in Gaza', *The Scotsman*, 16 March 2013: *https://www.scotsman.com/arts-and-culture/book-review-month-sea-encounters-gaza-1585260* (accessed 7 June 2023).
28 Murphy, *A Month by the Sea*, p. 19.
29 Murphy, *A Month by the Sea*, p. 26.
30 The international human rights NGO, Human Rights Watch, found both Hamas and Fatah to have committed 'serious violations of humanitarian law, in some cases amounting to war crimes' during the Battle of Gaza – Human Rights Watch, 'Gaza: armed Palestinian groups commit grave crimes', 12 June 2007: *https://www.hrw.org/news/2007/06/12/gaza-armed-palestinian-groups-commit-grave-crimes* (accessed 7 June 2023).
31 As evidenced in the so-called *Palestine Papers*, a cache of documents relating to the Israeli–Palestinian negotiations between 1999 and 2010 leaked to the news network Al Jazeera in 2011: *https://www.memopublishers.com/images/uploads/documents/the-palestine-papers-a-matter-of-public-interest.pdf* (accessed 7 June 2023). The papers are available here: *https://www.jewishvirtuallibrary.org/the-palestine-papers*
32 David Rose, 'The Gaza bombshell', *Vanity Fair*, 3 March 2008: *https://www.vanityfair.com/news/2008/04/gaza200804* (accessed 7 June 2023).
33 Israel Hayom, 'Egypt makes surprise move against Hamas and Iran', *Israel Hayom*, 2 November 2020: *https://www.israelhayom.com/2020/02/11/*

egypt-makes-surprising-move-against-hamas-and-iran/ (accessed 7 June 2023); Shlomi Eldar, 'Hamas must choose: Egypt or Iran?', *Al Monitor*, 10 January 2020: *https://www.al-monitor.com/pulse/originals/2020/01/israel-iran-hamas-egypt-qasem-soleimani-ismail-haniyeh-gaza.html* (accessed 7 June 2023); Al Monitor, 'Shadow war: Egypt and Iran battle for influence in Gaza', *Al Monitor*, 26 July 2019: *https://www.al-monitor.com/pulse/originals/2019/07/shadow-war-egypt-iran-battle-influence-gaza.html* (accessed 7 June 2023).

34 Murphy, *A Month by the Sea*, pp. 31–3.
35 Murphy, *A Month by the Sea*, pp. 97–8.
36 Murphy, *A Month by the Sea*, pp. 187–8.
37 Murphy, *A Month by the Sea*, pp. 195–6.
38 Murphy, *A Month by the Sea*, p. 61.
39 Murphy, *A Month by the Sea*, p. 61.
40 'When they started bombing Gaza I realised that the Gaza strip is about the same size as the coastline and water that I see from my garden in Llansteffan, so I was struck by the image of a million-and-a-half people down there with bombs and rockets falling on them.' Osi Rhys Osmond on *Ymateb/Response*, quoted on the weblog *Britain is No Country for Old Men*, 13 March 2015: *https://britainisnocountryforoldmen.blogspot.com/2015/03/wales-within-britain-is-no-longer.html* (accessed 7 June 2023). Once, I experienced a similar such aberration in Llansteffan, at the top of the little road called Water Lane where it meets the High Street. Crossing High Street, I was on my way to the beach, for Water Lane leads all the way to there. Unusually, a long queue of cars, lorries and vans had come to a standstill on High Street, filling the road. The traffic was being diverted from the dual carriageway some ten miles away, closed by the police following a fatal accident there in the early hours after midnight. As I crossed unto Water Lane the driver of a supermarket delivery van called out to me. He wanted to know whether I knew if the traffic was moving at all further up the village. As I talked, he listened attentively. Then he asked me where I was from. Obviously, I don't have a local accent. Ireland, I said. Yes, but which part, he asked, if I didn't mind saying. I said the north-west. Was he familiar with that part, I asked. He was, he said. Where exactly, he asked. Derry, I said, or Londonderry. I know about that, he said, for I was stationed there several times. With the army, I said, obviously. I was with the Paratroopers, he said. The British Army's Parachute Regiment was notorious in Derry for having shot dead thirteen unarmed civilians in the Bogside area of the city in the aftermath of a Civil Rights march on 30 January 1972, an event that has become known as Bloody Sunday (see *https://cain.ulster.ac.uk/events/bsunday/bs.htm*). I said to him that they have a reputation in the city. He said that he knew that, obviously. Moreover, he was there, he said, on Bloody Sunday. I wasn't sure

why he was telling me this, there at the top of Water Lane in Llansteffan on the way to the beach, fifty years and more later. I said to him that two of my uncles were also there on that day. They were both in the RUC. They were there as serving police officers. Did his countenance relax a little at that point, I couldn't be sure. We did a lot of work together, he told me. They were good guys. Then, all of a sudden, the traffic began to move. I didn't have time to tell him that they were both required to give evidence at the Saville Inquiry which, between 1998 and 2005, investigated the horrific happenings of that day (see *https://www.gov.uk/government/organisations/bloody-sunday-inquiry*), before publishing its monumental and wholly damning report in 2010 (see *https://www.gov.uk/government/publications/report-of-the-bloody-sunday-inquiry*). Instead, I watched the supermarket delivery van as it disappeared up High Street and through the village to some destination unknown to me. And then, as I walked the length of Water Lane on its way to the beach in Llansteffan, I was left thinking about my father too on the streets of the city of Derry, a civilian and unarmed, somewhere in the throng of a Civil Rights march as it descended into chaos.

41   Mission Gallery, *Hawk and Helicopter: Osi Rhys Osmond*, 15 January–20 March 2011: *https://www.missiongallery.co.uk/exhibitions/hawk-and-helicopter/* (accessed 7 June 2023).
42   Mission Gallery, *Hawk and Helicopter: Osi Rhys Osmond*, 15 January–20 March 2011: *https://www.missiongallery.co.uk/exhibitions/hawk-and-helicopter/* (accessed 7 June 2023).
43   Also known as Kalandia: *https://www.unrwa.org/where-we-work/west-bank/kalandia-camp* (accessed 6 June 2023).
44   United Nations Office for the Coordination of Humanitarian Affairs, *Occupied Palestinian Territory. Area C*: *https://www.ochaopt.org/location/area-c* (accessed 7 June 2023).
45   According to Article XI (3.c) of the Oslo II Accord it was intended that such territory eventually be transferred to Palestinian control: '"Area C" means areas of the West Bank outside Areas A and B, which, except for the issues that will be negotiated in the permanent status negotiations, will be gradually transferred to Palestinian jurisdiction in accordance with this Agreement': *https://israelipalestinian.procon.org/background-resources/1995-oslo-interim-agreement/* (accessed 7 June 2023).
46   See, for example, Adam Ramadan's study of the operation of power in the Palestinian refugee camps of Lebanon: Adam Ramadan, 'Spatialising the refugee camp', *Transactions of the Institute of British Geographers*, 38 (2013), 65–77.
47   Elior Levy, 'Qalandiya refugee camp: a "chaotic base for terror"', *ynetnews.com*, 16 July 2015: *https://www.ynetnews.com/articles/0,7340,L-4680672,00.html* (accessed 7 June 2023).

48 Levy, 'Qalandiya refugee camp'.
49 UNRWA – United Nations Relief and Works Agency for Palestinian Refugees in the Near East: https://www.unrwa.org (accessed 7 June 2023).
50 https://www.unrwa.org/where-we-work/west-bank/kalandia-camp (accessed 7 June 2023).
51 Palestinian Return Centre, '2 Palestinian youths injured by Israeli forces during clashes in Qalandia refugee camp', *Palestinian Return Centre*, 16 November 2020: https://prc.org.uk/en/news/3190/2-palestinian-youths-injured-by-israeli-forces-during-clashes-in-qalandia-refugee-camp (accessed 7 June 2023).
52 See, for example, Ahmed Alaqra, 'To subvert, to deconstruct: agency in Qalandiya refugee camp', *Jerusalem Quarterly*, 79 (2019), 63–76: https://www.palestine-studies.org/sites/default/files/jq-articles/Pages%20from%20JQ%2079%20-%20Alaqra.pdf (accessed 7 June 2023).
53 Dorota Woroniecka-Krzyzanowska, 'The right to the camp: spatial politics of protracted encampment in the West Bank', *Political Geography*, 61 (2017), 160–9.
54 Woroniecka-Krzyzanowska, 'The right to the camp', p. 160.
55 Alaqra, 'To subvert', p. 64.
56 Alaqra, 'To subvert', pp. 70–1.
57 For accounts of Free Derry, see the following: Eamonn McCann, *War and an Irish Town* (London: Pluto Press, 1980) and Niall Ó Dochartaigh, *From Civil Rights to Armalites: Derry and the Birth of the Irish Troubles* (Basingstoke: Palgrave Macmillan, 2005).
58 Brian Morrison, 'Rossville Flats', *Troubles Archive* (2014): http://www.troublesarchive.com/artforms/architecture/piece/rossville-flats (accessed 7 June 2023).
59 McCann, *Apeirogon*, p. 176.
60 McCann, *Apeirogon*, pp. 178–80.
61 Keenan, *An Evil Cradling*, p. 23.
62 I borrow the imagery from an opinion piece by Giles Fraser that argues against the analogy – Giles Fraser, 'Despite the murals, Belfast is not Bethlehem with rain', *The Guardian*, 16 April 2016: https://www.theguardian.com/commentisfree/belief/2016/apr/28/despite-the-murals-belfast-is-not-bethlehem-with-rain (accessed 7 June 2023).
63 For a discussion of the significance of this slogan, see Mac Giolla Chríost, *Jailtacht*, pp. 62–3, 119–21 and 144–6 in particular. Despite the much-changed political situation in Northern Ireland, this term carries much meaning. For example, the Fair Employment Tribunal in 2011 and in 2017 found the term to be of 'sectarian significance' and its use in the workplace to constitute sectarian abuse – *Halliday v Royal Mail Group Ltd Paul Corrigan Rory Culbert Case Refs: 165/09 FET, 47/10 FET*: https://www.casemine.com/

judgement/uk/5a8ff85760d03e7f57ebea6e; Helen Suzanne Scott v Stevenson & Reid Ltd Case Refs: 82/15 FET 2577/15 – Equality Commission for Northern Ireland, £20,000 *Tribunal Award in Fair Employment Case, 25/10/2017, Helen Scott v Stevenson & Reid Ltd*, Belfast: *https://www.equalityni.org/Footer-Links/News/Individuals/%C2%A320,000-Tribunal-award-in-Fair-Employment-case* and *https://www.equalityni.org/ECNI/media/ECNI/Cases%20and%20Settlements/OITFET%20online%20decisions%20as%20pdfs/Scott-v-StevensonReidLtd-Decision.pdf* (accessed 7 June 2023); The Irish Times, 'Woman awarded £20,000 after "tiocfaidh ár lá" shouted at her', *The Irish Times*, 25 October 2017: *https://www.irishtimes.com/news/ireland/irish-news/woman-awarded-20-000-after-tiocfaidh-%C3%A1r-l%C3%A1-shouted-at-her-1.3268337* (accessed 7 June 2023).

64 *https://www.youtube.com/watch?v=FCBjuFIUJ80* (accessed 7 June 2023).

65 The recording is a part of a major project on the political significance of the year 1968 in the history of NI, led by the Ulster Museum and Nottingham Trent University: *https://www.nmni.com/whats-on/voices-68* (accessed 7 June 2023).

66 The quotation is derived from the television documentary entitled 'Martin McGuinness' that was broadcast on the Irish-language channel *TG4* on 6 January 2021.

67 David Beresford, *Ten Men Dead* (London: HarperCollins, 1987).

68 This is a distortion of the intended meaning of Seamus Heaney's poem of the same title: Seamus Heaney, 'Whatever you say, say nothing', *North* (London: Faber and Faber, 1975).

69 It has been claimed by a retired MI5 operative, then active in NI, that Martin McGuinness had been very much opposed to the 1981 Irish republican hunger strike, to the extent that he prohibited any members of the IRA from Derry from taking part in it. Three Irish republicans from Derry did die on the hunger striker but they were members of the INLA, and not the IRA – Connla Young, 'Martin McGuinness "was opposed to the 1981 hunger strike"', *The Irish News*, 7 October 2019: *https://www.irishnews.com/news/northernirelandnews/2019/10/07/news/martin-mcguinness-was-opposed-to-the-1981-hunger-strike-1731703/* (accessed 7 June 2023).

70 Jeremy Sharon and Daniel K. Eisenbud, 'Massive haredi demonstration to take place in Jerusalem today', *The Jerusalem Post*, 2 March 2014: *https://www.jpost.com/National-News/Massive-haredi-demonstration-to-take-place-in-Jerusalem-today-343958* (accessed 7 June 2023).

71 Yair Ettinger, 'Hundreds of Haredim clash with police in Jerusalem over yeshiva student's arrest', *Haaretz*, 5 December 2013: *https://www.haaretz.com/.premium-yeshiva-student-arrest-sparks-riot-1.5297492* (accessed 7 June 2023); Ezra Taylor and Aaron Reich, 2020, 'Religious anti-draft protests

turn violent in Jerusalem, 38 arrested', *The Jerusalem Post*, 26 January 2020: https://www.jpost.com/israel-news/religious-anti-draft-protests-turn-violent-in-jerusalem-38-arrested-615432 (accessed 7 June 2023).

72 Literally translated, the term 'haredim' means 'those who tremble': https://www.britannica.com/topic/fundamentalism/The-Haredim (accessed 7 June 2023).

73 McCann, *Apeirogon*, p. 176.

74 McKittrick, Kelters, Feeney and Thornton, *Lost Lives*, p. 905.

75 Ulster Herald, 'Police to re-examine 1982 shooting of UDR man', *Ulster Herald*, 2 May 2014: https://ulsterherald.com/2014/05/02/police-to-re-examine-1982-shooting-of-udr-man/ (accessed 7 June 2023); Leona O'Neill, 'Victim's niece furious after "on-the-run" IRA murder suspect named as new Donegal mayor', *The Belfast Telegraph*, 9 June 2017: https://www.belfasttelegraph.co.uk/news/northern-ireland/victims-niece-furious-after-on-the-run-ira-murder-suspect-named-as-new-donegal-mayor-35804044.html (accessed 7 June 2023); Leona O'Neill, 'Relative of IRA murder victim hits out at potential Army prosecutions', *The Belfast Telegraph*, 6 March 2019 – https://www.belfasttelegraph.co.uk/news/northern-ireland/relative-of-ira-murder-victim-hits-out-at-potential-army-prosecutions-37883388.html (accessed 7 June 2023); https://m.facebook.com/dergvalley.victimsvoice/posts/hugh-cummings39-singleulster-defence-regimentmurdered-by-ira-terrorists-whilst-o/3577514188941713/ (accessed 7 June 2023); https://twitter.com/onthisdaypira/status/1007506335972380672?lang=en (accessed 7 June 2023).

76 Vincent Kearney, 'What do controversial On the Run letters actually say?', *BBC News*, 27 February 2014: https://www.bbc.co.uk/news/uk-northern-ireland-26376541 (accessed 7 June 2023); AgendaNI, 'The OTR dispute', *AgendaNI*, April 2014: https://www.agendani.com/the-otr-dispute/ (accessed 7 June 2023).

77 There were serious questions about the impartiality of HET in its handling of cases, and in particular it faced credible accusations of it being less rigorous in its approach to those cases in which the State was involved. In a damning inspection report in 2013, Her Majesty's Inspectorate of Constabulary concluded that 'HET is not conforming to current policing standards in a significant number of areas ... and the HET treats state involvement cases differently as a matter of policy', adding that this 'is entirely wrong' and that this has 'led to state involvement cases being reviewed with less rigour in some areas than non-state cases'. It is also concluded that 'HET's approach to state involvement cases is inconsistent with the UK's obligations under Article 2 ECHR': https://www.justiceinspectorates.gov.uk/hmicfrs/news/releases/0182013-hmic-inspection-of-the-historical-enquiries-team/ (accessed 7 June 2023).

The Seeing Places

78   The case of Lexie Cummings, a non-State case it should be explained, was taken up by TUV (Traditional Unionist Voice) MP Jim Allister: *https://tuv.org.uk/how-otr-deal-blighted-hets-work/*. The case was a matter of debate in the House of Commons, UK Parliament. See Hansard, 2012, Historical Enquiries Team, Volume 541, debated on Wednesday 7 March 2012: *https://hansard.parliament.uk/Commons/2012-03-07/debates/12030785000002/HistoricalEnquiriesTeam* (accessed 7 June 2023). See also Leona O'Neill, 'Fury of IRA victim's niece after "on-the-run" suspect joins Taoiseach during visit', *The Belfast Telegraph*, 16 October 2017: *https://www.belfasttelegraph.co.uk/news/northern-ireland/fury-of-ira-victims-niece-after-on-the-run-suspect-joins-taoiseach-during-visit-36229283.html* (accessed 7 June 2023).
79   Euskadi Ta Askatasuna, meaning Basque Homeland and Liberty. This paramilitary group is usually only known by the acronym ETA.
80   Paddy Woodworth, 'In 1973, I applauded an Eta killing. Not now', *The Irish Times*, 8 April 2017: *https://www.irishtimes.com/news/world/europe/in-1973-i-applauded-an-eta-killing-not-now-1.3039065* (accessed 7 June 2023).
81   *https://www.goli.org.uk/* (accessed 7 June 2023).
82   *https://apprenticeboysofderry.org/* (accessed 7 June 2023).
83   *http://royalblack.org/* (accessed 7 June 2023).
84   A common Hiberno-English idiomatic phrase meaning something that is common knowledge: *https://www.usingenglish.com/reference/idioms/even+the+dogs+in+the+street+know.html* (accessed 7 June 2023).
85   *https://www.belfastinterfaceproject.org/interfaces-map-and-database-overview* (accessed 13 March 2024).
86   McCann, *Apeirogon*, p. 175.
87   McCann, *Apeirogon*, p. 166.
88   Murphy, *A Month by the Sea*, p. 5.
89   Murphy, *A Month by the Sea*, p. 5.
90   Murphy, *A Month by the Sea*, p. 5.
91   Murphy, *A Month by the Sea*, p. 5.
92   Murphy, *A Month by the Sea*, p. 11.
93   Murphy, *A Month by the Sea*, p. 224.
94   Murphy, *A Month by the Sea*, p. 226.
95   Murphy, *A Month by the Sea*, p. 228.
96   Murphy, *A Month by the Sea*, p. 231.
97   Murphy, *A Month by the Sea*, p. 234.
98   Murphy, *A Month by the Sea*, p. 237.
99   Murphy, *A Month by the Sea*, p. 239.
100 McCann, *Apeirogon*, pp. 14, 65 and 280.
101 McCann, *Apeirogon*, p. 15.
102 McCann, *Apeirogon*, p. 65.

103 Edward W. Said, *After the Last Sky: Palestinian Lives* (London: Vintage, 1986), p. 17.
104 Osmond, *1986 Fieldnotes*, Monday 18 August 1986.
105 Ami Pedahzur and Arie Perliger, 'The changing nature of suicide attacks: A social network perspective', *Social Forces*, 84/4 (2006), 1987–2008: *http://www.jstor.org/stable/3844486* (accessed 7 June 2023).
106 Osmond, *1986 Fieldnotes*, Monday 18 August 1986.
107 Librarians and Archivists with Palestine, *Prisoners' Section, Nablus Public Library* (2013): *https://librarianswithpalestine.org/featured-projects-members/research-centers/prisoners-section-nablus-public-library/* (accessed 7 June 2023).
108 Lonely Planet, *Educational Bookshop and Café*: *https://www.lonelyplanet.com/israel-and-the-palestinian-territories/jerusalem/shopping/educational-bookshop-cafe/a/poi-sho/1030540/361047* (accessed 7 June 2023).
109 John NoNe, 'Derry's once radical bookshop has "gone to ground"', *indymedia Ireland. saormheáin éireann*, 25 April 2008: *http://www.indymedia.ie/article/87325* (accessed 7 June 2023).
110 Urry and Larsen, *The Tourist Gaze 3.0*.
111 Alaqra, 'To subvert', pp. 71–2.
112 Murphy, *A Month by the Sea*, pp. 83–4.
113 The Guardian, 'The Palestine Papers: Abbas admits refugee return "illogical"', *The Guardian*, 24 January 2011: *https://www.theguardian.com/world/palestine-papers-documents/4507* (accessed 7 June 2023).
114 Ian Black and Seumas Milne, 'Papers reveal how Palestinian leaders gave up fight over refugees', *The Guardian*, 24 January 2011: *https://www.theguardian.com/world/2011/jan/24/papers-palestinian-leaders-refugees-fight* (accessed 7 June 2023).
115 *https://www.unrwa.org/where-we-work/gaza-strip* (accessed 7 June 2023).

CHAPTER 6

The Suffering Subject

It wasn't as if he had never been there himself. That was not the reason Amos Oz[1] did not write about it. To the contrary, it was precisely because he had indeed been there that it was so. He simply could not, he said: 'I have almost never written about my experience as a soldier on the battlefield, because I tried, and I found that it is beyond my capacity to describe the battlefield … There is a stench on the battlefield … And this particular stench, which I remember very vividly, very physically, I remember the stench – this I simply cannot describe in words, and without the stench the description will be false'.[2] Write what you know?[3] It is not enough for a body to have suffered in a place that a voice may be given to experience. The field of conflict has many affective qualities that tend to paralyse the suffering subject. Too much of experience shrouds the senses. And yet, the witness cannot be voiceless; the body must be made to speak.

Afternoon tea

It is said that we know this of the twentieth century, 'the most terrible century in Western history',[4] that 'the human being suffering from trauma … became the very embodiment of our common humanity'.[5] This thought was in my mind of a Thursday afternoon as I watched the items being lifted from the tray and arranged on the glass-topped table before us by his daughter. A father and his daughter sharing tea with me in the family apartment on a nameless street in Ramallah. Or perhaps it was al-Bīrah, or Surda, for I cannot be certain of the exact location due to the manner of my transportation there. My gatekeeper in the West Bank would take me to the centre of Ramallah later on, along the main street that had been blocked by the throng of people that had turned out to welcome the father home from prison. Everyone had turned out that day: Hamas, Fatah, Islamic Jihad. It's on YouTube. Here: look.

Palestine is a country of fathers and daughters. Colum McCann introduces his readers to two such daughters of fathers in *Apeirogon*: 'Abir. From the ancient Arabic. The perfume. The fragrance of the flower';[6] 'Smadar. From the Song of Solomon. The grapevine. The opening of the flower'.[7] Their fathers introduce themselves, for they yet live. First of all, here is Bassam, father of Abir:

> My name is Bassam Aramin, I am the father of Abir. I'm a Palestinian, a Muslim, an Arab. I'm forty-eight years old. I've lived in many places – a cave near Hebron, seven years in prison, then an apartment in Anata, and these days in a house with a garden in Jericho near the Dead Sea. My father raised goats and other animals in the hills, my mother looked after fifteen brothers and sisters. They were both born near Sa'ir, a village close to Hebron, their parents, and their parents before them too. I lived in a cave but not a cave as you might think of it – we had shelves full of books, carpets on the walls, it was cool in summer, warm in winter, always alive with voices and good cooking, we were happy there, we had what we wanted.[8]

Then we have Rami, father of Smadar:

> My name is Rami Elhanan. I am the father of Smadar. I am a sixty-seven-year-old graphic designer, an Israeli, a Jew, a seventh-generation Jerusalemite. Also what you might call a graduate of the Holocaust. My mother was born in the Old City of Jerusalem, to an ultra-Orthodox family. My father came here in 1946. What he saw in the camps he seldom spoke about, except to my daughter Smadar when she was ten or eleven. I was a kid from a straightforward background – we weren't wealthy but we weren't poor. I got into some trouble at school, nothing big. I ended up in industrial school, then studied art, more or less an ordinary life.[9]

While *Apeirogon* is a novel, says McCann, neither of Bassam or Rami are fictional characters. They are real, and the words given in their voices here are also real in that they have been transcribed from a series of interviews between McCann and the two fathers conducted in Jerusalem, New York, Jericho and Beit Jala.[10] This is who they are, in their own words, as elicited by McCann. However, McCann advises that in the rest of the novel the two fathers have allowed him to 'shape and reshape their words and worlds'.[11] So, what we have in these two statements, presented side-by-side in the middle of the book, is the autobiographic subject. Their reality is at the heart of the novel's authenticity. Moreover, they are McCann's suffering subjects.[12] Each of them has lost his daughter to a violent death as a direct consequence of the Arab–Israeli conflict in Palestine. Abir was shot in the head with a rubber bullet by a member of the Israel Border Police on 16 January 2007 in the West Bank town of 'Anata. She died three days later in a hospital in Israel. She was ten years old. Ten years prior to that, Smadar was killed instantly in a suicide bombing by members of Hamas on Ben Yehuda Street, Jerusalem, on 4 September 1997. She was thirteen years of age.

The daughter filled the glass cups with an amber-red liquid. As she did so, steam rose from the cups filling the air between us with the aroma of sage.[13] It is a very traditional drink in Palestine. Her father watched her. As he watched, he spoke to me, the observant ethnographer. Timing is everything. You must put the herbs into the water at the right moment. Too much heat and the sage will leave a bitter taste. That is how it is done. Perfect, he said. I too signalled my appreciation of the craft. Having orchestrated the presentation of the tea and its accompanying pastries, the daughter retired to a seat behind her father and then we, men, talked.

How a father suffers the absence of a daughter. For it is best not told,[14] McCann shows us in two different ways; one:

> Every day since Abir was killed, Bassam has walked to the mosque in the hour before sunrise to join the optional pre-dawn prayers. Forty-eight years old, he moves through the dark with a slight limp, a cigarette cupped in the well of his hand. He is thin, slim, fit. His limp imprints him into the world: otherwise he might slip through almost unnoticed. Still, an agility lurks underneath, a wiry surprise, as if he might burst way from the limp at any moment and leave it abandoned behind him.[15]

Two:

> Show me, then. Convince me. Roll back the rock. Return Smadar. All of her. Gift her back to me, all sewn up and pretty and dark-eyed again. That's all I ask. Is that too much? No more whining from me, no more weeping, no more complaints. A heavenly stitch, that's all I ask.[16]

His daughter adjusted the headscarf where it rested in puce folds upon her. Another father who has been witness to such loss shows it in colour. How do I see it? There (Illustration 2), a father holds the body of his daughter to his chest. His hand, knuckles reddened, hooks her frame. Her face towards us, mouth unopened and eyes enigmatic in opaque shadow. Whose shadow? The long khimar is become her body and her father carries her to me. His eyes too are lidded by the darkness and behind him, where he has just been, a twilight blue sky gives birth to first stars of the night. There are seven. It is Gaza, and it is 2009. Yr awr las.[17]

Illustration 2 *Clwyf/Wound by Osi Rhys Osmond, 2009*

Nail clippings

It was the colour of the nails of her fingers that first drew my attention to what should have been, in truth, the most obvious thing about her father. As she sat back upon the small armchair, her hands came to rest upon her lap, pleated by her entwined fingers as if one. Her nails were freshly painted, I judged. The polish was wholly undimmed by the mundane frictions of everyday living. The colour seemed chosen to match the deep brown-purple of her hijab but when she adjusted the cloth where it rested at her neck, and as her fingers twisted there briefly, the nails seemed then blue-purple. Her father's hands parted and rose from his lap to hover over the tea just as hers were drawn away. The fingers of his left hand had no nails, while his right hand was missing three whole fingers.

Brian Keenan explains how having his nails tended by one of his captors, known as The Grim Reaper, was a means of maintaining his sanity, of showing to himself, and perhaps also to those who held him, that he was still a human being. We cannot know when exactly the event took place as all Keenan says is, 'My nails grew long and filthy, my beard unkempt. And I wondered would I ever be able to cut them'.[18] He may well have been a hostage for many months at that stage, or several weeks. Or perhaps it was a recurring event, an activity in which Keenan took refuge on a regular basis. His captors' lack of English and his lack of Arabic meant that communication was very challenging. In addition, there was concern, Keenan felt, that he might use the nail clippers upon himself, in an attempt to end his own life. In the end, none of that happened. Rather, there was nothing but silence between Keenan and The Grim Reaper, a silence broken only by the voices of unknown peoples passing along the streets unseen beyond the prison cell. Outside it is Belfast:

> It took many days to explain but eventually The Grim Reaper came with a pair of nail clippers. He would not let me cut my own nails, for fear that I might attempt to injure myself with the clippers. He held my hands and cut my nails in silence wondering what thoughts were running through his head and half convincing myself that there were probably none. Occasionally I would hear voices shouting from the street and

I spend time imagining that they were voices from my own streets in Belfast.[19]

Keenan, the hostage, is blinded, for he cannot see the street, and he is mute, for he does not call out to those who are calling to him – his eyes are veiled, his lips are sealed. This is the hostage on the edge of the abyss (Illustrations 3 to 6). Shades of the colour purple, dark and thick, bleed through the captive figure until the body is disappeared. Only the head remains, stilled, as if waiting, perhaps sensing the nearness of the whole self being lost. What are the walls of this prison? Only the colour purple. And what is the hostage too, other than the colour purple? See how the head is turned, the other cheek exposed, its skin naked to us. See how the body and the cell are become one. Beachcombing on Traeth Gwyn[20] in Llansteffan, like the wayward hound of Heracles[21] our artist stumbled upon guilty purple, the colour of captivity, the colour of Keenan's Lebanese shore. And yet all is not lost, Osmond seems to say. The witness may yet redeem the hostage. Perhaps I could cling to that feeling. I massaged the cold tips of my own fingers in the comfort of the palms of my hands, one after the other.

Keenan connects the activity of nail clipping with him having used his anger to break the spell of madness that had begun to envelop him, as it regularly did throughout his captivity: 'I needed anger to pull me back from these moments of madness'.[22] This madness seemed to descend upon him almost without warning, says Keenan. For example: 'I dreamt one day a bird came and landed on my raft from out of nowhere, suddenly this other living thing was sharing this floating raft with me.'[23] The raft was his mattress on the floor of the cell and he was adrift on an ocean of featureless water with no sight of land in prospect. An overwhelming sense of his own helplessness drove him to despair:

> As I think back on that dreaming raft and myself afloat and the bird that came to me, I remember other birds that came to that cell when my mind had taken flight in hallucinatory fantasy, yet not as in a dream for I remember being conscious of the place I was in. It was momentarily filled with birds flying erratically and crashing into the walls, to fall broken and bloodied at my feet and then they would gather themselves up again in furious flight, flinging themselves again into the wall. The cell seemed

to be littered with feathers and the dying and broken bodies of
birds. Their frightened flight seemed endless. These birds flew
backwards, flew upside down, with broken wings they would
seem to walk the walls and I would try to brush them away from
my head knowing that there was nothing there to brush away.[24]

These are the Mórrígan,[25] surely: how they drive the Irish imagination to despair. Their shape-shifting three-ness perches first, as one creature, upon the shoulder of those about to die, and then, multiplying, they swoop upon those yet living, driving them to maddened distraction. I fancied, irrationally, that I saw one of their number supping from the waters of the River Jordan, in the ancient ford by the Daughters of Jacob Bridge. But as I crossed over the figure turned, even as it remained stooped into the waters that swirled and eddied around it, and I could see that it was an old woman, darkly attired. From the posture, I fancied that she was washing garments, dyed incarnadine by the early morning sun as it crawled into the sky, bloody and raw.[26] With my gatekeeper, I had been seeking out a small place close by the deserted Arab village of Kafr 'Inān.[27] Once the home to several hundred Muslim souls, it was depopulated during the 1948 Arab–Israeli War. It remained unlived-in since then. Though, some thirty years afterwards, Zionist settlers did build a new village there for themselves and called it Kfar Hananya. The father with the maimed hands was a refugee from there, or some place near there, I believe, many decades ago. Then, he must have been a tiny child, a mere babe in arms, or even perhaps no more than an idea in his mother's womb. It was hard to say, to tell the truth of the matter, exactly.[28] However, on that day he could not travel with us to show me himself that place of origin, and without him neither could his daughter make the journey. Had I said something, the gatekeeper would have laughed at my mistake and said that no such bird is to be found here.

On crossing back over the bridge much later the same day, with the earth's own shadow brooding darkly on the far horizon, I saw that she had gone. Other creatures had settled upon the river: a conference of birds of various shapes.[29] My gatekeeper saw them too. He recognised the clumsy allusion, of course. Despite that he did not sense, however, that I too was already familiar with the poem, a miraculous Sufi lyric, as he launched into an elaborate description of the work. All of the birds in the whole world, lacking a sovran, meet to decide who amongst them

Illustration 3 *Hostage 1 by Osi Rhys Osmond, 2009*

Illustration 4 *Hostage 2 by Osi Rhys Osmond, 2009*

Illustration 5 *Hostage 3 by Osi Rhys Osmond, 2009*

Illustration 6 *Hostage 4 by Osi Rhys Osmond, 2009*

should be crowned so. The hoopoe bird, being the wisest of all birds, leads their discussion. The hoopoe explains that they will have to undertake an epic journey, crossing seven valleys, until they reach the place in which the solution to the problem will be revealed to them. Many birds will perish in these valleys. A few, very few, will reach that final destination, the place of revelation and enlightenment. We left the bridge and the river with its ford behind us, and we drove the deserted road into the sun, ebbing in the western sky. As the light of the descending sun faded from the earth, dark shapes slipped over its face: 'What shadow is ever separated from its maker?' Are they not one, the shadow and its maker?[30] As that night fell, I saw, once again, the father's hands and those of his daughter, this time entwined, her manicured nails pressing into his crippled flesh, and I looked at my own hands upon the steering wheel of the SUV that had been hired that morning in east Jerusalem.

Shopping

On another morning, as I was leaving the hotel, a hooded crow swooped down upon me. The glint of the chrome-finished spectacle case in the hard, mid-summer sun must have caught its eye. It knocked my hands just as I was opening the case and, without a pause, climbed the air to its perch high in a pine tree overlooking the front entrance to the hotel. Somewhat startled, I dropped the case and it clattered noisily upon the stone-slabbed ground at my feet. The crow had drawn blood. A small wound, where nail meets skin, cupped a bead of bright carmine, becoming darker still as it set within my flesh. The case retrieved, the chrome in my hands was aglow, incandescent with the colours of the sun. The crow called at me from the high tree. If only I knew the language of birds.[31] But such knowledge is a secret of the bird-poets alone. I knew that much from my neighbour in Bristol House.[32] I saw it in *Eglwysfach* (Illustration 7) where the poet[33] becomes hawk, becomes harrier, becomes falcon, becomes sea-eagle.[34] He senses the psychogeography[35] from the skies but at the same time is inscribed upon those earthy layers beneath. And when the artist met his poet at a protest rally they shared together the meaning of somewhere: 'While we marched together, Thomas expressed his views and canvassed mine on the subject of the rally, often returning to the question of the immigration of English-speakers and what this meant for the language, or the indifference of the Welsh as to the fate of their culture; we never talked about birds'.³⁶ They did not talk of birds. There was no need. And there was no need because everything on that matter was already known to them, both the poet and the artist being birds.³⁷ Perhaps the bird that first slipped into Keenan's mind had another meaning. Were he and the bird, in fact, the one and same creature, driven to that shape by some metamorphic madness?³⁸ Was not the poet-as-bird, the fallen king Sweeney, on his half-broken mind? Was it not the case when Keenan bade farewell to Belfast for Beirut, with his father dead,³⁹ that Seamus Heaney, poet laureate of the Irish trauma, had only recently unveiled his own version of Sweeney, the bird-poet?⁴⁰ By the time he was in his cell in Beirut Keenan knew the answer, of course, to Sweeney's most pressing question, 'what has befallen thee? Sad is thy voice;/ tell me what has marred thee/ in sense or form/'.⁴¹

Illustration 7 *Eglwys-fach by Osi Rhys Osmond, 2013*

That morning, I was on my way to meet with a contact in the Old City. Rather than following King David Street, passing the antique shops and the car hire offices, I took a small side-street that, upon reaching the desiccated grass space that was Bloomfield Park, transformed itself into a gravel pathway. I crossed through the park, passing a group of young men dressed in wedding clothes. One of them was calling at the others to strike some suitable postures for his camera. They paid me no attention. I followed the sloping path as it descended into the Yemin Moshe neighbourhood. There, the bride and her companions were stood on Pele Yoetz Street. One of her companions held a mobile phone in one hand while gesturing with the other in my direction. It was not me, of course, rather it was the arch of crimson coloured and purple flowers, rose and clematis, climbing the stone-dressed façade of the house at the corner of the street that had caught her eye. We crossed paths halfway along the street. Then I walked the full length of the street before crossing the road into another park. In the afternoon, Haredi children from the Old City would play in the fountains there, watched over by their mothers. They would sit together upon the thinly grassed slopes that surrounded the granite pavement through which the cascades of water would burst every few minutes for a short while. Then it would end, with no more warning than when it started, and the mothers would gather their children, stood in their drenched clothes, and return to the old City. During the remainder of the afternoon, the sun would dry the waters away as if neither the fountains nor the children had ever been that day. I entered the old City through Jaffa Gate and joined the throng of tourists jostling its way through the Three Markets. I paused to buy some fruit, cherries, fresh from Golan, and observed the scene for a few moments. Then I made for the café where we would meet. He ordered the coffee in Arabic. She hesitated. I thought for a moment that she was going to reply in her broken English, for she did not speak Hebrew. Could she tell that he was Jewish? I know people from the north who swear blind that they can tell a Catholic from a Protestant just by looking at them. My contact, I guess, had that look, and the more fluent the Arabic of a non-Arab Palestinian the more suspicions they arouse. It is well known, some said to me, that the only Zionists who learn Arabic that well are those who work for the Israeli security forces.[42] As he talks, I people-watch.

The Suffering Subject

'They arrived disguised as women', according to McCann.[43] Suicide bombers on an ordinary shopping street, as if it were an ordinary day. Yet, they were no one's daughters. They too were watchful; they knew to be: 'Witnesses said that the bombers made eye contact with each other from under their veils when they reached the area around Hillel Street'.[44] It was an ordinary day on an ordinary shopping street:

> The apartments above. The shop awnings below. The fruit stalls, the juice joints, the fashion stores. The cash registers. The loudspeakers. The jangle. The September throb. The flick of a lighter. The open clasp of a purse. The girls swaying arm in arm down the street. The laughter from a café. The pneumatic door hiss. A car door closing. The plimp of the bombers' soft-soled shoes. The swish of their dresses. The rub of the wide cloth sleeves.[45]

Smadar was shopping for clothes. And on another ordinary day Abir, too, had been shopping, this time for sweets:

> For two shekels Abir could have bought a bracelet with *He Loves Me, He Loves Me Not* imprinted along its rim. Instead she bought two *iswarit mlabase*: hard pills of pink, orange, yellow and light blue candy braceleted together on a string./ She slipped the money across the counter into the palm of the shop owner, who fished the bracelets out of a deep glass jar./ As they made their way out towards the school gates, Abir gave the second bracelet to her sister Areen.[46]

She had been shopping for sweets on a school day. When they looked in her school satchel after she had been shot dead this is what they found: 'Apart from the candy bracelet, her brown leather schoolbag contained two exercise books and three children's books, all Arabic, although Bassam had contemplated teaching her some words of Hebrew, which he had learned as a teenager, many years before, in prison in Hebron, locked away for seven years'.[47] But I already knew that. I knew that Bassam had learned Hebrew in prison. I had been told. He was well known for that. He had learned it there in order to survive, like them all. Sipping shay bil maramiya with another captive tongue in his living room in his apartment in Ramallah, I understood that he took no pride in this learning of Hebrew. It was no accomplishment; it was an act of retaliation; it was an act of hostility.[48]

It was an ordinary day on Ben Yehuda Street, until it was not: 'The sky was a radiant blue. The cobblestone street was crowded with September shoppers. Music was being piped from a raffia-fronted loudspeaker. The blasts ruptured the sound system. The silence afterwards was uncanny, a stunned interval, until the street erupted in screams'.[49] Perhaps he, her father, could make it so that it is always an ordinary day:

> What he wanted … was to somehow crawl inside time and rewind it, to upend chronology, reverse it and channel it in an entirely different direction – like a Borges story – so that the light was brighter, and the chairs were rights, and the street was ordered, the café was intact, and Smadar was suddenly walking along again, her hair short, her nose pierced, arm in arm with her school girl friends, sauntering past the café, sharing her Walkman, the smell of coffee sharp in her nostrils, caught in the banality of not caring what happens next.[50]

Borges: whither are we led? Into the labyrinth,[51] to confront our own monsters. Through McCann, Smadar's father shows us his demon. In the aftermath of the atrocity the ZAKA paramedics[52] arrived. ZAKA is an Israeli-based voluntary rescue and recovery organisation, largely staffed by Orthodox Jews, the aim of which is to provide first aid, rescue, recovery and identification services in the aftermath of major, public trauma such as terrorist attacks. Its activities grew rapidly during the Second Intifada, aka the Al-Aqsa Intifada. It is known to Israeli Jews for its 'true virtue',[53] the work of recovering for burial the body, however devastated, in accordance with the Halakha. What was once the person is gathered, piece by forensic piece, from the scene. He wanted her whole again, but not like that. Yet, he could still conjure her complete in his imagination: 'In Aramaic, *Talitha Kumi* means: Rise up, little girl, rise up'.[54] Why conjure her in Aramaic, the native tongue of Jesus? I was with another of my gatekeepers when I encountered one of the last speakers of Aramaic to live in the Old City. It is no longer a language of the Jewish people, and even Jesus now speaks Hebrew.[55] Rather, it is a language to re-fashion reality, to recover something lost beyond all meaningful recovery. It is the idiom of performative utterance.[56] Thus, McCann says of the father this: 'When he spoke he saw Smadar again. Her oval face. Her brown eyes. Her turn-to-the-shoulder laughter. In a garden. In Jerusalem. With a white band in her hair'.[57] A moment for the absence of unhappiness.[58] Not whole; yet complete.

Fruit

The afternoon passed quickly in his apartment on that unnamed street. He talked most fluently in broken English and then in Arabic when his English would not suffice. Many prisoners learned some English too whilst incarcerated.[59] His daughter brought a bowl of fresh cherries to the table, the sage tea and sweet pastries having been exhausted by then. The cherries were from Golan. She, his daughter, had purchased them in the market in Ramallah.[60] Dervla Murphy, then in Gaza, had also been shopping for fruit. It was much cheaper in al-Shati, she observed, than in Rimal.[61] She had been 'kidnapped'[62] from Gaza beach by members of the family of Hanaa, a septuagenarian grandmother, and taken to al-Shati to have lunch in her home there. Al-Shati is a refugee camp, also known as the Beach Camp.[63] It was created as a consequence of the 1948 Arab–Israeli War to house, temporarily, some 23,000 displaced Arab Palestinians. On a site comprised of an area of half a square kilometre, it is now the semi-permanent home of more than 85,000 people. It is also the only Palestinian camp in which she had been challenged and asked to confirm her identity.[64] She proffered her passport. I had an encounter of a similar sort in Qalandiya refugee camp. A figure called at us from a second-floor window, without fully showing himself, while at the same time a car, filling the narrow street, crept towards us. My gatekeeper shouted back at the figure in the gloomy window. The figure made no reply to us but merely fell away from the window-space into the shadow of the room inside. The two figures in the car, young, male, t-shirted, and leather-jacketed, eyeballed us as they passed by. At the top of the street the car turned right, to some other place in the depths of the camp.

Late that same afternoon, Hanaa sent Dervla Murphy shopping for fruit with some of her children and then on to meet Samira and her family. She would welcome the company of an international visitor. Samira made juice from the fruit brought by Murphy, and as they poured the juice for Samira's children, the children of other mothers appeared, as if on cue.[65] Between the buying of the fruit and the imbibing of the juice, Murphy learned of the horrendous casualties of Operation Cast Lead on Samira's family:

> In January 2009 two daughters, then aged ten and twelve, were playing on the roof when the shell came. The ten-year-old died instantly; her two older brothers having rushed up, momentarily mistook her twisted body for a big doll discarded the parapet. Her sister, Rana, lost both legs from the groin and will always be confined to a wheelchair.[66]

But Rana was not welcoming of the visitor. Murphy was quickly discomfited: 'At once I realised that my visit wasn't helping'.[67] Clearly, some knew only too well where the wounds that would not heal were to be found: 'I wondered then if Hamas had been using this tragedy in their legitimate campaign to publicise the criminality of Cast Lead'.[68] But there was no avoiding the suffering subjects of Gaza for, as Murphy left the house of Samira accompanied by a responsible male of the family, she witnessed them once again as he, Ya'qub, talked:

> As Ya'qub escorted me to a taxi route near the Gold Market he spoke of Cast Lead's long-term consequences: children blind, deaf, burn-scarred – young men paralysed – mothers maimed – homeless families with no possibility of replacing bombed dwellings – enfeebled grandparents left to succor disturbed orphans – orchards bulldozed, wells maliciously poisoned. Statistics can blur all this. So many killed, so many injured, the deaths usually fewer than the injuries. Too often we tend to focus on the heartbreaking finality of death, the desolation of the bereaved, and not to think enough about the injured and those who love them, the lives thwarted and distorted because 'wars' are no longer fought by warriors. Modern weaponry, callously deployed, makes nonsense of the concept of 'professional armies' fighting 'just wars'.[69]

The detail, this time, in its abstraction, was convincing. His words became her words too. But, lest statistics do indeed threaten to become a blurry storm over Operation Cast Lead and its multiple investigations,[70] let the following simple numbers stand witness, undiminished: 'Based on extensive field research, non-governmental organizations place the overall number of persons killed between 1,387 and 1,417. The Gaza authorities report 1,444 fatalities. The government of Israel provides a figure of 1,166';[71] amongst the dead were 'some 300 children'.[72] They say 'some' because, of all the statistics, that number cannot be counted.

While Keenan saw the cherries in the bowl that had just been placed before him, the oranges were the fruit from which he could not avert his eyes.

> But wait. My eyes are almost burned by what I see. There's a bowl in front of me that wasn't there before. A brown button bowl and in it some apricots, some small oranges, some nuts, cherries, a banana ... I lift an orange into the flat filthy palm of my hand and feel and smell and lick it. The colour orange, the colour, the colour, my God the colour orange .../ I cannot, I will not eat this fruit. I sit in quiet joy, so compete, beyond the meaning of joy .../ For days I sit in a kind of dreamy lethargy, in part contemplation and in part worship. The walls seem to be singing. I focus all of my attention on that bowl of fruit. At times I lift and fondle the fruits, at times I rearrange them, but I cannot eat them.[73]

This particular state of desire, this witness statement of primal longing barely restrained by self-denial, follows on from a short period of hunger strike that Keenan had undertaken some weeks previously. That hunger strike, it appeared to Keenan himself, called for little new effort on his part: 'I recall now that in those first few weeks I had eaten very little and felt little need to. Hunger never seemed to affect me. Perhaps the mind, constantly shifting and readjusting and falling back, grew so preoccupied that it never turned its attention to the needs of the body'.[74] Perhaps it was his decision to terminate his strike that transformed his state of hunger. He ended the strike when it was finally explained to him that he was being held because of the US bombing of Tripoli. The explanation was offered only after Keenan had forced a meeting with his kidnappers' bosses having threatened to prolong his strike. Even then these bosses remained inaccessible for they communicated with him solely through translation, even though Keenan was sure that they spoke English: 'the chiefs when they came would not let their voices be heard speaking English'.[75] The hunger strike ended, Keenan's mind turned upon the needs of his already debased body. To eat the fruit would be to destroy it. Allowing his body to consume the orange would reduce the fruit to his own degraded condition: 'I cannot relieve myself at a fixed and set time. I am reduced to sleeping in the smell of my own filth. Excrement, sweat, the perspiration of a body and a mind passing through waves of desperation. All of everything is in this room'.[76] As long as the orange held its colour, as long as the skin of the cherry remained unbroken, something of the world remained whole.

In his apartment on an unnamed street, I watched him as he watched his daughter clear the sage tea accoutrements from the low glass-topped table. He warned me. Inside. He said to me. The cherry stones. They contain cyanide. His daughter smiled at this, as if to ask who might ever be induced to do such a thing. I chose my piece of fruit, followed by the father, and then the daughter. We chose orange. She chose orange too. She tore off its skin with a deft incision of her finger nails and then placed it, almost whole, on a small plate that she had brought to the table. She then broke it into its segments. Ten, I counted. Before eating them, she cut the pips from each of them and placed them too on the plate. Keenan once said this about his ordeal: 'It was extremely difficult to write about I, because almost nothing happened in that time. Or, everything happened in the mind, while very little was going on in terms of external events'.[77] I thought of the secret held inside the cherry fruits, the skin of which not one of us had unsealed.

Amos Oz did, of course, write in the immediate aftermath of his first experience of the battlefield, namely the Six Day War of 1967.[78] He served in an IDF tank unit again in the 1973 Yom Kippur War, where he fought in the Golan Heights. The stench of war had barely subsided when Oz, all those years ago, penned his most imperishable words: 'Even unavoidable occupation is a corrupting occupation'.[79] A generation later, and with Oz dead, the State of Israel has lived over forty years of its sixty-year existence in occupation. How corrupt is the body of Palestine become, Oz might well ask. The artist presents the body, in

Illustration 8 *Aftermath by Osi Rhys Osmond, 2009*

full knowledge of the occupation, broken before the violence of the tank (Illustration 8). All seems awash in Tyrian purple. Sky and sea and earth are one. And yet the one who carries the suffering subject stares, zurq-eyed as Sycorax, in another direction. He looks not at us. Perhaps he is blind. Or perhaps he is like Zarqā' al-Yamāna, a harbinger of metamorphosis.[80] How might the body be redeemed, be transformed? In the aftermath, McCann, the chromatographer, halved the colour purple, extricating its shades one from the other, as if to clarify its essence: 'Sirens flashed red and blue against the white stone buildings. The night was raw with raised voices'.[81] This is how the body was recovered in the aftermath of the suicide bombings on Ben Yehuda Street:

> [T]he ZAKA set about their real work: to collect the body parts for burial. They paused a moment. Theirs was a concentration born from repetition. A form of prayer./ Silently they went about it. In small groups. Quick and terse through the scattered human jigsaw. A finger. An earlobe. A foot, still in its shoe, leaning, almost brazenly, against a rubbish bin./ They removed gutter grilles, combed the surfaces of manhole covers, pushed open jammed doors. They sifted the glass and debris, looking

for any sign of life or flesh. They reached into shattered glass with long tweezers to pick up a severed thumb. They picked bloody shrapnel from the windscreens of cars, shone torches on the underside of tables, climbed trees to scrape the skin of the victims from the branches, dabbed cartilage from the street signs, coiled intestines back into half-torsos, vacuumed up any available liquid from the pavement into portable machines./ They were meticulous. Rigorous. Precise.[82]

Amongst the detritus of the everyday, the proof of the depth of the trauma is in the forensic recovery of the body, of its reconstruction for burial. Moreover, this is no soulless act. Rather, it is prayerful. The street scene, prosaic on an ordinary shopping day, then rendered the place-space of political and politicised violence, now is made one with the suffering subject. McCann, in asserting that in this exercise '[s]pecial care was taken not to mix the blood of the victims and the bombers',[83] makes of it an act of *biopouvoir*[84] whereby the biotechnologies of the State, through its agents, are applied to restore its sense of order. The acquiescence of the citizenry in this ordering of things seems natural and inevitable, and perhaps even comforting. Perhaps there is a similar such comfort to be obtained in the act of unmaking the body of the suffering subject. Is it not the case that McCann also observes the following: 'Bassam replied, in Hebrew, that yes he understood./ The first doctor talked, then, about harvesting organs. Of creating life from life. Her liver, the kidneys, her heart .../ – We have a renowned eye transplant unit, you know .../ For a moment Abir's eyes seemed to hover in the room: large, brown, copper-flecked at the core'.[85] Here too there is life after death. Yet, here too it seems that biology is underwritten by politics for Bassam's reply is so obviously made 'in Hebrew', in his captive tongue. Bassam's language reveals that the hospital and the prison are one.

Elsewhere, in that apartment on that unnamed street, I listened as the father there too spoke in his captive tongue, giving voice to those who had held him once, both in prison and in hospital. As he spoke, he worded his story with his body and his maimed hands too. The scent of sage tea was still in the room. What does it mean when a man survives his own suicide bomb? Bio-pouvoir, while innate and pervasive, seems to be unthought of in our everyday. But in that particular moment it spilled into the space between us, and its mystery was laid bare in all of its darkness. I had an answer to his question, but I would not let it pass my lips. She was still in the room. I would write it later. After all, fieldnotes are only ever for an audience of one.[86]

Notes

1. *https://www.jewishvirtuallibrary.org/amos-oz* (accessed 7 June 2023).
2. Amos Oz quoted in interview with Johann Hari in *The Independent*, 19 March 2009: *https://www.independent.co.uk/news/world/middle-east/israels-voice-of-reason-amos-oz-on-war-peace-and-life-as-an-outsider-1648254.html* (accessed 7 June 2023).
3. Bret Anthony Johnston, 'Don't write what you know', *The Atlantic* (2011): *https://www.theatlantic.com/magazine/archive/2011/08/dont-write-what-you-know/308576/* (accessed 7 June 2023).
4. Isaiah Berlin quoted in Eric Hobsbawm, *Age of Extremes: The Short Twentieth Century, 1914–1991* (London: Michael Joseph, 1994), p. 1.
5. Fassin and Rechtman, *The Empire of Trauma*, p. 23.
6. McCann, *Apeirogon*, p. 35.
7. McCann, *Apeirogon*, p. 35.
8. McCann, *Apeirogon*, p. 231.
9. McCann, *Apeirogon*, p. 217.
10. McCann, *Apeirogon*, 'Author's Note'.
11. McCann, *Apeirogon*, 'Author's Note'.
12. The suffering subject is a trope commonplace in ethnography. See, for example, Alan Rumsey, *Ethnographic Macro-tropes and Anthropological Theory*, and, Daniel, *Charred Lullabies*. As with Oz, Daniel too found writing about violence, this time in the context of Sri Lanka's civil war, most challenging: '[E]very ethnography of violence is also its anthropography … I have not tamed violence by and into the representations of writing. Indeed one cannot. But neither can one overcome the will to try nor forget the fact of one's trials in so willing' (p. 9). In his own efforts to do so, he produced the suffering subject.
13. Shay bil maramiya – Palestinian sage-scented tea.
14. 'Don't tell me the moon is shining; show me the glint of light on broken glass' – an apocryphal quotation often attributed to Aonton Chekov and probably paraphrased from Avrahm Yarmolinsky, *The Unknown Chekov: Stories and Other Writings Hitherto Untranslated by Anton Chekov* (New York: Noonday Press, 1954), p. 14.
15. McCann, *Apeirogon*, p. 11.

16 McCann, *Apeirogon*, p. 35.
17 The Welsh language term for L'heure Bleue – The Blue Hour: https://earthsky.org/earth/what-is-the-blue-hour (accessed 6 June 2023) and Götz Hoeppe, *Why the Sky is Blue: Discovering the Color of Life* (Princeton, NJ: Princeton University Press, 2007).
18 Keenan, *An Evil Cradling*, p. 75.
19 Keenan, *An Evil Cradling*, p. 75.
20 Literally 'the White Beach': its English language name is Scott's Bay.
21 According to Julius Pollux, second century CE, *Onomasticon*, the divine hero Heracles discovered the colour purple whilst observing his dog consuming a sea snail on a Lebanese beach.
22 Keenan, *An Evil Cradling*, p. 75.
23 Keenan, *An Evil Cradling*, p. 74.
24 Keenan, *An Evil Cradling*, pp. 74–5.
25 Sometimes known as the three Morrígna – see, for example, Ó hÓgáin, *Myth, Legend and Romance*.
26 See 'Washer at the ford', in James MacKillop, *A Dictionary of Celtic Mythology* (Oxford: Oxford University Press, 2004) and *Bruiden Da Choca* or *Togail Bruidne Da Choca* (The destruction of Da Coca's hostel): https://www.vanhamel.nl/codecs/Bruiden_Da_Choca (accessed 7 June 2023). In Celtic mythology, the bean-nighe is to be found at water's edge washing the blood from the burial shrouds of those who are about to die.
27 See Rochelle A. Davis, *Palestinian Village Histories: Geographies of the Displaced* (Stanford, CA: Stanford University Press, 2011).
28 Walid Khalidi, *All that Remains: The Palestinian Villages Occupied and Depopulated by Israel in 1948* (Beirut: Institute for Palestinian Studies, 1992) – not wholly accurate, but yet true.
29 Farīd ud-Dīn Attar, *The Conference of the Birds, Parable of the King's Mirror*, Translated by Sholeh Woplé (New York: W. W. Norton and Company, 2017).
30 Farīd ud-Dīn Attar, *The Conference of the Birds*.
31 From the Qur'ān 27:16 (the inspiration for *The Conference of the Birds*): 'And David was succeeded by Solomon, who said, "O people! We have been taught the language of birds, and been given everything we need."'
32 The former place of residence of the artist Osi Rhys Osmond, in the village of Llansteffan.
33 The poet Osi Rhys Osmond has in mind is R. S. Thomas: https://www.poetryfoundation.org/poets/r-s-thomas (accessed 7 June 2023).
34 See p. 49 in Osi Rhys Osmond, 'The ornithologist-poet as a bird', in John Barnie (ed.), *Encounters with R. S.* (Swansea: The H'mm Foundation, 2013), pp. 48–54.

35 Siân Lewis, *'Graphic Essays' by Osi Rhys Osmond, Reflecting on the Poet R.S. Thomas* (2016): *https://vimeo.com/97257826* (accessed 7 June 2023).
36 Osmond, 'The ornithologist-poet', p. 52.
37 Iwan Bala, *The Hawk has Flown – A Tribute to Osi Rhys Osmond*, 13 March 2015: *https://www.iwa.wales/agenda/2015/03/the-hawk-has-flown-a-tribute-to-osi-rhys-osmond/* (accessed 7 June 2023). See also: *https://osirhysosmond.wordpress.com/2015/04/08/maer-hebog-wedi-hedfan-the-hawk-has-flown/* (accessed 7 June 2023).
38 Pascale Amiot-Jouenne, *Les Métamorphoses de Sweeney dans la Littérature Irlandaise Contemporaine* (Caen: Presses Universitaires de Caen, 2011).
39 Joanna Moorhead, 'Life is sweet for Brian Keenan', *The Guardian*, 12 September 2009: *https://www.theguardian.com/lifeanstyle/2009/sep/12/brian-keenan-dublin-hostage* (accessed 7 June 2023).
40 Seamus Heaney, *Sweeney Astray: A Version from the Irish* (Derry and Dublin: Field Day Publications, 1983).
41 James George O'Keeffe, *The Adventures of Suibhne Geilt, a Middle-Irish Romance* (London: The Irish Texts Society, 1913), section 101 (47): *https://archive.org/stream/builesuibhnethef12okee/builesuibhnethef12okee_djvu.txt101* (accessed 7 June 2023).
42 Yonatan Mendel, *The Creation of Israeli Arabic: Political and Security Considerations in the Making of Arabic Language Studies in Israel* (Basingstoke: Palgrave Macmillan, 2014).
43 McCann, *Apeirogon*, p. 270.
44 McCann, *Apeirogon*, p. 270.
45 McCann, *Apeirogon*, pp. 270 and 271.
46 McCann, *Apeirogon*, p. 11.
47 McCann, *Apeirogon*, p. 22.
48 According to the Israeli Ministry of Foreign Affairs, members of Hamas are advised to 'learn Hebrew until they speak it fluently' in preparation for the kidnapping of 'Zionist soldiers' who may then be used as leverage for the release of Palestinian prisoners: *https://mfa.gov.il/MFA/ForeignPolicy/Terrorism/Palestinian/Pages/The-Kidnapper-Handbook-by-Hamas.aspx* (accessed 7 June 2023). Also, according to Hamas spokespeople in Gaza, learning Hebrew is required of recruits to their military wing so as to 'improve the outcome of military confrontation with Israeli soldiers' – Rasha Abou Jalal, 2015, 'Palestinians learning Hebrew for strategic advantage', *Al Monitor*, 22 September 2015: *http://www.al-monitor.com/pulse/originals/2015/09/gaza-hamas-teach-hebrew-israel-conflict.html* (accessed 7 June 2023).
49 McCann, *Apeirogon*, p. 40.
50 McCann, *Apeirogon*, pp. 39 and 40.

51 Ana Maria Barrenechea, *Borges: The Labyrinth Maker* (New York: New York University Press, 1965).
52 *http://www.zaka.org.il* (accessed 7 June 2023).
53 *https://www.zaka.us/Chesed_Shel_Emet* (accessed 7 June 2023).
54 McCann, *Apeirogon*, p. 47.
55 Jeffrey Heller, 'Hebrew or Aramaic? Pope, Netanyahu spar over Jesus' native language', *Al Arabiya*, 26 May 2014: *https://english.alarabiya.net/en/News/middle-east/2014/05/26/Hebrew-or-Aramaic-Pope-Netanyahu-spar-over-Jesus-native-language* (accessed 7 June 2023).
56 John Langshaw Austin, *How to do Things with Words* (Oxford: Clarendon Press, 1962).
57 McCann, *Apeirogon*, p. 47.
58 A performative utterance, if wholly coherent and efficacious, is said to be 'happy'.
59 Ben Lorber, '"A needle in the binding": the legacy of Palestinian prisoner self-education in Israeli prisons', *Mondoweiss*, 29 November 2011: *https://mondoweiss.net/2011/11/'a-needle-in-the-binding'-the-legacy-of-palestinian-prisoner-self-education-in-israeli-prisons/* (accessed 7 June 2023); lawrenceofcyberia, 27 July 2004, *Jibril Rajoub*: *https://lawrenceofcyberia.blogs.com/palestinian_biographies/jibril-rajoub-biography.html* (accessed 7 June 2023).
60 Miriam Berger, 'Shopping with the enemy: why West Bank Palestinians can't avoid Israeli goods', *Newsweek*, 8 January 2017: *https://www.newsweek.com/why-hard-west-bank-palestinians-boycott-israeli-goods-539953* (accessed 7 June 2023).
61 Murphy, *A Month by the Sea*, p. 63.
62 Murphy, *A Month by the Sea*, p. 61.
63 *https://www.unrwa.org/where-we-work/gaza-strip/beach-camp* (accessed 7 June 2023).
64 Murphy, *A Month by the Sea*, p. 62.
65 Murphy, *A Month by the Sea*, pp. 63 and 66.
66 Murphy, *A Month by the Sea*, p. 65.
67 Murphy, *A Month by the Sea*, p. 65.
68 Murphy, *A Month by the Sea*, p. 65.
69 Murphy, *A Month by the Sea*, p. 67.
70 Richard Goldstone, *Human Rights in Palestine and Other Occupied Arab Territories. Report of the United Nations Fact-finding Mission on the Gaza Conflict* (2009): *https://www2.ohchr.org/english/bodies/hrcouncil/docs/12session/A-HRC-12-48.pdf* (accessed 7 June 2023); Richard Falk, *Report of the Special Rapporteur on the Situation of Human Rights in the Palestinian Territories Occupied by Israel since 1967* (2009): *https://www.un.org/unispal/document/auto-insert-189696/* (accessed 7 June 2023); and Amnesty International, *Israel/Gaza. Operation 'Cast Lead': 22*

Days of Death and Destruction (London: Amnesty International, 2009): https://www.amnesty.org/download/Documents/48000/mde150152009en.pdf (accessed 7 June 2023).
71 Goldstone, *Human Rights in Palestine*, p. 17.
72 Amnesty International, *Israel/Gaza*, p. 1.
73 Keenan, *An Evil Cradling*, pp. 68–9.
74 Keenan, *An Evil Cradling*, p. 55.
75 Keenan, *An Evil Cradling*, p. 57.
76 Keenan, *An Evil Cradling*, p. 67.
77 Brian Keenan quoted in interview with Stephen Phelan, 'Shadow of the gunmen: an interview with Brian Keenan', *The Sunday Herald*, May 2004: https://www.stephenphelan.co.uk/articles/brian-keenan/ (accessed 7 June 2023).
78 He contributed to the volume edited by Avraham Shapira and published in 1968, entitled *Siah Lohamim: Pirkei Hakshavah Ve-hitbonenut* (Tel Aviv: Group of Young Members of the Kibbutz Movement). It was subsequently published in English as Avraham Shapira, *The Seventh Day: Soldiers Talk about the Six-day War* (London: Steimatzky's Agency and André Deutsch, 1970).
79 Quotation from Amos Oz, *The Defence Minister and Lebensraum*, 22 August 1967: https://www.nli.org.il/he/newspapers/?olive_path=%2fOlive%2fAPA%2fNLI_Heb%2fSharedView%2eArticle%2easpx&olive_query=parm%3d7aitscnbC65aSRfl7IWLhrnh%252FLzKJuiuN%252BbpE9RJeiCZh2kSh8z5bGbRF%252FODv6f1Yw%253D%253D%26mode%3dimage%26href%3dDAV%252f1967%252f08%252f22%26page%3d4%26rtl%3dtrue (accessed 7 June 2023). See also, Mitch Ginsburg, 'In forgotten article after the Six Day War, Amos Oz warned of "eternal annexation"', *The Times of Israel*, 31 December 2018: https://www.timesofisrael.com/in-forgotten-article-after-six-day-war-amos-oz-warned-of-eternal-annexation/ (accessed 7 June 2023).
80 Kristina Richardson, 'Blue and green eyes in the Islamicate Middle Ages', *Annales Islamologiuqes*, 48/1 (2014), 13–29.
81 McCann, *Apeirogon*, p. 52.
82 McCann, *Apeirogon*, p. 53.
83 McCann, *Apeirogon*, p. 53.
84 Biopower is the usual English language translation for this term. The usage I derive here is from Michel Foucault, *Security, Territory, Population* (Basingstoke: Palgrave Macmillan, 2007) and Foucault, *The Birth of Biopolitics*.
85 McCann, *Apeirogon*, p. 56.
86 Following Roger Sanjek in 'A vocabulary for fieldnotes', pp. 92–121 in Roger Sanjek (ed.), *Fieldnotes: The Makings of Anthropology* (Ithaca, NY: Cornell University Press, 1990), in which he records this observation: '"What are fieldnotes?" George Bond asks. He answers that they are first, certainly, texts; they are documents with "the security and concreteness that writing lends to

observation ... immutable records of some past occurrence." Yet, fieldnotes are written, usually, for an audience of one. So they are also "*aides-mémoire* that stimulate the re-creation, the re-newal of things past," Bond explains. All writing is like this' (p. 92).

CHAPTER 7

Conclusions

Until recently it was a commonly held view, and quite uncontroversial too, that art, while it ought to make us feel something about the world, does not tell us what to do about any given issue in that realm. Hence, as Iris Vidmar and Elvio Baccarini put it, 'narrative art' is conceived of as possessing the quality of 'moving' its audience and of 'involving' it in a particular story, but no more than that:[1] the artist pays attention; her art draws attention. The poet Derek Mahon, reflecting upon the relationship between the northern poets and the Troubles of NI, says that we ought to keep our expectations of art in this context low. In his seminal poem *The Snow Party*, it is a time of barbarism, of the boiling to death of those arbitrarily accused by an emperor of heresy. But it is also the occasion of a party marked by the ritual consumption of tea to observe the coming of snow. In the voice of one who attended that party, the voice of another poet, Bashō, from seventeenth century Japan,[2] Mahon says this: 'Snow is falling on Nagoya/ And further south/ On the tiles of Kyoto.// Eastward, beyond Irago,/ It is falling/ Like leaves on the cold sea'.[3] I am no poet but I think of my own tea party in a place by Jerusalem in Palestine, where it rarely snows, but when it does it must be remarked upon. It has its meaning, this falling snow. And it snowed in Jerusalem that year, once. Mahon calls to mind the dis-anchored universality of James Joyce and of Wallace Stevens: 'It was evening all afternoon/ It was snowing/ And it was going to snow/ The blackbird sat/ In the cedar-limbs';[4] the snowflakes 'falling softly upon the Bog of Allen and, farther westward, softly falling into the dark mutinous Shannon waves ... falling faintly through the universe and faintly falling, like the descent of their last end, upon all the living and the dead'.[5] The snow falls; the tea is drunk; the poet composes; barbarity remains unchecked, Mahon cautions in his poem. However, a mood has been current in the creative arts for a few years now that suggests more ought to be asked of artists and their audiences than this. By way of notable example, artist Olafur Eliasson says in relation to the art of

Ai Weiwei that 'a good work of art' may move us to act, to take action, and in so doing 'art can engage with the world to change the world'.[6]

Furthermore, on the occasion of the COP26 climate crisis conference in Glasgow in 2021, Eliasson, in conversation with Kumi Naidoo, a leading anti-apartheid, Greenpeace and Amnesty International activist, asserts that activism and art have in common the task of making 'something invisible, visible'; that is to not merely draw attention to a problem but that '[a]rt and activism are able to take it from a narrative, a thought, into a physical way of addressing something'.[7] In other words, art, in its various forms, ought to be a means acting in the world and of bringing about social change. As we have seen in this book, the testimonies of our Celtic quadrumvirate, the Irish triad and a sole Welsh witness to Palestine, whether in the form of literary fiction, travel writing, autobiography or visual art, can be read as rhetoric; they demonstrate commitment to social purpose. The question then arises, as to what the implications of this might be in practice, in the realm of the world as it is lived rather than as it is imagined. The events of 7 October 2023 and the subsequent Israel–Hamas War bring to this an urgent and searing intensity.

'If I must die ... let it be a tale'[8] – beyond the suffering subject

The death of Refaat Alareer[9] in Gaza on 7 December 2023 as a result of an Israeli airstrike gave poetic voice to the trauma of the Israel–Hamas War due to the simple fact that on 1 November 2023 he, in an act of creative expression that proved tragically prophetic, posted on X (formerly known as Twitter) his English-language poem *If I Must Die*.[10] Killed alongside him were his brother, his sister, three of her children, and a nephew. The poem's opening and closing lines seem to be what strikes most of its readers. The opening lines read as follows: 'If I must die,/ you must live/ to tell my story'. And its closing lines read thus: 'If I must die/ let it bring hope,/ let it be a tale'. Despite some criticism of both poem and poet, such as in the magazine *Tablet* where Maxim D. Shrayer confesses to 'being moved' by the poem while also claiming that the poet glorifies the political violence of Hamas's military wing, the IQB,[11] what a tale it has become. For example, remarkably, the poem as posted by Alareer on his account on X, *Refaat in Gaza@itranslate123*, has been viewed over 31 million times.¹² Writing in *Le Monde*, Clothilde Mraffko better captures the prevailing mood when she describes the poem as 'an epitaph and bulwark against the permanent shadow of death in the enclave'.¹³ Remarkable too is the impact of the reading of the poem by the actor Brian Cox for the Palestine Festival of Literature,¹⁴ also posted on X,¹⁵ of which there have been almost 14 million views. Less than 50 days since the death of the poet, *If I Must Die* had already been translated into several hundred different languages, including Welsh and Irish.¹⁶ A Welsh version of the opening and closing lines reads as follows: 'Os oes rhaid imi farw,/ rhaid i tithau fyw/ er mwyn adrodd fy hanes … os oes rhaid imi farw/ boed i obaith dyfu o'r peth/ boed iddo droi'n stori i'w hadrodd'.¹⁷ And here is an Irish rendering of the same: 'Má tá orm bás a fháil,/ caithfidh tú mairreachtáil/ chun mo scéal a insint … Má tá orm bás a fháil/ go dtabharfaidh sé dóchas/ lig scéal a bheith ann'.¹⁸ His death brought renewed attention to the other poets of Gaza and of the West Bank such as Mosab Abu Toha. On Christmas Day 2023, in one of a series of several pieces in *The New Yorker*, this international prize-winning poet recounts the story of his flight to Egypt from Gaza, bringing with him from his personal library just a single book, and reflecting upon what that means for him as a creative practitioner:

> I have come into Egypt with only one book, a worn-out copy of my poetry collection. Since I last read it, I have lived a lot of new poems, which I still have to write. After weeks of typing on my phone, in streets and in schools, I am not used to opening my laptop without worrying about when I can charge it. I am not used to being able to close the door. But one morning I sit at my friend's beautiful wooden desk, in a room full of light, and write a poem. It is addressed to my mother. I hope that the next time we speak I can read it to her.¹⁹

Similarly, early in the New Year of 2024, the renowned poet Najwan Darwish deploys art in the face of the violence in his interview with Alexia Underwood in *The Guardian*. There, Darwish laments the death not only of Alareer but of others as well such as the poet Saleem al-Naffar and the loss of the poetry they would have written in the future. Moreover, when asked whether, as an artist, he has an answer to the violence and the loss, he responds,

Before October 7, I used to have certain, more solid thoughts and beliefs. And after that, things changed: I feel like I've lost my ability to feel. I see things, I see atrocities, but I don't feel them. I know that with time, the feelings will come back and I'll be able to recognise what's happening ... Since early November, I've been in this process of trying to remember so I can rewrite at least some lines, and also trying to forget about it so I can live my life again.[20]

And yet, this is more than a mere suffering subject. Darwish asserts that he will write again, it is only a matter of time, and that his words will be 'a testimony for history'.[21] Certain words uttered by Refaat Alareer in an interview given a short time before he was killed, signal something beyond that – they bring to mind the work of Costica Bradatan on those remarkable intellectuals who were prepared to die for an idea, and indeed did so:[22] 'What should we do? ... Drown? Commit mass suicide? Is this what Israel wants? We have nothing to lose'.[23] That is, nothing to lose but his life: here is the poet made a martyr-philosopher.[24]

Illustration 9 *Gaza by Osi Rhys Osmond, n.d.*

'my kite you made, flying up above'[25] – together

At the centre of Alareer's poem *If I Must Die* is the making of a kite and its flight: 'you must live/ to tell my story/ to sell my things/ to buy a piece of cloth/ and some strings/ (make it white with a long tail)/ so that a child, somewhere in Gaza/ while looking heaven in the eye/ ... sees the kite, my kite you made, flying up/ above/ and thinks for a moment an angel is there/ bringing back love'. For me, it is reminiscent of Seamus Heaney's poem *A Kite for Michael and Christopher* and it invokes in my mind the two boys of that poem sharing in the task of constructing and flying a kite: 'take it in your two hands, boys, and feel/ the strumming, rooted, long-tailed pull of grief./ ... Stand in here in front of me/ and take the strain'.[26] Working together. Whether there is a two-state solution, a one-state solution, or perhaps even a two-state-confederation solution,[27] Jerusalem will be shared. The ideology of revisionist Zionism, through the Jerusalem Law of 1980 declares Jerusalem, 'united in its entirety', to be the capital of the State of Israel.[28] The Palestinian Authority through PNA Basic Law declares Jerusalem to be the capital city of a future Palestinian state.[29] Currently, it remains the policy of both the UN and the EU that Jerusalem be the capital city of both the State of Israel and of a Palestinian state.[30] Indeed, the UN has recognised for many years a number of alternative proposals for the sharing of Jerusalem as the capital city of two states.[31] Jerusalem, an obsession: magnificent and horrific. Susan Abulhawa, child of Palestinian refugees of 1967, has a vocabulary for this. She puts it as follows:

> I have always found it difficult not to be moved by Jerusalem, even when I hated it – and God knows I have hated it for the sheer human cost of it. But the sight of it, from afar or from inside the labyrinth of its walls, softens me. Every inch of it holds the confidence of ancient civilisations, their deaths and their birthmarks pressed deep into the city's viscera and onto the rubble of its edges. The deified and the condemned have set their footprints in its sand. It has been conquered, razed, and rebuilt so many times that its stones seem to possess life, bestowed by the audit trail of prayer and blood ... It possesses me, no matter who conquers it, because its soil is the keeper

of my roots, of the bones of my ancestors, because it knows the private lust that flamed the beds of all my foremothers.[32]

Amos Oz, born in Jerusalem in 1939 to Ashkenazim immigrants, puts it like this:

> Many things have happened in Jerusalem. The city has been destroyed, rebuilt, destroyed and rebuilt again. Conqueror after conqueror has come, ruled for a while, left behind a few walls and towers, some cracks in the stone, a handful of potsherds and documents, and disappeared. Vanished like the morning mist down the hilly slopes. Jerusalem is an old nymphomaniac who squeezes lover after lover to death before shrugging him off with a yawn, a black widow who devours her mates while they are still penetrating her.[33]

The connection is carnal, primal in its immediacy and in its urgency. They write that Jerusalem lays claim to them, yet the claim is theirs, and they are claiming Jerusalem absolutely. In so far as ownership is in question, it is they together who own the city, obsessively, compulsively, instinctively.

I stand before the Golden Gate.[34] The sun is arisen high and the day is already long. Beneath lies the Kidron Valley wherein Yahweh will sit in judgment. Facing us, the grave slabs of the Mount of Olives rest in silent anticipation. A male Haredi is moving amongst them, alone. It feels like a page from Simon Sebag Montefiore's 'biography' of the city is being performed before us:

> It is now one hour before dawn on a day in Jerusalem. The Dome of the Rock is open: Muslims are praying. The Wall is always open: the Jews are praying. The Church of the Holy Sepulchre is open: the Christians are praying in several languages. The sun is rising over Jerusalem, its rays making the light Herodian stones of the Wall almost snowy ... and then catching the glorious gold dome of the Dome of the Rock that glints back at the sun. The divine esplanade where Heaven and Earth meet, where God meets man, is still in a realm beyond human cartography. Only the rays of the sun can do it and

finally the light falls on the most exquisite and mysterious edifice in Jerusalem. Bathing and glowing in the sunlight, it earns its auric name. But the Golden Gate remains locked, until the coming of the Last Days.[35]

Later, alone then in the city too, I am swept up by the multitude of the faithful on their way to prayers. Later again, it is dusk and the setting sun bathes the stone streets of the Old City in red, becoming deeper and darker and more intense as the sun falls over the edge of the world in the west. And tomorrow it will resurrect itself.

From Damascus Gate (in Arabic, Bab al-Amud – an Arabic-speaking tourist once asked me where they could find the gate) I pass along Hagai Street.[36] It is known to the faithful as Al-Wad. Both names are translated into English as /the valley/: everything has at least two names in Jerusalem.[37] The street descends into this urban combe as it traverses the Muslim Quarter of the city before it ascends on the approach to the Haram as-Sharif, where the Dome of the Rock and Al-Aqsa stand in waitful expectation. As I turn with the milling crowd into Ala'e-Din Street I am stopped by the MAGAV, the Israeli Border Police.[38] They shout at me in Arabic. One of them, heavily armed and nervous, approaches me. He speaks to me again in Arabic. He seems to be a Druze. He thinks that I am a fish out of water. I am spread against the wall. The ancient stones feel cool against the palms of my hands. The Magavnikim crowd around me now. I am searched. They speak Arabic and Hebrew with each other. I am turned around again to face them. Behind them, unsettled, the faithful pass by, glancing at me, absorbing the scene. It feels like home, disturbingly. I am as if again upon the streets of Derry, once upon a time. They direct me to retrace my steps and return along Hagai, the street that 'encapsulates Jerusalem', that is a 'microcosm' of the conflict.[39] Derry, my own city: 'microcosm' of the Troubles.[40]

Once,[41] one of my contacts from East Jerusalem told me of the fatal stabbing that had occurred on Hagai the previous autumn. Muhannad Shafeq Halabi, a Palestinian, fatally wounded Nehemia Lavi and Aharon Banita, both Jews. They later died in hospital. The assailant was killed on the street by the MAGAV. In the wave of violence that followed, Elia Kahvedjian, an Armenian storekeeper in the neighbourhood, said that 'people have somehow lost their humanity. Instead of looking at one another as human beings, we are looking at people as eternal enemies ... Let people start looking at the human being on the other side, and then possibly things will start being resolved'.[42] My contact was similarly agitated. As he spoke, I thought of who he was in illegally occupied East Jerusalem. According to the research he might be an Israeli Arab, an Arab Israeli, an Arab citizen of Israel, a Palestinian Israeli, an Israeli Palestinian, a Palestinian in Israel, or a Palestinian citizen of Israel, or Palestinian by nationality and Israeli by citizenship, or simply Palestinian – he prefers this, by far.[43] But I reflect on the notion that it is this complexity of identity that Brian Keenan saw on the streets of Belfast and of Beirut. In his appeal to common humanity Keenan undertook a project on his subjective transformation whereby he became Irish himself, thereby erasing the ethno-political difference that, for him at least, was at the heart of the Troubles of NI. In turn, this created for Keenan the potential for erasing the conflict itself. Indeed, such a thing has come to pass for under the terms of the Good Friday Agreement (a document also known as the Belfast Agreement) it is 'the birthright of all the people of Northern Ireland to identify themselves and be accepted as Irish or British, or both, as they may so choose' and they have a 'right to hold both British and Irish citizenship'.[44] I note here that I too have availed myself of this resolution.

'thy children shall come again to their own border'[45] – a state for all

Whether there is a two-state solution, a one-state solution, or a confederate-state solution, the Palestinian refugees must have a place they are content to call home. Most refugees are not stateless peoples: it is known to whom their citizenship pertains.[46] From that connection flows the rights that belong to all human beings. To be stateless is to be cast adrift from those rights, and to be stateless is a graver problem than that of being a refugee. Tragically, many Palestinians are both refugees and stateless.[47] Sitting in the front room of his apartment in Ramallah, or perhaps it was al-Bīrah, or Surda, he, the survived suicide bomber, asked me to name the airport of my arrival. I thought it a trick question. I said Ben Gurion, knowing what this name would mean to him. He then asked me to name the town to which the airport is adjacent. I named it Lod. He nodded knowingly. His own family, he said, came from that place when it was known as Lydda. His parents, he said, were refugees of the war of 1948. According to the 1945 population survey, 16,780 individuals were recorded as being residents of Lydda. Of those, 14,910 were Muslims, 1,840 were Christians, and 20 were Jews.[48] As of 2020, the population of Lod, totalling 80,931 individuals, is comprised of 50,789 Jews, 24,142 Arabs, and 6,000 others.[49] His parents, he said, were participants in the Lydda Death March, one of the most notorious events of al-Nakba.[50] The order by the IDF to expel the Arab population was signed on 12 July 1948 by Yitzhak Rabin, who would become Prime Minister of Israel twice, for the first time between 1974 and 1977, and then from 1992 until his assassination in office in 1995: 'The inhabitants of Lydda must be expelled quickly without attention to age. They should be directed towards Beit Nabala ... Implement immediately'.[51] They were expelled and they never returned. It will appear ironic, surely, to some readers that the logo on the coat of arms of the city of Lod reads as follows: 'The children will return to their country'. The wording is drawn from Jeremiah 31: 17. I am familiar with the verse from the King James Version: 'And there is hope in thine end, saith the Lord, that thy children shall come again to their own border'.[52]

The right of return of Palestinian refugees was conceded by PNA negotiators to Israel in talks held variously between 1999 and 2010. That much was revealed as a fact in documents known as 'The Palestine Papers' that were leaked to *Al Jazeera* and *The Guardian* and published by them in 2011. Therein, '[Mahmoud] Abbas was recorded as arguing that Israel could not be asked to accept a return of even one million refugees, since it would mean the end of Israel. This, despite the fact that he himself was a 1948 refugee from Safad'.[53] This compromise on the matter of the Palestinian right of return was described as 'the most striking concession'.[54] One of the sources of the leak, Ziyad Clot, said that he had chosen to resign from his position as an adviser to the Palestinian negotiation team over the right of return issue, saying that the PNA/PLO 'was not in a position to represent all Palestinian rights and interests' and that the negotiations excluded 'the great majority of the Palestinian people: the seven million Palestinian refugees'.[55] In contrast, the position put forward by Chris Gunness on behalf of UNRWA in 2011 is that 'the voluntary return of refugees to their country of origin has come to be recognized by refugees, states and international agencies as the optimal solution to the plight of refugees'.[56] While the country of origin in the case of Palestinians ceased to exist in 1948, the specific places of origin remain. In seeking a place that they are content to call home, responsibility for the stateless condition in which many Palestinian refugees find themselves lies not just with the State of Israel but with others too.

Up until very recently, while 140 of the member states of the United Nations recognise the State of Palestine, few western countries had done so.[57] None of Canada, the USA, the UK, Australia and New Zealand, for example, recognise Palestine. Also, up until as recently as April 2024, of the twenty-seven member states of the EU, only nine recognised Palestine – Malta, Cyprus, the Czech Republic, Slovakia, Hungary, Romania, Bulgaria, Poland and Sweden. Of them, only Sweden recognised Palestine whilst a member state of the EU; the eight other states had already recognised Palestine prior to joining the EU. Somewhat paradoxically, the reason these EU states have held this position regarding the recognition of Palestine is because they see it as being tied to the successful conclusion of comprehensive negotiations between Israel and Palestine for the creation of a two-state solution. Such negotiations have been non-existent for decades. In the meantime, the national parliaments of many EU member states, including Belgium (2015), France (2014), Greece (2015), Italy (2018), Ireland (2014), Portugal (2014) and Spain (2014), tabled non-binding declarations calling for the recognition of the State of Palestine.[58] More recently again, in May 2024, one of the effects of the ongoing Israel–Hamas War has been to cause Ireland, along with Spain and Norway, to finally recognise the State of Palestine.[59] Similarly, and also in May 2024, the war in Gaza caused Senedd Cymru, the parliament of Wales, to call upon the UK to recognise the State of Palestine.[60] This official declaration followed the rejection by Senedd Cymru of two public petitions calling upon Wales to recognise the State of Palestine on that grounds that '[a]nything to do with the recognition of a state' is a matter that is exclusively in the power of the UK government and is not 'something' for which either Senedd Cymru or the Welsh government is 'responsible'.[61]

Beyond the challenges pertaining to Palestinian statehood and Palestinian citizenship, many of the countries in which Palestinians find themselves as refugees do not allow a straightforward pathway for them to attain local citizenship.[62] Indeed, most Arab states that neighbour Israel have 'strongly opposed resettlement and naturalisation of the refugees. Instead, they adopted policies and procedures aimed at preserving the Palestinian identity of the individuals and their status as refugees'.[63] The Casablanca Protocol signed by the member states of the League of Arab States in 1965 aimed at providing support to the Palestinian refugees resident in their countries is the basis of these policies.[64] Similarly also, in the absence of a permanent solution to the conflict between Israel and Palestine, the effect of the policies pursued by the UNRWA, responsible for the Palestinian refugees in the Gaza Strip, Syria, Lebanon, Jordan, the West Bank,[65] and the UNHRC, responsible for them elsewhere in the world,[66] has been, unfortunately, to keep these people in a state of suspended animation as perpetual refugees. Thus, the condition of being a Palestinian refugee is passed on, inherited. As a result, there now exists a fourth generation of Palestinian refugees.[67] Significantly, perhaps, for the children of this fourth generation in the camps of Lebanon, the principal source of dissatisfaction with their lot is not merely their inability to return to Palestine but rather their lack of social, economic and political rights, and the routine discrimination they face in their daily lives:

> Young Palestinians hardly ever made statements like, 'The problems we are facing are because we, the Palestinians, have been expelled from our homes …' as I heard from members of former generations. Young Palestinians, instead, made statements along the lines of, 'The problems we are facing are because we, the Palestinians, do not have rights in Lebanon.' Quite often it was not return that was proposed as the solution for Palestinians in Lebanon, but the right to work and civil rights in general … A return to Palestine did not appear to be the most pressing solution for the young Palestinians' problem of prospectlessness, but rather emigration to any other country. When I asked young Palestinians where they would travel if they could go anywhere, the answers were, contrary to my expectations, hardly ever Palestine but predominantly Europe, America and, more rarely, African or Asian countries.[68]

Against this sense of despair, the plea made by the UN Secretary General to this very generation to 'not lose hope'[69] during a visit to Lydda school in Tripoli, Lebanon (sponsored by the UNRWA) seems rather disengaged, complacent even. In retrospect, that the frustrations of Palestinians both in the State of Israel and in the Occupied Palestinian Territories too regularly boil over throughout 2021 and 2022, such as the Arab population currently resident in Lod becoming embroiled in violent confrontation with the Israeli security forces during the crisis of 6–21 May in which 256 Palestinians were killed and Al-Aqsa stormed by the MAGAV,[70] seems a prelude to the events of 7 October 2023. Until there is a negotiated solution to the case of the Palestinian refugees comprised of a mixture of return, restitution and compensation, in accordance with international law and public policy norms, the principle that one day the children of Lydda might return must endure.

'facts on the ground'[71] – to unsettle the settlements

It is before 7 October 2023 and I am in Ma'ale Adumim. I am with a Soviet-era refusnik[72] who had been imprisoned in the gulag for learning Hebrew.[73] The dramatised autobiography *The Voice of Silence* by Ephraim Kholmyansky (2021) is an exemplar of such a story of language learning resulting in incarceration.[74] We share coffee and apple cake and honey cake. On the journey from Jerusalem to Ma'ale Adumim, and also as I walk with my company along the city's clean streets in the glare of a midday sun in midsummer, I recall some of my reading material on the city:

> Ma'ale Adumim has all the advantages of a city: an enclosed mall and several strip malls, a municipal government center, intra-city transportation, an extensive library, health services, an art museum, sports and recreational facilities, a lake, a music conservatory, parks and more … clean and pleasant, surrounded by palm trees and a breathtaking desert view, and is only 20 minutes from downtown Jerusalem.[75]

For Jews considering making aliyah, this is how it is. Aliyah is a Hebrew language term that means 'ascent or rise, or going up'. It refers to a worshipper in a Jewish congregation being called up to the bimah, a raised reading platform situated in the centre of a synagogue, to read an assigned passage from the Torah. However, since the foundation of the State of Israel and the passing of the Law of Return in 1950,[76] in which the term is inscribed, aliyah has become widely understood to refer to the act of immigration by Jews to Israel. As we walk up the street towards our meeting place, all of this seems real. The honey cake is finished. The conversation moves out of the gulag and into the West Bank. Ma'ale Adumim is the Jewish settlement that has broken the two-state solution, says Larry Derfner.[77] That was as long ago as 2012, and in the same piece he quotes the mayor of Ma'ale Adumim as asserting that the town, which, by now, has a population of around 38,000,[78] was built for the express purpose of 'break[ing] Palestinian contiguity'.[79] Palestinian activists agree with this particular assessment: '[t]he settlement severs the West Bank at a strategic point, dividing it into two cantons, thus making it impossible to establish a viable Palestinian state with reasonable territorial contiguity'.[80] Together with Givat Ze'ev (population c.18,000)[81] and Efrat (population c.11,000),[82] it forms part of a ring of settlements around the eastern half of Jerusalem that the State of Israel considers provides strategic protection to the city as an integral part of its territory, both militarily and politically.

None of these settlements existed before the Six Day War of 1967. Ma'ale Adumim, for example, was '[l]aunched by 23 pioneer families on the seventh night of Chanukah in 1975'.[83] And after that, the State of Israel did the rest. We know this from Shlomo Hillel, then the Minister of Public Security in the Israeli government. Drawing upon an interview with Hillel, Ronald Ranta describes the evidence as follows: 'Hillel explains that the decision [to develop Ma'ale Adumim] was taken in the light of the need to create facts on the ground in response to the Rabat Summit'.[84] Facts on the ground mean a substantial, resident Jewish population. The significance of the Rabat Summit of 1974 was that it was the occasion at which the Arab League declared the PLO to be the 'sole legitimate representative of the Palestinian people'.[85] In terms of situating this development in terms of Israeli political ideology, it is worth noting that there is a broad consensus in the scholarly literature that Israel has been driven from its political left as well as from its right on the creation of settlements such as Ma'ale Adumim. Also, this process was motivated by a sense of strategic vulnerability, shared by Israelis irrespective of political ideology, whether left or right, that was exposed by the Yom Kippur War of 1973 during which the State of Israel was almost overwhelmed.[86] As the human rights' organisation B'Tselem says,

'Most settlements were built on area that was declared state land or on land that was requisitioned – ostensibly temporarily – for military purposes',[87] indeed it is argued by some that such settlers are 'warriors'.[88] I draw to mind here Osi Rhys Osmond, uncompromising pacifist, and how he presents the warrior. The body (Illustration 10), standing in shadowless light falling in striated columns, is genderless, its back turned upon us, its head lowered, its limbs drawn in upon itself. This warrior is washed in enigmatic blue. Dark blue, almost black, a concealed red seeps through. Where is the fight? The figure seems inactive, peculiarly passive. Has the violence been and gone? After death, the body turns blue. Livor mortis: the bruises of death. Is this warrior a study in lividity? A zombie? How brutalised is the landscape of this corpse? As of 2021, a total of 475,481 Jews are resident in the West Bank.[89] It is well known, of course, that the greater part of the international community considers these settlements to be illegal under international law[90] and that in their permanence they constitute a type of colonisation[91] and that in their ethnic exclusivity they make for a type of apartheid.[92] Yet,

Illustration 10 *Rhyfelwr/Warrior by Osi Rhys Osmond, n.d.*

almost all Israelis expect that these settlements will be retained by Israel as a part of any agreement to end the conflict. Moreover, and perhaps rather more surprisingly, successive teams of Palestinian negotiators have regularly conceded that places such as Ma'ale Adumim, termed 'consensus settlements' in the vocabulary of Israel–Palestine negotiations up to this point,[93] will remain an integral part of the State of Israel whatever the shape of a final peace agreement.[94] I might add here that Israel removed all of the Jewish settlements from Gaza in 2005, a sum of twenty-one settlements with a total population of around 8,000;[95] similar such Jewish settlements in the Sinai Peninsula were all removed in 1982.[96] In the case of the latter, the forced evacuation of the settlement of Yamit[97] was especially traumatic for Israelis and the case engendered extensive coverage in the media. Images of some of its two to three thousand residents, amongst them children, being carried from their homes by the IDF were the cause of considerable angst amongst Israelis. As I walked through Ma'ale Adumim prior to 7 October 2023 I tried to imagine Yamit there, but I could not. Then, afterwards, when once more in Ma'ale Adumim, I found that I could: settlements may be unsettled.

'an extraordinary series of events'[98] – ending the occupation

All military occupations are ugly. According to the so-called Hague Conventions of 1899 and 1907 governing the conduct of war and its immediate aftermath, '[t]erritory is considered occupied when it is actually placed under the authority of the hostile army'.[99] Such military occupation has 'two classic features', says Adam Roberts: 'first, a formal system of external control by a force whose presence is not sanctioned by international agreement; and second, a conflict of nationality and interest between the inhabitants, on the one hand, and those exercising power over them, on the other'.[100] In addition to this, military occupation is not and cannot be a permanent condition or state of affairs. The public discourse of political representatives of the State of Israel in the context of the Israel–Hamas War betrays that the occupation no longer 'represents a specific type of control in which the sovereignty of the occupied territory is not usurped, and in which foreign rule is temporary'[101] but instead seems akin to colonisation. The ugliness of military occupation is characterised in a number of ways. In the case of Palestine, that quality is described by Neve Gordon (2007) as follows: 'The military ... imposed curfews, deported leaders, demolished homes, carried out arrests, tortured detainees, and restricted movement both immediately after the 1967 war and in the wake of the new millennium'.[102] She notes elsewhere evidence of a further dimension to this ugliness whereby 'some of the occupied inhabitants have been reduced to what the Italian political philosopher Giorgio Agamben has called *homo sacer*, people who can be killed without it being considered a crime'.[103] The Israeli occupation of Palestine is indeed ugly but might it be said that it is less ugly than some other military occupations? Neve Gordon (2008) again:

> It is also worth noting that, when comparing the Israeli occupation with other military occupations, the number of Palestinians killed is relatively small. During the USA's military occupation of Iraq, for example, on average more civilians have been killed per day than were killed during a whole year in the West Bank and Gaza Strip between 1967 and 1987. Moreover, the United Nations reports that during the four-month period May to August 2006, 12,417 Iraqi civilians were killed, much more than the number of Palestinians killed during four decades of Israeli military rule.[104]

This much held true prior to 7 October 2023, and then it would have been reasonable to contend that perhaps it is the qualitative aspect of ugliness that ought rightly be kept to the fore here, not the quantitative. Subsequently, reporting as the hundredth day of the Israel–Hamas War approached, Oxfam International noted that 'Israel's military is killing Palestinians at an average rate of 250 people a day which massively exceeds the daily death toll of any other major conflict in recent years'.[105] Another threshold crossed, surely.

Growing up under conditions of military occupation in NI, I never thought to precisely gauge its ugliness, nor the suffering caused by it, through counting the number of checkpoints I ever passed through. By the time I first visited the West Bank in 2016 I was completely familiar with the routine horridness of the border crossing. Whether I had as my companion a Palestinian, a retired member of the IDF, an American citizen, or a pro-Palestinian activist, it always felt the same: grim and dully violent. That said, growing up, I was for a long time not wholly alert to the proper nature of military occupation: I had known nothing else; nor did it occur to me that any other state was likely to come to pass. I spent the summer of 1987 doing research in England. Up until that time this was the longest period I had spent outside NI – previously, I had only ever been away for a few days at a time. Walking through Oxford, my senses were assaulted by the posters, flyers, stickers (all the usual activist paraphernalia) that festooned the streets in the immediate aftermath of a Troops Out Movement (TOM) protest that had earlier taken place in the city, TOM being an organisation founded in London in 1973 with the express aim of the immediate and unconditional withdrawal of the British Army from NI.[106] This wholly random event had the effect of creating for me a new sense of the potential impermanence of the military presence in NI. It was a polite notice.

The whole ugliness did not overwhelm me until later that academic year when, during a period of 14 days in March 1988, the city of Belfast was convulsed by 'an extraordinary series of events', comprised of 'a string of singularly savage killings'.[107] On 6 March, three members of an IRA active service unit, Mairéad Farrell, Seán Savage and Danny McCann, natives of Belfast, were shot dead by the SAS in Gibraltar. This particular event 'came to be regarded as one of the most controversial and publicised incidents of the troubles',[108] with eyewitnesses saying that the three IRA members had been 'attempting to surrender and that they were "finished off" while lying on the ground'.[109] Peers of mine, fellow students of the Irish language at the Queen's University Belfast, protested the failure of our university to recognise the death of one of its students, namely Mairéad Farrell. She had enrolled as a first-year undergraduate student in the September of that academic year, having just been released after serving a long prison sentence for planting a bomb at the Conway Hotel. On 16 March at the joint funeral of Farrell, Savage and McCann in Milltown Cemetery in Belfast (I watched as the three funerals converged on the Falls Road), a lone gunman affiliated to the loyalist paramilitary organisations the UDA and the UFF attacked the mourners with seven RGD-5 fragmentation grenades and two handguns: one a Browning 9mm pistol and the other a Ruger .357 Magnum. The details seem important. He killed three: Thomas McErlean, John Murray (from Palestine Street in the

Holylands area of Belfast; I lived just around the corner) and Caoimhín Mac Brádaigh (also known as Kevin Brady, an IRA member who had learned the Irish language, and thereby adopted the Irish language version of his name, because of his Irish republican ideological sympathies). On 19 March, at the funeral of Mac Brádaigh (I decided against witnessing this funeral), two British Army corporals, plain-clothed and in an unmarked car, each carrying a Browning 9mm pistol, were killed by the IRA after having driven their car into the cortège. It was a Volkswagen Passat P-2: the detail seems important. Quickly surrounded, the corporals were dragged from the car and hauled to their deaths in a 'brutal' and 'harrowing'[110] fashion. And all was captured on film by a British Army helicopter that was all the while overhead. I felt physically sick. Not long after that I left Belfast for Wales.

Shocked by its ugliness, McCann, in the voice of Rami Elhanan, calls for the immediate and unconditional ending of the military occupation of Palestine by the State of Israel. The author quotes Rami, word for word, in section 500 in the first half of *Apeirogon*:

> I tell the story over and over again. We must end the Occupation and then sit down together to figure it out. One state, two states, it doesn't matter at this stage – just end the Occupation, and then begin the process of rebuilding the possibility of dignity for all of us. It's as clear to me as the noonday sun.[111]

Shocked by its ugliness, McCann, in the voice of Bassam Aramin, calls for the immediate and unconditional ending of the military occupation of Palestine by the State of Israel. The author quotes Bassam, word for word, in the other section 500, in the second half of *Apeirogon*:

> Rumi, the poet, the Sufi, said something that I will never forget: *Beyond right and wrong there is a field, I'll meet you there*. We were right and we were wrong and we met in a field. We realised that we wanted to kill each other to achieve the same thing, peace and security. Imagine that, what an irony, it's crazy. We sat in the Everest Hotel and talked about ending the Occupation. Even the word *occupation* makes most Israelis tremble. Of course, each one had a different point of view – they are the occupiers and we are the ones under occupation, so it looks different to them.

> But in the end we were all dying, we were killing each other, over and over and over.[112]

All military occupations are ugly, and they must come to an end. In explaining his response to this ugliness in an interview with V. Mahesh in *The Hindu* newspaper, McCann argues that because '[t]he Israeli government want one particular narrative and one only', '[i]t is our job – as artists and students and activists – to help swerve the narrative in a different direction'.[113] At another point in the same interview, he indicates the nature of that alternative narrative in the following terms, saying:

> (Mahesh) In Apeirogon, you make a brief allusion to Mahatma Gandhi's salt march. In that context, you point to 'satyagraha' and say that "the civility of the disobedience was part of its power." Does the Hamas's resort to rocket attacks on Israel diminish its "moral" edge?
>
> (McCann) Who is to say where things begin? ... There is an imbalance of power. There is an occupier and an occupied. There are certain fundamentals that are right and wrong, and there are some very clear injustices here. The Occupation is fundamentally and undeniably unjust. Of course, targeting civilians diminishes the moral edge – on all sides.[114]

There is no moral argument for military occupations that mutate into a state of permanence. The challenge is practical: how to end them.

The question is unbearably simple, but the answer painfully elusive. Unconditional withdrawal by the occupying power very rarely happens. More to the point, it is the aim of occupying powers to end military occupation only when their strategic goals have been accomplished. And for the State of Israel that includes, primarily, according to Roberts, meeting certain 'understandable security concerns'.[115] The end also happens, says Roberts, along with 'the gradual emergence (or re-emergence) of autonomous political institutions within the territory, which assume increasing responsibilities culminating in sovereignty and independence'.[116] In regard to these two things, some in the State of Israel admire the 38-year-long military occupation of NI, named Operation Banner by the British Army. For example, the Israeli military historian

Martin van Creveld, whose Dutch parents made aliyah, evading capture by Nazis, eventually reaching Israel in 1950, is quoted in the conclusions to the review by the UK Ministry of Defence of Operation Banner:

> Martin van Creveld has said that the British army is unique in Northern Ireland in its success against an irregular force. It should be recognised that the Army did not 'win' in any recognisable way; rather it achieved its desired end-state, which allowed a political process to be established without unacceptable levels of intimidation. Security force operations suppressed the level of violence to a level which the population could live with, and with which the RUC and later the PSNI could cope. The violence was reduced to an extent which made it clear to the PIRA that they would not win through violence … that success is unique.[117]

How close is the State of Israel, therefore, to accomplishing its strategic goals? As long ago as 1990 the occupation of Palestine was described as having been of 'unusual duration'[118] and 'exceptional' in its length.[119] It has not been a static phenomenon, it has evolved, and 'dramatically' so according to Neve Gordon.[120] Thus, Gordon organises the period of occupation from 1967 up until 2007, when her work was published, into five distinctive phases, as follows:

1967–1980: the military government,
1981–1987: civil administration,
1988–1993: the first intifada,
1994–2000: the Oslo years, and
2001–2007: the second intifada.[121]

Up until 7 October 2023, one might have said that the strategic goals of the State of Israel had been achieved in terms of securing the integrity of the national territory of the country against the possibility of an overwhelming, surprise attack. Ergo, East Jerusalem was formally annexed through the Jerusalem Law of 1980; the Golan Heights were formally annexed through the Golan Heights Law of 1981;[122] the wall separating the occupied West Bank from the State of Israel had been effectively completed; the blockade of the Gaza Strip by both

Conclusions

the State of Israel and the Arab Republic of Egypt was understood to have effectively corralled the political power of Hamas. But the wholly unexpected, startling nature of the attack on Israel on 7 October 2023 led by Hamas's military wing, the IQB, has shattered that illusion. One of the meanings of that event in and of itself is that security is not the solution to the existential fears of the State of Israel: the military occupation has failed; it does not aid the State of Israel in achieving its strategic goals. By now, that which Adam Roberts[123] said of the occupation of Palestine in 1990, that it remains both long and violent and with apparently limited prospects for it being brought to an end any time soon, no longer stands so certainly. A point of inflection has been reached; a crossroads arrived at: I, like Ilan Pappé, have a sense of the beginning of the end.

It is a departure that is very significant for the relationship between art in all of its forms and social activism that, as a matter of policy, the nominees for the Turner Prize in 2021 were comprised only of collectives that have helped to 'inspire social change through art'.[124] The Turner Prize is widely understood to be 'the highest honour in the British art world'.[125] In announcing the Turner Prize exhibition in Coventry in 2021, Hammad Nasar, the lead curator of the event, declared of the nominated artists that '[they are] engaged in constructing pocket utopias – exercises in the real world that deploy the artistic imagination to propose new, more equal, more hopeful futures'.[126] In making sense of all of this, art journalist and academic Tom Seymour noted at the time that for supporters of the Turner Prize this is 'a new vision for art … which is useful, utilitarian and utopic in concept … capable of helping us not just consider but surmount the challenges we face'. This is a daunting ambition for art. It causes us to examine art and its testimonies closely and asks that our reading of these testimonies ought to provide us with insight to two things: (1) justice, the moral heart of things; and (2) action, that which ought to be done to rectify wrong in the world. In addressing both of these concerns, it can be said that the testimonies that have drawn our attention in this book are engaged together in the task of that which anthropologist Joel Robbins describes as 'the cultural construction of the good',[127] echoing philosopher Charles Larmore's claim of morality as a 'social institution'.[128] Each of Keenan, Murphy, McCann and Osmond, in their testimonies *An Evil Cradling, A Month by the Sea, Apeirogon* and *Ymateb/Response*, provide a vision of the moral heart of things that is both constructed in and communicated through their art form. In this sense, our creative practitioners do more than offer 'accounts of trauma' that show to us all the vulnerabilities we share in common.[129] Rather, they offer convincing notions of justice that may be put into practice.[130]

Putting the good into practice, however, raises a special sort of challenge. Art, after all, 'real art' says the art critic Jonathan Jones, is complex, nuanced, ambiguous, elusive, mysterious and difficult.[131] Having said that, it seems that the silhouettes of the solutions to the most intractable of the issues in the conflict in Palestine – the case of the city of Jerusalem, the Palestinian refugees, the Israeli settlements, and the military occupation – can already be discerned, the witness of our creative practitioners showing us that their outline form has been glimpsed, if only through a glass, darkly.[132] The analysis conducted here shows that their testimonies are a little constrained in their potential as authoritative sources due to the affordances of their respective crafts, to the necessary complexity of their testimonies as works of art, as artefacts of creative practice. It is, of course, the case that Givoni asserts that the witness and their testimony has only had limited success in bringing about the social change on behalf of which they advocate:

> When examined through the prism of the vigorous reflections and debates about witnessing and testimony, the history of witnessing in the previous century appears less like a steady trail of modest victories over violent and oppressive regimes and more like a multifaceted struggle that, while better orchestrated and more finely tuned than ever, is still trying to find its bearings.[133]

However, one might ask whether Givoni's assertion is too pessimistic. At the very least, the testimonies of Celtic Palestine present to us the most painful trauma without, as Sarah O'Connell puts it in her review of the literary aesthetics of the topic of trauma, overwhelming us with it.[134] They allow us to look upon the Gorgon without being paralysed by it. It may be said that the testimonies of Keenan, Osmond, Murphy and McCann affirm Callard's claim that 'art is for seeing evil'.[135] In their aesthetic interrogation of violence, as Robert Applebaum says of this field, they survey the damage; they contemplate redemption.[136] As trauma memoirs, the autobiography and biography of people, places and events, driven by the ethical imperative to bear witness,[137] they point directly to social activism.

I think here of some of the things I too once witnessed and of the damage wrought: a child stunned mute by the sight of a soldier shot before him on the street – his tongue held captive by the trauma. Like a body by Osmond (Illustration 10), a figure, solitary, standing upon the shore, bathed in the light of that moment of witnessing which casts no shadow. Or of being linguistically cleansed: it cannot have been ethnic cleansing for my family, parents and siblings, was of the same ethnicity as those doing the cleansing. Returning home from another visit to the Irish-speaking stronghold of the Donegal Gaeltacht in the early 1970s we were confronted by the sight of our house having been attacked by our neighbours, hostile to all things Irish including the language. It was a warning: the Irish language does not belong here. The warning was heeded. We moved from there a little after that.[138] By now the Irish language in Northern Ireland is officially recognised by law.[139] The Irish language lobby group, An Dream Dearg (literally translated as 'the Angry Crew/Gang/Crowd'), welcomed the Act receiving royal assent by paying tribute to those who had played a part in the struggle for the language, saying, 'To all those who walked this path with us, today belongs to you. For all those willing to continue the work we have started, let us walk that path together. Ar aghaidh linn le chéile (literally translated as "forward together")'.[140] Sadly, my parents, both long since passed, did not see that day.

This much can be said with certainty: the testimonies of creative practitioners stand as revelations of justice, of moral conscience. In considering the relative merits of the creative practitioner as witness and as rhetorician, Zuleikha Chaudhari says this of the relationship between her own creative practice and one of those non-creative disciplines, namely the field of law:

> Both law and art assert productions of truth and reality; the construction of narratives; a historical frame of reference and the creation of alternative conditions and visions of the present. In considering this parallel between law and art, the project

hopes to develop a set of arguments and judgments that are an exploration into whether art can allow for a legal paradigmatic shift.[141]

By her work, therefore, she premises 'art as evidence and artists as witnesses'.[142] Thus, one may conclude, simply, but powerfully nonetheless: should one be moved by art to change the world? The response is this: yes, absolutely. Indeed, it seems to be the case that this is truer now than it has been because it would appear that one of the consequences of the global pandemic has been to infuse art in all its forms with a renewed and more urgent sense of social purpose.[143] Thus, creative practitioners say that they are increasingly committed to 'getting [their] hands dirty'.[144] A consequence of this commitment is, it would appear, that public art has come to be more broadly defined, to be more inclusive, to be less prescriptive.[145] Let our expectations of the creative practitioner, the artist, as witness be laid out in the following terms: as once was the colonisation and dispossession of Ireland by England, and surely there are few greater acts of witness to that than Seán Ó Tuama and Thomas Kinsella's magisterial anthology of the poetry of those centuries,[146] the occupation by Israel of Palestine is now become an epochal and universal trauma. And the agony of its pain is underwritten by the Jewish experience of the holocaust. And for all the while we bear witness to it, it shall be re-represented once more and over again. Herein lies the unique strength of artistic witness: it never tires of the story; its truths are manifold; it shows without telling; it says without exhortation; it explicates without reduction. Art is without question, in all its forms, a morally authoritative and persuasive witness.[147]

Notes

1. Iris Vidmar and Elvio Baccarini, 'Art, knowledge and testimony', *Synthesis Philosophica*, 50/2 (2010), 351–66.
2. This is the bardic name of Matsuo Munefusa, b. 1644, d. 1694, master of the haiku.
3. From the poem 'The snow party', from the eponymous volume of 1975.
4. From the poem 'Thirteen ways of looking at a blackbird', from *The Collected Poems of Wallace Stevens* (1954).
5. From the closing paragraph of the short story 'The dead', from the collection *Dubliners*, first published in 1914.

6 Olafur Eliasson, 'Why art has the power to change the world', *World Economic Forum*, 18 January 2016: *https://www.weforum.org/agenda/2016/01/why-art-has-the-power-to-change-the-world/* (accessed 8 June 2023).
7 *Olafur Eliasson and Kumi Naidoo – On Art and Activism*, 17 November 2021: *https://vimeo.com/642793738*, embedded at *https://olafureliasson.net/* (accessed 8 June 2023).
8 'If I must die', a poem by Refaat Alareer, first published in 2011: *https://www.worldliteraturetoday.org/blog/poetry/bilingual-poem-gaza-refaat-alareer* and *https://www.thenationalnews.com/arts-culture/books/2023/12/13/brian-cox-refaat-alareer-poem-if-i-must-die-palestine/* (accessed 8 January 2024).
9 Since, his daughter, Shaima Refaat Alareer, has been killed in an IDF airstrike in Gaza City, along with her husband and baby son. See, for example: *https://twitter.com/sananoorhaq/status/1784325098133946412* (accessed 30 April 2024).
10 *https://twitter.com/itranslate123/status/1719701312990830934* (accessed 9 January 2024).
11 Maxim D. Shrayer, 'If I must die … on the intifada generation that sacrificed its poets', *Tablet*, 19 December 2023: *https://www.tabletmag.com/sections/arts-letters/articles/if-i-must-die* (accessed 8 January 2024).
12 *https://twitter.com/itranslate123/status/1719701312990830934* (accessed 9 January 2024).
13 Clothilde Mraffko, 'The final verses of Gaza's poet Refaat Alareer', *Le Monde*, 18 December 2023: *https://www.lemonde.fr/en/m-le-mag/article/2023/12/18/the-final-verses-of-gaza-s-poet-refaat-alareer_6354443_117.html* (accessed 11 January 2024).
14 Farah Andrews, 'Succession actor Brian Cox reads Refaat Alareer poem for Palestine Festival of Literature', *N Arts & Culture*, 13 December 2023: *https://www.thenationalnews.com/arts-culture/books/2023/12/13/brian-cox-refaat-alareer-poem-if-i-must-die-palestine/* (accessed 8 January 2024).
15 *https://twitter.com/PalFest/status/1734707506977337538* (accessed 11 January 2024). The accompanying post incorrectly claims that '[t]his was the last poem he published'.
16 A corpus of very many of these ad hoc translations of the poem is to be found here: *https://ifimustide.net* (accessed 8 January 2024).
17 I prefer this translation, by Iestyn Tyne Hughes, from the Wales website of the writers' organisation PEN, 'Cerdd gadwyn – I gofio Refaat Alareer // A chain poem – in memory of Refaat Alareer', *Wales PEN Cymru*, 10 December 2023: *http://walespencymru.org/cerdd-gadwyn-i-gofio-refaat-alareer-a-chain-poem-in-memory-of-refaat-alareer/* (accessed 9 January 2024).
18 This translation is by @RosCatha and is from the aforementioned corpus of ad hoc translations: *https://ifimustide.net* (accessed 8 January 2024).

19 Mosab Abu Toha, 'A Palestinian poet's perilous journey out of Gaza', *The New Yorker*, 25 December 2023: *https://www.newyorker.com/magazine/2024/01/01/a-palestinian-poets-perilous-journey-out-of-gaza* (accessed 11 January 2024).

20 Alexia Underwood, 'Palestinian poet Najwan Darwish: "We can't begin to comprehend the loss of art"', *The Guardian*, 4 January 2024: *https://www.theguardian.com/world/2024/jan/04/najwan-darwish-palestinian-poet-israel-gaza-war* (accessed 11 January 2024).

21 Underwood, 'Palestinian poet Najwan Darwish'.

22 Costica Bradatan, *Dying for Ideas: The Dangerous Lives of the Philosophers* (London: Bloomsbury, 2015).

23 Quoted by Abeer Salman and Sana Noor Haq, 'Palestinian poet and writer Refaat Alareer killed in Gaza, friends and colleagues say', *CNN*, 8 December 2023.

24 Bradatan, *Dying for Ideas*.

25 Alareer, 'If I must die'.

26 The poem is from Heaney's volume *Station Island* (London: Faber and Faber, 1984).

27 This option is advocated by a small minority such as the group ALFA – this is the acronym for 'A Land for All', described as meaning 'Two States One Homeland'. See *https://www.alandforall.org/english/?d=ltr* (accessed 8 February 2024). It differs from the two-state solution in that it envisages the two states sharing institutions of a confederate nature wherein also Israelis will be allowed, as a matter of right, to live in Palestine as citizens of Israel but as residents of Palestine and that Palestinians will be allowed, as a matter of right, to live in Israel as residents of Israel but as citizens of Palestine. ALFA held its first joint-board meeting on 10 October 2023, three days after the start of the Israel–Hamas War.

28 The proper title is as follows: Basic Law – Jerusalem, the Capital of Israel (1980). For an English language version of the text see here: *https://mfa.gov.il/mfa/foreignpolicy/mfadocuments/yearbook4/pages/113%20basic%20law-%20jerusalem-%20knesset%20resolution-%2030%20j.aspx* (accessed 8 June 2023). Basic Law is understood to mean texts with constitutional status in the State of Israel. See *https://m.knesset.gov.il/en/activity/pages/basiclaws.aspx* (accessed 8 June 2023). See also *https://m.knesset.gov.il/EN/activity/documents/BasicLawsPDF/BasicLawJerusalem.pdf* (accessed 29 May 2024).

29 Palestinian Basic Law too is held to have constitutional significance. For an English version of the pertinent law, see *https://www.palestinianbasiclaw.org/basic-law/2002-basic-law* (accessed 8 June 2023).

30 UN, 'Jerusalem must be capital of both Israel and Palestine, Ban says', *UN News*, 28 October 2009: *https://news.un.org/en/story/2009/10/*

319482-jerusalem-must-be-capital-both-israel-and-palestine-ban-says (accessed 8 June 2023).
31 UN, *The Status of Jerusalem* (1997): *https://www.un.org/unispal/wp-content/uploads/2016/07/The-Status-of-Jerusalem-Engish-199708.pdf* (accessed 8 June 2023).
32 Susan Abulhawa, *Mornings in Jenin* (London: Bloomsbury, 2011), p. 140.
33 Amos Oz, *A Tale of Love and Darkness*. Translated from the Hebrew by Nicholas de Lange (London: Vintage, 2005), p. 26.
34 This is from a field visit during 2017.
35 Simon Sebag Montefiore, *Jerusalem: The Biography* (London: Weidenfeld and Nicolson, 2011), p. 628.
36 This is from a field visit during 2018.
37 Bernard Spolsky and Robert L. Cooper, *The Languages of Jerusalem* (Oxford: Oxford University Press, 1991).
38 Much of the Old City of Jerusalem is policed by the MAGAV, and not by the IDF: *https://www.gov.il/en/departments/publications/reports/ie_17_border_police* (accessed 8 June 2023).
39 Nir Hasson, 'The street that encapsulates Jerusalem', *Haaretz*, 11 November 2015: *https://www.haaretz.com/the-street-that-encapsulates-jerusalem-1.5420287* (accessed 8 June 2023).
40 John Hume (a native of Derry who would become leader of the political party the SDLP in 1979), quoted in 'Northern Ireland: power in Derry', *Time*, 4 September 1978: *https://content.time.com/time/subscriber/article/0,33009,912116-2,00.html* (accessed 24 January 2024). See also Henry Patterson, 'Unveiling a truer likeness of John Hume', *Policy Exchange*, 15 July 2022: *https://policyexchange.org.uk/blogs/unveiling-a-truer-likeness-of-john-hume/* (accessed 24 January 2024). To describe the city as a microcosm of the conflict is so commonplace by now as to be a cliché. In each of the following, for example, the city is so described: Margo Shea, *Derry City: Memory and Political Struggle in Northern Ireland* (Notre Dame, IN: University of Notre Dame Press 2020); Adrian Grant, *Derry: The Irish Revolution, 1912–23* (Dublin: Four Courts Press, 2018); Bonnie Weir, 'Brexit and a border town: troubles ahead in Northern Ireland?', *The New York Review*, 11 April 2019: *https://www.nybooks.com/online/2019/04/11/brexit-and-a-border-town-troubles-ahead-in-northern-ireland/* (accessed 24 January 2024); Kate Van Liere, 'Northern Ireland's fragile peace', *Historical Horizons. Calvin University Historical Studies Department Blog*, 20 September 2019: *https://historicalhorizons.org/2019/09/20/northern-irelands-fragile-peace/* (accessed 24 January 2024); Simon Basketter, 'October 1968 – when Derry dared to revolt against British imperialism', *Socialist Worker*, 2624 (2 October 2018): *https://socialistworker.co.uk/features/october-1968-when-derry-dared-to-revolt-against-british-imperialism/* (accessed 24 January 2024).

41 This is from a field visit during 2016.
42 Hasson, *Haaretz*.
43 Ilan Peleg and Dov Waxman, *Israel's Palestinians* (Cambridge: Cambridge University Press, 2011); Sherry Lowrance, 'Identity, grievances, and political action: recent evidence from the Palestinian community in Israel', *International Political Science Review*, 27/2 (2006), 167–90.
44 See 1(vi), p. 2, in HM Government, *The Belfast Agreement: An Agreement Reached at the Multi-Party Talks on Northern Ireland* (London: The Stationery Office 1998): *https://www.gov.uk/government/publications/the-belfast-agreement* (accessed 8 June 2023). See also *https://www.nidirect.gov.uk/articles/about-northern-ireland#toc-2* (accessed 8 June 2023).
45 Jeremiah, 31:17, KJV.
46 According to the UNHCR, of the 22.5 million refugees in 2016, just over 6.5 million were understood to be stateless, says Jason Tucker, 'Why here? Factors influencing Palestinian refugees from Syria in choosing Germany or Sweden as asylum destinations', *Comparative Migration Studies*, 6/29 (2018).
47 Institute on Statelessness and Inclusion, *The World's Stateless: Deprivation of Nationality* (Tilburg: Institute on Statelessness and Inclusion, 2020), pp. 114–16. See also Francesca P. Albanese and Lex Takkenberg, *Palestinian Refugees in International Law* (Oxford: Oxford University Press, 2020).
48 *http://users.cecs.anu.edu.au/~bdm/yabber/census/VSpages/VS1945_p30.jpg* (accessed 8 June 2023).
49 *https://www.cbs.gov.il/en/settlements/Pages/default.aspx?mode=Yeshuv* (accessed 8 June 2023).
50 The expulsion of the Arab population of Lydda is described as such by Paul Thomas Chamberlin, *The Global Offensive: The United States, the Palestine Liberation Organization, and the Making of the Post-Cold War Order* (Oxford and New York: Oxford University Press, 2012), p. 27, and by Tom Fraser, 'Arab-Israeli wars', in R. Holmes, C. Singleton and S. Jones (eds), *The Oxford Companion to Military History* (Oxford: Oxford University press, 2001), p. 64.
51 Benny Morris, *The Birth of the Palestinian Refugee Problem, 1947–1949*, (Cambridge, New York and Melbourne: Cambridge University Press, 1987), p. 207.
52 Jeremiah 31:17, KJV.
53 Clayton E. Swisher, *The Palestine Papers (Politics): The End of the Road?* (London: Hesperus Press Ltd, 2011), p. 11.
54 Swisher, *The Palestine Papers*, p. 10.
55 Ziyad Clot, 'Why I blew the whistle about Palestine', *The Guardian*, 14 May 2011: *https://www.theguardian.com/commentisfree/2011/may/14/blew-the-whistle-about-palestine?CMP=twt_g* (accessed 8 June 2023).

Conclusions

56 Ma'an New Agency, *Exploding the Myths: UNRWA, UNHCR and the Palestinian Refugees*, UNRWA, 27 June 2011: https://www.unrwa.org/newsroom/features/exploding-myths-unrwa-unhcr-and-palestine-refugees (accessed 8 June 2023).

57 UN General Assembly Security Council, *Question of Palestine: Admission of New Members to the United Nations*, 9 April 2024: https://documents.un.org/doc/undoc/gen/n24/097/67/pdf/n2409767.pdf?token=YQ6sSaMUd0Gl5UL0rF&fe=true (accessed 29 May 2024). Since then, Bahamas, Barbados, Jamaica, as well as Trinidad and Tobago, have recognised the State of Palestine.

58 Chiara Loda and John Doyle, 'Parliamentary recognition', in G. Visoka, J. Doyle and E. Newman (eds), *Routledge Handbook of State Recognition* (Abingdon and New York: Routledge, 2020), pp. 317–51.

59 Al Jazeera, 'EU states announce formal recognition of Palestinian state', *Al Jazeera*, 28 May 2024: https://www.aljazeera.com/news/2024/5/28/palestinian-state-the-only-route-to-peace-says-spanish-pm (accessed 29 May 2024).

60 *Statement of Opinion on Recognising the State of Palestine by Senedd Cymru*, 16 May 2024: https://record.assembly.wales/StatementOfOpinion/387 (accessed 28 May 2024). For the response of Welsh pacifism to the official position of Wales, see the following: Linden Peach, 'When Wales said no: Palestine, parch and personalism', *Planet. The Welsh Internationalist*, 253 (2024), 23–31.

61 The petitions date to 2021 and to 2024, as follows: *Petition for the Welsh Government to Recognise the State of Palestine*, 19 May 2021: https://petitions.senedd.wales/petitions/244825#:~:text=Rejected%20petition%20For%20the%20Welsh%20Government%20to%20diplomatically (accessed 28 May 2024); and *Petition for Senedd Cymru to Recognise the State of Palestine*, 22 May 2024: https://petitions.senedd.wales/petitions/246253#:~:text=We%20the%20undersigned%20would%20like%20to%20show%20solidarity (accessed 28 May 2024).

62 There is some evidence that amongst Palestinian refugees Germany and Sweden rank highly as preferred destinations due to there being fewer obstacles to gaining citizenship. See Tucker, *Comparative Migration Studies*.

63 Human Rights Watch, *Treatment and Rights in Arab Host States*, 23 April 2002: https://www.hrw.org/news/2002/04/23/treatment-and-rights-arab-host-states (accessed 8 June 2023).

64 https://unispal.un.org/UNISPAL.NSF/0/E373EB5C166347AE85256E36006948BA (accessed 8 June 2023).

65 https://www.unrwa.org/where-we-work (accessed 8 June 2023).

66 https://www.un.org/unispal/document/auto-insert-197289/ (accessed 8 June 2023).

67 Zaher Abu Hamdah, 'A fourth generation of Palestinians living in Lebanon "on the fringes of the law"', *Raseef22*, 6 December 2021: https://raseef22.net/article/1085578-a-fourth-generation-of-palestinians-living-in-lebanon-on-the-fringes-of-the-law (accessed 8 June 2023).

68 Fiorella Larissa Erni, *Tired of Being a Refugee* (Geneva, Graduate Institute ePapers, eCahier de l'Institut, 2013), paragraphs 13–14 in '6. Changing patterns in social identification': https://books.openedition.org/iheid/591?lang=en (accessed 8 June 2023).

69 UNRWA, 'UN Secretary-General Guterres to Palestine refugees in Lebanon: do not lose hope', *UNRWA*, 21 December 2021: https://www.unrwa.org/newsroom/press-releases/un-secretary-general-guterres-palestine-refugees-lebanon-do-not-lose-hope (accessed 8 June 2023).

70 For contemporaneous reporting on this in the international media, see, for example, BBC News, 'Israel declares emergency in Lod as unrest spreads', *BBC News*, 12 May 2021: https://www.bbc.co.uk/news/world-middle-east-57081848 (accessed 8 June 2023).

71 Writing in the wake of the publication in 1983 of *Israel in Lebanon: The Report of the International Commission to Enquire into Reported Violations of International Law by Israel during its Invasion of Lebanon* under the chairpersonship of Seán MacBride, Edward Said says that, while the report declares 'the facts speak for themselves', it is the case that for the Palestinians 'the facts have never done so' – Edward W. Said, 'Permission to narrate', *Journal of Palestinian Studies*, 13 (1983/84), 27–48, at 29. Then, writing in 1998 on the occasion of the fiftieth anniversary of the creation of the State of Israel, Said reminds us that 'Palestine and Palestinians remain … there is no getting away from the fact that, as an idea, a memory, and as an often buried or invisible reality, Palestine and its people have simply not disappeared … the sheer fact of our existence has foiled, where it has not defeated, the Israeli effort to be rid of us completely' – Edward W. Said, 'Palestine has not disappeared', *Le Monde Diplomatique*, 1 May 1998: https://mondediplo.com/1998/05/01said (accessed 24 January 2024). Fact: these words retain their truth.

72 https://www.refusenikproject.org/; https://www.nli.org.il/en/a-topic/987007529443005171 (accessed 8 June 2023).

73 Yaakov Schwartz, 'Family of refusenik puts on display the world's only photos of Soviet gulag life', *The Times of Israel*, 30 May 2018: https://www.timesofisrael.com/family-of-refusenik-puts-on-display-worlds-only-photos-of-soviet-gulag-life/ (accessed 8 June 2023).

74 Ephraim (Alexander) Kholmyansky, *The Voice of Silence: The Story of the Jewish Underground in the USSR* (Boston, MA: Academic Studies Press, 2021).

75 https://www.nbn.org.il/life-in-israel/community-and-housing/community-guide/maale-adumim/ (accessed 8 June 2023).

76 https://www.knesset.gov.il/laws/special/eng/return.htm (accessed 8 June 2023).

77 Larry Derfner, 'The settlement that broke the two-state solution', *Foreign Policy*, 26 December 2012: https://foreignpolicy.com/2012/12/26/the-settlement-that-broke-the-two-state-solution/ (accessed 8 June 2023).

Conclusions

78 The Jewish Virtual Library claims a population of 49,725 in 2021 for the Ma'ale Adumim 'bloc' – Jewish Virtual Library, n.d., *The 'Consensus' Settlements*: https://www.jewishvirtuallibrary.org/the-ldquo-consensus-rdquo-settlements (accessed 8 June 2023).
79 Derfner, *Foreign Policy*.
80 B'Tselem, 'The hidden agenda: the establishment and expansion plans of Ma'ale Adummim and their human rights ramifications', *B'Tselem* (2009): https://www.btselem.org/publications/summaries/200912_maale_adummim (accessed 8 June 2023). See also Nir Shalev, *The Hidden Agenda: The Establishment and Expansion Plans of Ma'ale Adummim and their Human Rights Ramifications* (Jerusalem: Bimkom and B'Tselem, 2009), pp. 47, 54, 55 and 58.
81 The Jewish Virtual Library claims a population of 35,195 in 2021 for the Givat Ze'ev 'bloc' – Jewish Virtual Library, *The 'Consensus' Settlements*.
82 The Jewish Virtual Library claims a population of 36,086 in 2021 for the 'bloc' of which Efrat is a part, namely the Gush Etzion bloc – Jewish Virtual Library, *The 'Consensus' Settlements*.
83 Jewish Virtual Library, n.d., *Geography of Israel: Ma'ale Adumim*: https://www.jewishvirtuallibrary.org/ma-ale-adumim (accessed 8 June 2023).
84 Ronald Ranta, *Political Decision Making and Non-decisions: The Case of Israel and the Occupied Territories* (Basingstoke: Palgrave Macmillan, 2015), p. 152.
85 Seventh Arab League Summit Conference, *Resolution on Palestine*, Rabat, Morocco, 28 October 1974: https://unispal.un.org/UNISPAL.NSF/0/63D9A930E2B428DF852572C0006D06B8 (accessed 8 June 2023).
86 Idith Zertal and Akiva Eldar, *Lords of the Land: The War over Israel's Settlements in the Occupied Territories, 1967–2007* (New York: Bold Type Books, 2007); Neve Gordon, *Israel's Occupation* (Berkeley and Los Angeles, CA: University of California Press, 2008); Gershom Sorenberg, *The Accidental Empire: Israel and the Birth of the Settlements, 1967–1977* (London: Macmillan, 2006).
87 B'Tselem, *The Hidden Agenda*.
88 Flore de Preneuf, 'Settlers are reluctant warriors for Sharon', *Tampa Bay Times*, published 2 February 2001 and updated 9 September 2005: https://www.tampabay.com/archive/2001/02/02/settlers-are-reluctant-warriors-for-sharon/ (accessed 8 June 2023) and *On the Spot: Warriors. Jewish Settlers*, a European television series from 2013: https://www.imdb.com/title/tt11116770/plotsummary?ref_=tt_ov_pl (accessed 8 June 2023).
89 Yaakov Katz, *West Bank Jewish Population Stats* (Bet El Institutions, 2021): http://westbankjewishpopulationstats.com/ (accessed 8 June 2023).
90 See 'Chapter 3: Israeli settlements and international law', in Amnesty International, *Destination: Occupation* (London: Amnesty International, 2019): https://www.amnesty.org/en/latest/campaigns/2019/01/chapter-3-israeli-settlements-and-international-law/ (accessed 8 June 2023).

91 UN Department of Operational Support, *Israel's Illegal Occupation of Palestinian Territory, Tantamount to 'Settler-colonialism': UN expert*, 27 October 2022: *https://operationalsupport.un.org/en/israels-illegal-occupation-of-palestinian-territory-tantamount-to-settler-colonialism-un-expert* (accessed 14 January 2024).
92 Human Rights Watch, *A Threshold Crossed.*
93 See Martin Blecher, *Israeli Settlements: Land Politics beyond the Geneva Convention* (Lanham, MD: The Rowman and Littlefield Publishing Group, Inc., 2018).
94 See the section entitled 'Settlement blocs', in Alan Dowty (ed.), *The Israel/Palestine Reader* (Cambridge: Polity Press, 2019). See also Jewish Virtual Library, *The 'Consensus' Settlements.*
95 Jewish Virtual Library, *The 'Consensus' Settlements.*
96 Erik Cohen, 'The removal of the Israeli settlements in Sinai: an ambiguous resolution of an existential conflict', *The Journal of Applied Behavioral Science*, 23/1 (1987), 139–49.
97 *https://www.jewishvirtuallibrary.org/the-yamit-evacuation* (accessed 8 June 2023).
98 McKittrick, Kelters, Feeney and Thornton, *Lost Lives*, pp. 1105 and 1106.
99 Article 42, Convention (IV) respecting the Laws and Customs of War on Land and its annex: regulations concerning the Laws and Customs of War on Land. The Hague, 18 October 1907: *https://ihl-databases.icrc.org/applic/ihl/ihl.nsf/Article.xsp?action=openDocument&documentId=01D426B0086089BEC12563CD00516887* (accessed 8 June 2023).
100 Adam Roberts, 'Prolonged military occupation: the Israeli-occupied territories since 1967', *The American Journal of International Law*, 84/1 (1990), 44–103, at 44.
101 Jeremy E. Taylor, 'The changing face of "occupation studies"', *The Occupation Studies Research Network*, 6 November 2021: *https://fasos-research.nl/occupationstudies/the-changing-face-of-occupation-studies/* (accessed 8 June 2023).
102 Neve Gordon, 'Of dowries and brides: a structural analysis of Israel's occupation', *New Political Science*, 29/4 (2007), 453–78, at 461.
103 Neve Gordon, 'From colonization to separation: exploring the structure of Israel's occupation', *Third World Quarterly*, 29/1 (2008), 25–44, at 37.
104 Gordon, 'From colonization to separation', p. 28.
105 Oxfam International, *Daily Death Rate in Gaza Higher Than Any Other Major 21st Century Conflict*, 11 January 2024: *https://www.oxfam.org/en/press-releases/daily-death-rate-gaza-higher-any-other-major-21st-century-conflict-oxfam* (accessed 14 January 2024). The UN Office for the Coordination of Humanitarian Affairs provides regularly updated data on the number of casualties resulting from the conflict in Palestine, including the Israel–Hamas War: *https://www.ochaopt.org/data/casualties* (accessed 14 January 2024).
106 For a history of the movement by an insider, see Aly Renwick, 'Something in the air: the rise of the Troops Out Movement', in G. Dawson, J. Dover and

S. Hopkins (eds), *The Northern Ireland Troubles in Britain: Impacts, Engagements, Legacies and Memories* (Manchester: Manchester University Press, 2016), pp. 111–26.
107 McKittrick, Kelters, Feeney and Thornton, *Lost Lives*, pp. 1105 and 1106.
108 McKittrick, Kelters, Feeney and Thornton, *Lost Lives*, p. 1112.
109 McKittrick, Kelters, Feeney and Thornton, *Lost Lives*, p. 1112.
110 McKittrick, Kelters, Feeney and Thornton, *Lost Lives*, p. 1121.
111 McCann, *Apeirogon*, p. 226.
112 McCann, *Apeirogon*, pp. 237–8.
113 V. Mahesh, '"The Israeli Occupation is fundamentally and undeniably unjust": Colum McCann', *The Hindu*, 29 May 2021: *https://www.thehindu.com/books/books-authors/the-occupation-is-fundamentally-and-undeniably-unjust-colum-mccann/article34664100.ece* (accessed 8 June 2023).
114 Mahesh, *The Hindu*.
115 Roberts, 'Prolonged military occupation', p. 61.
116 Roberts, 'Prolonged military occupation', p. 102.
117 Paragraph 855 in Ministry of Defence, *Operation Banner: An Analysis of Military Operations in Northern Ireland* (London: Ministry of Defence, 2006).
118 Roberts, 'Prolonged military occupation', p. 61.
119 Roberts, 'Prolonged military occupation, p. 44.
120 Gordon, 'From colonization to separation', p. 26.
121 Gordon, 'Of dowries and brides', p. 467.
122 *https://www.knesset.gov.il/review/data/eng/law/kns10_golan_eng.pdf* (accessed 8 June 2023) and *https://www.mfa.gov.il/mfa/foreignpolicy/peace/guide/pages/golan%20heights%20law.aspx* (accessed 8 June 2023).
123 Roberts, 'Prolonged military occupation'.
124 *https://coventry2021.co.uk/what-s-on/turner-prize/* (accessed 8 June 2023).
125 John M. Cunningham, 'Turner Prize. British arts award', *Britannica* (2021): *https://www.britannica.com/art/Turner-Prize* (accessed 8 June 2023).
126 Tom Seymour, 'Northern Irish activist collective wins Turner Prize 2021 with a "pub without permission"', *The Art Newspaper*, 1 December 2021: *https://www.theartnewspaper.com/2021/12/01/northern-irish-activist-collective-wins-turner-prize-2021* (accessed 8 June 2023).
127 Robbins, 'Beyond the suffering subject', p. 457.
128 Larmore, 'The right and the good', p. 28.
129 Robbins, 'Beyond the suffering subject', p. 455.
130 Robbins, 'Beyond the suffering subject', p. 458.
131 Jonathan Jones, 'Britain's best-loved artwork is a Banksy. That's proof of our stupidity', *The Guardian*, 26 July 2017: *https://www.theguardian.com/commentisfree/2017/jul/26/britain-artwork-banksy-art-girl-with-balloon?CMP=fb_gu* (accessed 8 June 2023).

132 Corinthians 13:12, KJV.
133 Givoni, *The Care of the Witness*, p. 11.
134 Sarah J. O'Connell, 'Review; Literary aesthetics of trauma: Virginia Woolf and Jeanette Winterson by Reina van der Wiel', *The Journal of the Midwest Modern Language Association*, 48/1 (Spring 2015), 255–8.
135 Callard, *Art is for Seeing Evil*.
136 Robert Applebaum, *The Aesthetics of Violence: Art, Fiction, Drama, and Film* (Washington, DC: Rowman and Littlefield, 2017).
137 Here, I paraphrase Reina van der Wiel, *Literary Aesthetics of Trauma: Virginia Woolf and Jeanette Winterson* (Basingstoke: Palgrave Macmillan, 2014).
138 See also p. 12 in Mac Giolla Chríost, *Jailtacht*.
139 Identity and Language (Northern Ireland) Act 2022: https://www.legislation.gov.uk/ukpga/2022/45/section/2/enacted (accessed 20 April 2024).
140 An Dream Dearg, *Northern Ireland's Irish Language Legislation becomes Law after receiving Royal Assent*, 7 December 2022: https://www.dearg.ie/ga/nuacht/cartlann/091202-legislation-becomes-law (accessed 20 April 2024).
141 The Visible Award, *Zuleikha Chaudhari, Landscape as Evidence: Artists as Witness* (2019): https://www.visibleproject.org/blog/project/landscape-as-evidence-artist-as-witness/ (accessed 8 June 2023).
142 The Visible Award, *Zuleikha Chaudhari*.
143 See, for example, Judith Wielander and Matteo Lucchetti (eds), *Collectively Annotated Bibliography on Artistic Practices in the Expanded Field of Public Art* (Hälsingegatan: Public Art Agency Sweden, 2020).
144 The Visible Award, *'Getting Our Hands Dirty', a Conversation between Nida Sinnokrot and Nat Muller on Sakiya – Art/Science/Agriculture* (2017): https://www.visibleproject.org/blog/getting-our-hands-dirty-a-conversation-between-nida-sinnokrot-and-nat-muller-on-sakiya-artscienceagriculture/ (accessed 8 June 2023). This, Sakiya, is a project that brings together 'visual art, ecological preservation, sustainable agriculture and food justice' in Palestine. See p. 218 in Wielander and Lucchetti, *Collectively Annotated Bibliography*.
145 Wielander and Lucchetti, *Collectively Annotated Bibliography*.
146 Seán Ó Tuama and Thomas Kinsella, *An Duanaire, 1600–1900: Poems of the Dispossessed* (Dublin: Dolmen Press, 1981).
147 The alternative, it could be said, is the current state of affairs in Germany. There, the voice of the artist on the matter of Palestine is struggling to be heard. Against a backdrop in which the Deutscher Bundestag, the German parliament, on 17 May 2019, adopted a resolution stating that 'the pattern of argument and methods of the BDS movement are anti-Semitic', Jason Farago of *The New York Times* writes that '[t]he arts scene in Germany – and especially Berlin – has been turned upside down by Hamas's attacks in Israel on October 7, and the siege and bombardment of Gaza. Prizes have been

rescinded, Conferences called off. Plays taken off the boards. Government cultural officials have suggesting tying funding to what artists and institutions say about the conflict, and media – both traditional and social – bubble with public denunciation of this writer, that artist, this D.J., that dancer' – see 'Berlin was a beacon of artistic freedom. Gaza changed everything', *The New York Times*, 6 April 2024: *https://www.nytimes.com/2024/04/06/arts/design/berlin-israel-gaza-art-scene.html* (accessed 10 April 2024). For the primary source on the Deutscher Bundestag resolution on BDS, see *https://www.bundestag.de/dokumente/textarchiv/2019/kw20-de-bds-642892* (accessed 10 April 2024).

Select Bibliography

Abbott, A., 'Against narrative: a preface to lyrical sociology', *Sociological Theory*, 25/1 (2007), 67–99.

Alaqra, A., 'To subvert, to deconstruct: agency in Qalandiya refugee camp', *Jerusalem Quarterly*, 79 (2019), 63–76.

Albanese, Francesca P. and Takkenberg, Lex, *Palestinian Refugees in International Law* (Oxford: Oxford University Press, 2020).

Amiot-Jouenne, Pascale, *Les Métamorphoses de Sweeney dans la Littérature Irlandaise Contemporaine* (Caen: Presses Universitaires de Caen, 2011).

Anwar, A., 'Foreword. To Osi: the colourful internationalist druid', in Bala and Osmond, *Encounters with Osi*, pp. 2–5.

Applebaum, Robert, *The Aesthetics of Violence: Art, Fiction, Drama, and Film* (Washington, DC: Rowman and Littlefield, 2017).

Aran, Amnon, *The Middle East: Intractable Conflict?: The Israeli-Palestinian Impasse: Will This Time be Different?* (LSE IDEAS, London School of Economics and Political Science, London UK, 2009): *http://eprints.lse.ac.uk/43643/1/The%20Middle%20East_the%20Israeli-Palestinian%20impasse(lsero).pdf*

Aretxaga, Begoña, *Shattering Silence: Women, Nationalism, and Political Subjectivity in Northern Ireland* (Princeton, NJ: Princeton University Press, 2001).

Austin, John L., *How to Do Things with Words* (Oxford: Clarendon Press, 1962).

Bala, I., 'Worker of the word and the image', in Bala and Osmond, *Encounters with Osi*, pp. 9–18.

Bala, Iwan and Osmond, Hilary Rhys (eds), *Encounters with Osi* (Swansea: H'mm Foundation, 2015).

Barnie, J., 'Planet essays', in Bala and Osmond, *Encounters with Osi*, pp. 188–91.

Bawarshi, Anis S. and Reiff, Mary Jo, *Genre: An Introduction to History, Theory, Research, and Pedagogy* (West Lafayette, IN: Parlor Press).

Bazerman, C., 'The life of genre, the life in the classroom', in W. Bishop and H. Ostrom (eds), *Genre and Writing: Issues, Arguments, Alternatives* (Portsmouth: Boynton/Cook, 1997), pp. 19–26.

Beaulieu, A., 'From co-location to co-presence: shifts in the use of ethnography to the study of knowledge', *Social Studies of Science*, 49/3 (2010), 453–70.

Bell, J. Bowyer, *Terror out of Zion: The Fight for Israeli Independence 1929–1949: Irgun Zvia Leumi, Lehi, and the Palestine Underground* (Dublin: Academy Press, 1979).

Bercovitch, J., and Kadayifci, S. A., 'Conflict management and Israeli-Palestinian conflict: the importance of capturing the "right moment"', *Asia-Pacific Review*, 9/2 (2002), 113–29.

Beresford, David, *Ten Men Dead* (London: HarperCollins, 1987).

Berger, John, *Hold Everything Dear: Dispatches on Survival and Resistance* (London: Verso, 2007).

Bird, Dúnlaith, *Travelling in Different Skins: Gender Identity in European Women's Oriental Travelogues, 1850–1950* (Oxford: Oxford University Press, 2012).

Blecher, Martin, *Israeli Settlements: Land Politics beyond the Geneva Convention* (Lanham, MD: The Rowman and Littlefield Publishing Group, Inc., 2018).

Bloom, M., 'Mother. Daughter. Sister. Bomber', *Bulletin of the Atomic Scientists*, November/December (2005), 54–62.

Bradatan, Costica, *Dying for Ideas: The Dangerous Lives of the Philosophers* (London: Bloomsbury, 2015).

Bruhn, T. and Doona, J., 'Serious grappling with satire: rhetorical genre affordances and invitations to participation in public controversy', *Javnost – The Public. Journal of the European Institute for Communication and Culture*, 29/3 (2022), 284–300.

Buchanan, Allen and Powell, Russell, *The Evolution of Moral Progress: A Biocultural Theory* (New York: Oxford University Press, 2018).

Butler, J., 'What is critique? An essay on Foucault's virtue', in D. Ingram (ed.), *The Political: Blackwell Readings in Continental Philosophy* (Malden, MA: Blackwell, 2002), pp. 212–26.

Carey, J., 'The three sails, the twelve winds, and the question of Early Irish colour theory', *Journal of the Warburg and Courtauld Institutes*, 72 (2009), 221–32.

Catani, C., 'Mental health of children living in war zones: a risk and protection perspective', *World Psychiatry*, 17/1 (2018), 104–5.

Chamberlin, Paul Thomas, *The Global Offensive: The United States, the Palestine Liberation Organization, and the Making of the Post-Cold War Order* (Oxford and New York: Oxford University Press, 2012).

Code, Lorraine, 'Rhetoric and social epistemology', in MacDonald, *The Oxford Handbook of Rhetorical Studies*, pp. 721–32.

Cohen, E., 'The removal of the Israeli settlements in Sinai: an ambiguous resolution of an existential conflict', *The Journal of Applied Behavioral Science*, 23/1 (1987), 139–49.

Collins, Larry and Lapierre, Dominique, *O Jerusalem!* (London: The History Book Club, 1972).

Cook, David, *Contemporary Muslim Apocalyptic Literature* (Syracuse, NY: Syracuse University Press, 2005).

Cowper-Coles, Minna, *Gender and Political Support: Women and Hamas in the Occupied Palestinian Territories* (London: Routledge, 2022).

Crompton, L., 'Fragments from our past', in Bala and Osmond, *Encounters with Osi*, pp. 153–5.

Danesi, M., 'Visual rhetoric and semiotic', in *Oxford Research Encyclopedia of Communication* (published online, 2017): *https://oxfordre.com/communication/view/10.1093/acrefore/9780190228613.001.0001/acrefore-9780190228613-e-43*

Daniel, Errol Valentine, *Charred Lullabies: Chapters in an Anthropography of Violence* (Princeton, NJ: Princeton University Press, 1996).

Davies, L., 'My brother', in Bala and Osmond, *Encounters with Osi*, pp. 180–1.

Davis, Rochelle A., *Palestinian Village Histories: Geographies of the Displaced* (Stanford, CA: Stanford University Press, 2011).

Donahaye, Jasmine, *Whose People? Wales, Israel, Palestine* (Cardiff: University of Wales Press, 2012).

Dowty, Alan (ed.), *The Israel/Palestine Reader* (Cambridge: Polity Press, 2019).

Dugard, J. and Reynolds, J., 'Apartheid, international law, and the Occupied Palestinian Territory', *European Journal of International Law*, 24/3 (August 2023), 867–913.

Elfyn, M., 'Auspicious', in Bala and Osmond, *Encounters with Osi*, pp. 192–3.

Erni, Fiorella Larissa, *Tired of Being a Refugee* (Geneva: Graduate Institute ePapers, eCahier de l'Institut, 2013).

Fahnestock, J. and Secor, M., 'The rhetoric of literary criticism', in C. Bazerman and J. Paradis (eds), *Textual Dynamics of the Professions: Historical and Contemporary Studies of Writing in Professional Communities* (Madison, WI: University of Wisconsin Press, 1991), pp. 77–96.

Fassin, Didier and Rechtman, Richard, *The Empire of Trauma: An Inquiry into the Condition of Victimhood* (Princeton, NJ: Princeton University Press, 2009).

Felski, R., 'Sociological writing as resonant writing', *The Sociological Review*, 70/4 (2022), 656–65.

Foucault, Michel, *Security, Territory, Population* (Basingstoke: Palgrave Macmillan, 2007).

Foucault, Michel, *The Birth of Biopolitics* (Basingstoke: Palgrave Macmillan, 2008).

Francis, K., 'Notes, prose and poetry. An essay of sorts', in Bala and Osmond, *Encounters with Osi*, pp. 68–79.

Fraser, T., 'Arab-Israeli wars', in R. Holmes, C. Singleton and S. Jones (eds), *The Oxford Companion to Military History* (Oxford: Oxford University press, 2001), p. 64.

Frisch, H., 'Motivation or capabilities? Israeli counterterrorism against Palestinian suicide bombings and violence', *Journal of Strategic Studies*, 29 (2006), 843–69 and *Mideast Security and Policy Studies*, 70 (2006): https://besacenter.org/wp-content/uploads/2006/12/MSPS70.pdf.

Givoni, M., 'The ethics of witnessing and the politics of the governed', *Theory, Culture and Society*, 31/1 (2013), 123–42.

Givoni, Michal, *The Care of the Witness: A Contemporary History of Testimony in Crises* (Cambridge: Cambridge University Press, 2016).

Givoni, M., 'Indifference and repetition: occupation testimonies and left-wing despair', *Journal of Cultural Studies*, 33/4 (2019), 595–631.

Gordon, N., 'Of dowries and brides: a structural analysis of Israel's occupation', *New Political Science*, 29/4 (2007), 453–78.

Gordon, N., 'From colonization to separation: exploring the structure of Israel's occupation', *Third World Quarterly*, 29/1 (2008), 25–44.

Gordon, Neve, *Israel's Occupation* (Berkeley and Los Angeles, CA: University of California Press, 2008).

Gornick, Vivian, *The Situation and the Story: The Art of Personal Narrative* (New York: Farrar, Strauss and Giroux, 2001).

Grant, Adrian, *Derry: The Irish Revolution, 1912–23* (Dublin: Four Courts Press, 2018).

Hannerz, U., 'Being there… and there… and there! Reflections on multi-site ethnography', *Ethnography*, 4/2 (2003), 201–16.

Harker, M., 'The ethics of argument: rereading kairos and making sense in a timely fashion', *College Composition and Communication*, 59/1 (2007), 77–97.

Harlow, B., '"Be it resolved …": Referenda on recent scholarship in the Israel–Palestine conflict', *Cultural Critique*, 91/Fall (2015), 190–205.

Helmer, D., 'Hezbollah's employment of suicide bombing during the 1980s: the theological, political, and operational development of a new tactic', *Military Review*, July–August (2006), 71–82.

Hemming, J., 'Pale horses and green dawns: elusive colour terms in early Welsh heroic poetry', *North American Journal of Celtic Studies*, 1/2 (November 2017), 189–223.

Hobsbawm, Eric, *Age of Extremes: The Short Twentieth Century, 1914–1991* (London: Michael Joseph, 1994).

Honderich, Ted (ed.), *The Oxford Companion to Philosophy* (Oxford: Oxford University Press, 1995).

Hopwood, M., 'Mewn heddwch', in Bala and Osmond, *Encounters with Osi*, pp. 200–3.

Horowitz, M. C., 'The rise and spread of suicide bombing', *Annual Review of Political Science*, 18 (2015), 69–84.

Huddleston, R., 'Arts in society "Poetry makes nothing happen". W. H. Auden's struggle with politics', *Boston Review*, 25 February 2015.

Ignatieff, M., 'Is nothing sacred? The ethics of television', *Daedalus* (1985), 57–78.

Jarratt, S. and Reynolds, N., 'The splitting image: contemporary feminisms and the ethics of ethos', in J. S. Baumlin and T. F. Baumlin (eds), *Ethos: New Essays in Rhetorical and Critical Theory* (Dallas, TX: Southern Methodist University Library, 1994), pp. 37–63.

Jazeel, T. and Mookherjee, N., 'Aesthetics, politics, conflict', *Journal of Material Culture*, 20/4 December (2015), 353–9.

Kamberelis, G., 'Genre as institutional informed social practice', *Journal of Contemporary Legal Studies*, 6 (1995), 117–71.

Keenan, Brian, *An Evil Cradling* (London: Hutchison, 1992).

Kemp, M., 'The psychoanalytic encounter with settler colonialism in Palestine/Israel', *International Journal of Applied Psychoanalytic Studies*, 17/2 June (2020), 93–125.

Khalidi, Walid, *All That Remains: The Palestinian Villages Occupied and Depopulated by Israel in 1948* (Beirut: Institute for Palestinian Studies, 1992).

Kilby, J. and Gilloch, G., 'Sociography: writing differently', *The Sociological Review*, 70/4 (2022), 635–55.

Kinsey, C., 'On painting', in Bala and Osmond, *Encounters with Osi*, pp. 57–60.

Kirby, R. P., 'A fourth rhetorical device: the role of kairos in narrative discourse', *Medium*, 27 April 2020: *https://medium.com/age-of-awareness/a-fourth-rhetorical-device-the-role-of-kairos-in-narrative-discourse-6b78f2415e7f*

Knauft, B., 'Good anthropology in dark times: critical appraisal and ethnographic application', *The Australian Journal of Anthropology* (2018), 1–15.

Kress, Gunther and van Leeuwen, Theo, *Reading Images: The Grammar of Visual Design* (New York: Routledge, 1996).

Larmore, C., 'The right and the good', *Philosophia*, 20/1–2 (1990), 15–32.

Lefebvre, Henri, *The Production of Space* (Oxford: Blackwell, 1974, translated by D. Nicholson-Smith, 1991).

LeFevre, Karen Burke, *Invention as a Social Act* (Carbondale, IL: Southern Illinois University Press, 1987).

Lejeune, Philippe, *On Autobiography* (Minneapolis, MN: University of Minnesota Press, 1988).

Lencek, Lena and Bosler, Gideon, *The Beach: The History of Paradise on Earth* (London: Secker and Warburg, 1998).

Lentin, R., 'Expected to live: women shoah survivors' testimonials of silence', *Women's Studies International Forum*, 23/6 (2000), 689–700.

Levine, Caroline, *Forms: Whole, Rhythm, Hierarchy, Network* (Princeton, NJ: Princeton University Press, 2015).

Levine, C., 'Forms, literary and social', *Dibur Literary Journal*, 2/Spring (2016), 75–9.

Loda, C., and Doyle, J., 'Parliamentary recognition', in G. Visoka, J. Doyle and E. Newman, *Routledge Handbook of State Recognition* (Abingdon and New York: Routledge, 2020), pp. 317–51.

Louvet, Marie-Violaine, *Civil Society, Post-colonialism and Transnational Solidarity: The Irish and the Middle East Conflict* (Basingstoke: Palgrave Macmillan, 2016).

Lowrance, S., 'Identity, grievances, and political action: recent evidence from the Palestinian community in Israel', *International Political Science Review*, 27/2 (2006), 167–90.

MacDonald, Michael J. (ed.), *The Oxford Handbook of Rhetorical Studies* (Oxford: Oxford University Press, 2014).

Maguire, Anne, *For Brian's Sake: The Story of the Keenan Sisters* (Belfast: Blackstaff Press Ltd, 1992).

Masalha, Nur, *Palestine: A Four Thousand Year History* (London: I. B. Tauris, 2018, new edition 2022).

Masood, K. M. S., 'Manifestations of nature and politics in Mahmoud Darwish's metaphors', *Journal of Literature, Languages and Linguistics*, 66 (2020), 53–66.

McCann, C., 'Two stories, so many stories', in M. Chabon and A. Waldman (eds), *Kingdom of Olives and Ash: Writers Confront the Occupation* (London: HarperCollins, 2017), pp. 389–404.

McCann, Colum, *Apeirogon: A Novel* (London: Bloomsbury, 2020).

McCann, Eamonn, *War and an Irish Town* (London: Pluto Press, 1980).

McDowell, Sara and Braniff, Máire, *Commemoration as Conflict: Space, Memory and Identity in Peace Processes* (Basingstoke: Palgrave Macmillan, 2014).

McKittrick, David, Kelters, Seamus, Feeney, Brian and Thornton, Chris, *Lost Lives: The Stories of the Men, Women and Children Who Died as a Result of the Northern Ireland Troubles* (Edinburgh and London: Mainstream Publishing, 1999).

Mendel, Yonatan, *The Creation of Israeli Arabic: Political and Security Considerations in the Making of Arabic Language Studies in Israel* (Basingstoke: Palgrave Macmillan, 2014).

Miller, C. R., 'Genre as social action', *Quarterly Journal of Speech*, 70/2 (1984), 151–67.

Miller, Rory, *Ireland and the Palestine Question: 1948–2004* (Dublin: Irish Academic Press, 2005).

Mollerup, N. G., *'Being There', Phone in Hand: Thick Presence and Anthropological Fieldwork with Media* (EASA Media Anthropology Network E-Seminar Series, 2017): *https://comm.ku.dk/staff/?pure=en%2Fpublications%2Fbeing-there-phone-in-hand(58d7d7f1-e042-4006-95d4-30bcc2d4d116)%2Fexport.html*

Montefiore, Simon Sebag, *Jerusalem: The Biography* (London: Weidenfeld and Nicolson, 2011).

Mookherjee, N., 'Aurality of images in graphic ethnographies: sexual violence during wars and memories of the feelings of fear', *The Sociological Review*, 70/4 (2022), 686–99.

Morris, Benny, *The Birth of the Palestinian Refugee Problem, 1947–1949* (Cambridge, New York and Melbourne: Cambridge University Press, 1987).

Mulqueen, J. and Smyth, J., '"The Che Guevara of the IRA": the legend of "Big Joe" McCann', *History Ireland*, 18/1 (2010): https://www.historyireland.com/the-che-guevara-of-the-ira-the-legend-of-big-joe-mccann/

Mundye, C., 'Outside the Imaginary Museum: mythology and representation in the poetry of Lynette Roberts and Keidrych Rhys', *Pn Review*, 40/2 (2013), 23–9.

Murphy, Dervla, *Full Tilt: Ireland to India with a Bicycle* (London: John Murray, 1965).

Murphy, Dervla, *A Month by the Sea: Encounters in Gaza* (London: Eland, 2013).

Murphy, Dervla, *Between River and Sea: Encounters in Israel and Palestine* (London: Eland, 2015).

O'Connell, S. J., 'Review; Literary aesthetics of trauma: Virginia Woolf and Jeanette Winterson by Reina van der Wiel', *The Journal of the Midwest Modern Language Association*, 48/1 (Spring 2015), 255–8.

Oddo, J., 'Variation and continuity in intertextual rhetoric: from the "war on terror" to the "struggle against violent extremism"', *Journal of Language and Politics*, 13/3 (2014), 513–38.

Oddo, John, *Intertextuality and the 24-hours News Cycle: A Day in the Rhetorical Life of Colin Powell's UN Address* (East Lansing, MI: Michigan State University Press, 2014).

Ó Dochartaigh, Niall, *From Civil Rights to Armalites: Derry and the Birth of the Irish Troubles* (Basingstoke: Palgrave Macmillan, 2005).

Olmert, J., 'A half century of occupation: Israel, Palestine, and the world's most intractable conflict by Gershon Shafir (Oakland: University of California Press, 2017), reviewed by Josef Olmert', *Israel Journal of Foreign Affairs*, 12/1 (2018), 113–15.

Oosthuizen, A., 'Osi Rhys Osmond: educator, creator, thinker, friend. An interview with Ann Oosthuizen', in Bala and Osmond, *Encounters with Osi*, pp. 206–29.

Ortner, S., 'Dark anthropology and its others: theory since the eighties', *Hau: Journal of Ethnographic Theory*, 6/1 (2016), 47–73.

Osmond, L., 'Encounters with Osi', in Bala and Osmond, *Encounters with Osi*, pp. 146–7.

Osmond, O. R., 'The ornithologist-poet as a bird', in John Barnie (ed.), *Encounters with R. S.* (Swansea: The H'mm Foundation, 2013), pp. 48–54.

Pappé, Ilan, *The Ethnic Cleansing of Palestine* (London: Oneworld Publications, 2006).

Patterson, David, *A Genealogy of Evil: Anti-Semitism from Nazism to Islamic Jihad* (Cambridge: Cambridge University Press, 2011).

Paul, J., 'The use of kairos in Renaissance political philosophy', *Renaissance Quarterly*, 67/1 (2014), 43–78.

Peach, L., 'When Wales said no. Palestine, parch and personalism', *Planet. The Welsh Internationalist*, 253 (2024), 23–31.

Pedahzur, A. and Perliger, A., 'The changing nature of suicide attacks: A social network perspective', *Social Forces*, 84/4 (2006), 1987–2008.

Peleg, Ilan and Waxman, Dov, *Israel's Palestinians* (Cambridge: Cambridge University Press, 2011).

Pender, K., 'Kairos and the subject of expressive discourse', *Composition Studies*, 31/2 (2003), 91–106.

Pennebaker, J. W. and Beall, S. K., 'Confronting a traumatic event: towards an understanding of inhibition and disease', *Journal of Abnormal Psychology*, 95/3 (1986), 274–81.

Pink, S., Horst, H., Postill, J., Hjorth, L., Lewis, T. and Tacchi, J., *Digital Ethnography: Principles and Practice* (London: SAGE Publishing, 2015).

Postill, J., *Digital Ethnography: 'Being There' Physically, Remotely, Virtually and Imaginatively* (published online, 2015): https://johnpostill.wordpress.com/2015/02/25/digital-ethnography-being-there-physically-remotely-virtually-and-imaginatively/

Ramadan, A., 'Spatialising the refugee camp', *Transactions of the Institute of British Geographers*, 38 (2013), 65–77.

Ranta, Ronald, *Political Decision Making and Non-decisions: The Case of Israel and the Occupied Territories* (Basingstoke: Palgrave Macmillan, 2015).

Reed-Danahay, Deborah (ed.), *Auto/ethnography: Rewriting the Self and the Social* (Oxford: Berg, 1997).

Reed-Danahay, D., 'Participating, observing, witnessing', in S. Coleman, S. B. Hyatt and A. Kinsolver (eds), *The Routledge Companion to Contemporary Anthropology* (London: Routledge, 2016), pp. 57–71.

Regan, S., 'Seamus Heaney and the making of "Sweeney Astray"', *Hungarian Journal of English and American Studies*, Fall 21/2 (2015), 317–39.

Renwick, Aly, 'Something in the air: the rise of the Troops Out Movement', in G. Dawson, J. Dover and S. Hopkins (eds), *The Northern Ireland Troubles in Britain: Impacts, Engagements, Legacies and Memories* (Manchester: Manchester University Press, 2016), pp. 111–26.

Reynolds, N., 'Ethos as location: new sites for discursive authority', *Rhetoric Review*, 11/2 (1993), 325–38.

Rhys-Martin, S., 'Osi, not just my mother's husband', in Bala and Osmond, *Encounters with Osi*, pp. 142–3.

Rich, D., 'The very model of a British Muslim Brotherhood', in B. Rubin (ed.), *The Muslim Brotherhood: The Organization and Policies of a Global Islamist Movement* (New York: Palgrave Macmillan, 2010), pp. 117–36.

Richardson, K., 'Blue and green eyes in the Islamicate Middle Ages', *Annales Islamologiques*, 48/1 (2014), 13–29.

Robbins, J., 'Beyond the suffering subject: toward an anthropology of the good', *Journal of the Royal Anthropological Institute*, 19/3 (2013), 447–62.

Roberts, A., 'Prolonged military occupation: the Israeli-occupied territories since 1967', *The American Journal of International Law*, 84/1 (1990), 44–103.

Robinson, D. N., 'Rhetoric and character in Aristotle', *The Review of Metaphysics*, 60/1 (2006), 3–15.

Ronald, K., 'A re-examination of personal and public discourse in classical rhetoric', *Rhetoric Review*, 90/1 (1990), 36–48.

Rumsey, A., 'Ethnographic macro-tropes and anthropological theory', *Anthropological Theory*, 4/3 (2004), 267–98.

Rye, G., 'The ethics of aesthetics of trauma fiction: memory, guilt and responsibility in Louise L. Lambrichs's Journal d'Hannah', *Journal of Romance Studies*, 9/3 (Winter 2009), 48–59.

Said, Edward W., 'Permission to narrate', *Journal of Palestinian Studies*, 13 (1983/84), 27–48.

Said, Edward W., *After the Last Sky: Palestinian Lives* (London: Vintage, 1986).

Said, Edward W., *The Question of Palestine* (revised edition, New York: Penguin Random House, 1992; originally published 1979).

Sailer, S. S. 'Leaps, curses and flight: Suibne Geilt and the roots of early Irish culture', *Études Celtiques*, 33 (1997), 191–208.

Sanjek, Roger (ed.), *Fieldnotes: The Makings of Anthropology* (Ithaca, NY: Cornell University Press, 1990).

Sanjek, R. and Tratner, S. W. (eds), *eFieldnotes: The Makings of Anthropology in the Digital World* (Philadelphia, PA: University of Pennsylvania Press, 2016).
Sartwell, Crispin, *Political Aesthetics* (Ithaca, NY: Cornell University Press, 2010).
Schmertz, J., 'Constructing essences: ethos and the postmodern subject of feminism', *Rhetoric Review*, 18/1 (1999), 82–91.
Schwalm, H., 'Autobiography', in P. Hühn et al. (eds), *The Living Handbook of Narratology* (Hamburg: Hamburg University, 2014): https://www-archiv.fdm.uni-hamburg.de/lhn/node/129.html
Schwarz, D. R., 'The consolation of form: the theoretical and historical significance of Frank Kermode's "the Sense of an Ending"', *The Centennial Review*, 28/4–29/1 (Fall 1984–Winter 1985), 29–47.
Sharpe, Christina, *Ordinary Notes* (London: Daunt Books, 2023).
Shea, Margo, *Derry City: Memory and Political Struggle in Northern Ireland* (Notre Dame, IN: University of Notre Dame Press, 2020).
Siewers, A. K., 'The bluest-greyest-greenest eye: colours of martyrdom and colours of the winds as iconographic landscape', *Cambrian Medieval Celtic Studies*, 50 (Winter 2005), 31–66.
Slote, M., 'Right action', in Honderich, *The Oxford Companion to Philosophy*, pp. 774–6.
Smith, D., 'Osi: a palimpsest in persona', in Bala and Osmond, *Encounters with Osi*, pp. 61–5.
Smith, G., 'Fiction in Goffman', *The Sociological Review*, 70/4 (2022), 711–22.
Smyth, J., 'Dermot Seymour. A load of old Boellix', in J. Hurley et al. (eds), *Contemporary Art from Ireland, 19 May 2005–12 August 2005* (Frankfurt am Main: European Central Bank, 2005), pp. 62–3.
Sorenberg, Gershom, *The Accidental Empire: Israel and the Birth of the Settlements, 1967–1977* (London: Macmillan, 2006).
Spolsky, Bernard and Cooper, Robert L., *The Languages of Jerusalem* (Oxford: Oxford University Press, 1991).
Sutton, J., 'Kairos', in Th. O. Sloan (ed.), *Encyclopedia of Rhetoric* (New York: Oxford University Press, 2001), pp. 413–17.
Swisher, Clayton E., *The Palestine Papers (Politics): The End of the Road?* (London: Hesperus Press Ltd, 2011).
Thabet, A. A. M., 'Post-traumatic stress reactions in children of war', *Journal of Child Psychology and Psychiatry*, 40/3 (1999), 385–91.

Thabet, A. A. M., Abed, Y. and Vostanis, P., 'Emotional problems in Palestinian children living in a war zone: a cross-sectional study', *Lancet*, 359/9320 (2002), 1801–4.

Thrift, N., 'Space: the fundamental stuff of human geography', in N. Clifford, S. Holloway, S. P. Price and G. Valentine (eds), *Key Concepts in Geography* (London: SAGE Publications, 2008), pp. 95–107.

Tilche, A. and Simpson, E., 'On trusting ethnography: serendipity and the reflexive return to the fields of Gujarat', *Journal of the Royal Anthropological Institute*, 23 (2017), 690–708.

Tucker, J., 'Why here? Factors influencing Palestinian refugees from Syria in choosing Germany or Sweden as asylum destinations', *Comparative Migration Studies*, 6/29 (2018): *https://comparativemigrationstudies.springeropen.com/articles/10.1186/s40878-018-0094-2*

Urry, John and Larsen, Jonas, *The Tourist Gaze 3.0* (London: Sage, 2011, third edition).

van den Hengel, L., 'Zoegraphy: per/forming posthuman lives', *Biography*, 35 (2012), 1–20.

van der Wiel, Reina, *Literary Aesthetics of Trauma: Virginia Woolf and Jeanette Winterson* (Basingstoke: Palgrave Macmillan, 2014).

van Eck, C., 'Rhetoric and the visual arts', in MacDonald, *The Oxford Handbook of Rhetorical Studies*, pp. 461–74.

van Leeuwen, Th., 'Rhetoric and semiotics', in MacDonald, *The Oxford Handbook of Rhetorical Studies*, pp. 673–82.

Vicary, S., 'Knowing Osi', in Bala and Osmond, *Encounters with Osi*, pp. 126–7.

Vidmar, I. and Baccarini, E., 'Art, knowledge and testimony', *Synthesis Philosophica*, 50/2 (2010), 351–66.

Viterbo, H., 'Security Prisoners', in O. Ben-Naftali, M. Sfard, and H. Viterbo (eds), *The ABC of the OPT: A Legal Lexicon of the Israeli Control over the Occupied Palestinian Territory* (Cambridge: Cambridge University Press, 2018), pp. 383–98.

Vivian, Bradford, *Commonplace Witnessing: Rhetorical Invention, Historical Remembrance, and Public Culture* (Oxford: Oxford University Press, 2017).

Walzer, A. E., 'Parrēsia, Foucault, and the classical rhetorical tradition', *Rhetoric Society Quarterly*, 43/1 (2013), 1–21.

Watson, A., 'The familiar strange of sociological fiction', *The Sociological Review*, 70/4 (2022), 723–32.

Weintraub, S., 'The Yellow Book: a reappraisal', *The Journal of General Education*, 16/2 (July 1964), 136–52.
Wenger, Étienne, *Communities of Practice: Learning, Meaning and Identity* (Cambridge: Cambridge University Press, 1999).
Wielander, Judith and Lucchetti, Matteo (eds), *Collectively Annotated Bibliography on Artistic Practices in the Expanded Field of Public Art* (Hälsingegatan: Public Art Agency Sweden, 2020).
Wieviorka, Annette, *L'ère du Témoin* (Paris: Hachette Littératures, 2002).
Wilder, L., '"The rhetoric of literary criticism" revisited: mistaken critics, complex contexts, and social justice', *Written Communication*, 22/1 (2005), 76–119.
Williams, N., 'Where is war poetry? Part one', *Wales Arts Review* (2019) https://www.walesartsreview.org/where-is-war-poetry-part-one/
Wilson, S., 'Cheese on toast', in Bala and Osmond, *Encounters with Osi*, pp. 119–20.
Woroniecka-Krzyzanowska, D., 'The right to the camp: spatial politics of protracted encampment in the West Bank', *Political Geography*, 61 (2017), 160–9.
Zertal, Idith and Eldar, Akiva, *Lords of the Land: The War over Israel's Settlements in the Occupied Territories, 1967–2007* (New York: Bold Type Books, 2007).

Select Other Sources

Al Arabiya
Al Jazeera
Al Monitor
Art Newspaper
Arutz Sheva. Israel National News
Atlantic
BBC News
BBC Radio Cymru
Belfast Telegraph
Blue Nib Literary Magazine
Booklist
Carnegie Endowment for International Peace
Channel 4
Christian Science Monitor

CNN
Conversation
Daily Mail
Daily Review
Daily Star (Lebanon)
Electronic Intifada
EU Observer
Fair Observer
Financial Times
Foreign Policy
Forward
Golwg 360
Guardian
Haaretz
Hindu
Honest Ulsterman
Independent
Indymedia
Irish Examiner
Irish Independent
Irish Literary Supplement
Irish News
Irish Post
Irish Times
Israel Hayom
Jerusalem Post
Jewish Book Council
Jewish Telegraphic Agency
Jewish Virtual Library
Kirkus
Kirkus Reviews
Le Monde
Le Monde Diplomatique
Los Angeles Review of Books
Los Angeles Times
Middle East Eye
Middle East Monitor
Mondoweiss

National News
New Internationalist
New Statesman
New York Review
New York State Writers' Institute
New York Times
Newsweek
Occupation Studies Network
Painting Imperative. International Painting Magazine
Pembroke and Pembroke Dock Observer
Policy Exchange
Prospect Magazine
Reuters
RT
Scotsman
Signs: Journal of Women in Culture and Society
Socialist Worker
Spiegel International
Star Tribune
Sunday Herald
Sunday Times
Tampa Bay Times
TG4
Times of Israel
Times Literary Supplement
Toronto Star
Ulster Herald
UN News
Vanity Fair
Walesonline
Washington Institute for Near East Policy
Washington Post
Washington Report on Middle East Affairs
Waterstones
Western Telegraph
Women in Islam Journal
WYPR – 88.1 FM Baltimore
Ynetnews

Index

A

Abbas, Mahmoud 37, 54, 148, 183
Abbott, Andrew 3, 22
Abulhawa, Susan 93, 108, 112, 179, 201
activism 13, 15, 20, 64, 66, 71, 81, 85, 117, 176, 195, 197, 199
activist 10, 36, 64, 67, 71, 81, 93, 101, 106, 134, 138, 187, 191, 193, 207
Adair, Tom 115, 117, 124, 141
affordance 9, 20, 26, 91–2, 196
Agamben, Giorgio 190
Alareer, Refaat 176, 178, 179, 199, 200
Albanese, Francesca P. 38, 202
al-Naffar, Saleem 177
Alsalem, Reem 102
Anderson, Terry 40
apartheid 37, 54, 55, 64, 66, 82, 83, 124, 135, 176, 188
Applebaum, Robert 197, 208
Arafat, Yasser 35, 128
Aretxaga, Begoña 106, 117
art 2–5, 7, 8–10, 12–14, 16, 20, 22, 23, 25, 41, 45, 47, 48, 65, 68, 69, 71, 72, 91, 97, 99, 112–15, 123, 150, 175, 176, 177, 186, 195–200, 207, 208
Arthur, Paul 132
artist 5, 7, 8, 10, 13, 18, 20, 26, 27, 44, 47, 60, 63, 64, 66, 68, 69, 71–3, 92, 95, 96, 98–100, 106, 113–15, 137, 154, 158, 159, 166, 170, 175, 177, 193, 195, 198, 208, 209

Atkins, Ellen 90, 109
audience 7, 9, 13, 15–16, 41, 49, 67–8, 72, 73, 81–2, 122, 127, 169, 174–5
Auque, Roger 41
autobiography 3, 18, 20, 98, 107, 176, 186, 197

B

Baccarini, Elvio 175, 198
Bala, Iwan 69, 84–6, 171
Barghouti, Marwan 34, 52
Barnie, John 73, 86, 170
BDS 37, 54, 64, 81, 82, 88, 112, 131, 208, 209
Behan, Rosemary 124, 141
Beirut 5–7, 9, 16, 17, 40, 41, 43, 49, 57, 62, 75, 76, 77, 80, 86, 97, 99, 122, 131, 140, 159, 182
Belfast 5, 6, 9, 11, 16, 18, 21, 25, 33, 49, 50, 62, 76, 80, 87, 93–8, 107, 130, 131, 135, 144, 153, 154, 159, 182, 191, 192, 202
Berg, Anastasia 2, 22
Berger, John 69, 70, 71, 84, 85
biography 3–4, 15, 106, 107, 180, 197
Bird, Dúnlaith 103, 116
Bloom, Mia 100, 115
bomb 6, 7, 25, 46–7, 92, 106, 142, 168, 191
bombardment 208
bomber 7, 10, 19, 46, 58, 89, 99–100, 161, 168, 182
bombing 6, 20, 43, 47, 99, 142, 151, 165, 167

Bradatan, Costica 178, 200
Bramley, Ellie Violet 95, 113
Bright, Martin 108, 118
Brown, Terence 78
Burns, Anna 106, 107
Butler, Judith 13, 28, 68, 84, 103

C

Callard, Agnes 2, 22, 196, 208
Carson, Ciarán 93, 112
Carton, Marcel 41
Chaudhari, Zuleikha 197, 208
Cicippio, Joseph 40
Code, Lorraine 107, 118
colonial 38, 64, 76, 101
colonialism 54
colonialist 39
colonisation 21, 135, 139, 188–9, 198
coloniser 20, 94
Cordner, Anthea E. 106, 117, 118
Cowper-Coles, Minna 102, 115
crime 35, 37, 38, 53, 55, 103, 116, 141, 190
criminal 35, 51, 128
criminality 164
Crompton, Lynne 72, 85
Cummings, Hugh 'Lexie' 133–4, 146–7

D

damage 2, 3, 93, 106, 126, 197
Danesi, Marcel 16, 29
Daniel, Errol Valentine 1, 2, 3, 18, 21, 22, 30, 169
Darwish, Mahmoud 47, 123, 139, 140, 141, 177, 178, 200
Darwish, Najwan 177, 200
daughter 19, 32, 73, 104, 105, 107, 123, 149–52, 155, 158, 161, 163, 164, 166, 199

Deane, Seamus 77
dead 1–2, 22, 33, 36, 45–6, 48, 59, 97, 107, 119, 122, 132, 142, 159, 161, 165–6, 175, 191, 198
death 7, 33, 73, 81, 82, 94, 122, 128, 133–4, 151, 164, 168, 175–7, 179–80, 181, 188, 190–2
Derfner, Larry 187, 204
Derry 1, 2, 21, 32–3, 36, 45, 46, 48, 51, 53, 59, 69, 77, 84, 86, 130–2, 134, 137, 138, 142–5, 147–8, 171, 181, 201
dispositio 15, 92, 122
Donahaye, Jasmin 25
drawing 47, 69, 70, 127
Dugard, John 37, 55
Dunne, Aidan 96, 113

E

East, Ben 90, 109, 111
Egypt 99, 125, 126, 141, 142, 177, 195
Elfyn, Menna 71, 85
Eliasson, Olafur 175, 176, 199
Eribon, Didier 4
ethical 5, 10, 14, 31, 63, 66, 67, 73–4, 78, 82, 97, 197
ethics 3, 66, 67, 74
ethnic cleansing 39, 197
ethos 13, 14, 67, 68, 73, 83, 84, 117
exploded 7, 90
explosive 7, 125

F

Fahnestock, Jeanne 16, 28, 29
Fatah 34, 37, 42, 54, 125, 128, 129, 141, 149
father 1, 19, 54, 99, 103, 123, 131, 132, 143, 149, 150–3, 155, 158, 159, 162–3, 166, 168
Faulks, Sebastian 40, 57
Felski, Rita 3, 4, 22

Index

fieldwork 6–8, 11, 17–8, 24, 34
Finch, Charles 90, 109
Fontaine, Marcel 41
Foucault, Michel 26, 28, 30, 73, 74, 173
form 2–4, 9–12, 14–17, 20, 32, 41, 61, 63, 64, 65, 68, 71, 72, 74, 89–119, 159, 167, 176, 187, 195, 196, 198

G

Gaza 7, 8, 10, 17, 19, 20, 26, 35–40, 42, 46–9, 53, 55–7, 62, 63, 72, 81, 98–105, 114–16, 118, 124–7, 136, 139, 141, 142, 148, 152, 163–5, 171–3, 176–9, 184, 185, 189, 190, 194, 199, 200, 206, 208, 209
genre 4, 8–9, 42, 80
Gilloch, Graeme 5, 22, 23
Givoni, Michal 13, 14, 28, 63, 68, 73–5, 80–2, 84–8, 196, 208
Glass, Charles 40
Golan 66, 160, 163, 166, 194, 207
Goodman, Michael John 95, 113
Gordon, Neve 190, 194, 205–7
Gornick, Vivian 14, 28, 76, 86
grave 44, 180
graveyard 122
gulag 6, 11, 186, 187, 204

H

Hamas 19, 36, 37, 39, 42, 53, 54, 61, 94, 102, 105, 115, 125, 126, 128, 141, 142, 149, 151, 164, 171, 176, 184, 189, 190, 193, 195, 200, 206, 208
Hannerz, Ulf 17, 29
Harlow, Barbara 16, 29
Heaney, Seamus 31, 50, 51, 77, 78, 87, 93, 145, 159, 171, 179, 200

Hebrew language 6, 11, 24, 34, 35, 36, 53, 64, 82, 83, 160, 161, 162, 168, 171, 172, 181, 186, 201
Hebron 131, 150, 161
Hopwood, Mererid 71, 85
Horwell, Veronica 81, 88
hostage 6, 9, 16, 18, 19, 24, 40, 41, 42, 49, 62, 75, 77, 79, 94, 97, 98, 103, 116, 140, 153, 154, 156, 157, 171

I

IDF 6, 24, 35, 36, 39, 43, 56, 58, 65, 115, 133, 137, 166, 183, 189, 190, 199, 201
Ignatieff, Michael 66, 83
incarceration 6, 34, 49, 186
injustice 2, 3, 8, 16, 21, 39, 63, 67, 119, 193
IQB 36, 176, 195
IRA 1, 7, 21, 32, 33, 34, 51, 131, 133, 145, 146, 147, 191, 192, 194
Ireland 5, 7, 11, 12, 16–18, 21, 34, 37, 49, 65, 76, 77, 79, 80–2, 87, 96, 98, 106, 117, 122, 124, 133, 134, 136, 142, 184, 194, 197, 198, 201
Islamic Jihad 5, 6, 24, 61, 104, 149

J

Jacobsen, David 40
Jarratt, Susan 67, 83
Jazeel, Tariq 92, 111
Jericho 70, 92, 150, 151
Jerusalem 10, 11, 17, 24, 37, 47, 53, 54, 65, 70, 75, 92, 93, 121, 123, 128–30, 132, 133, 136, 138, 145, 146, 150, 151, 158, 163, 176, 179, 180–2, 186, 187, 194, 196, 200, 201

Jones, Jonathan 196, 207
justice 2, 16, 20, 21, 29, 65, 117,
 195, 196, 197, 208

K
kairos 12, 31, 48, 49, 50
Kauffmann, Jean-Paul 41
Keenan, Brian 5–7, 9, 12, 13–16,
 18–21, 26, 30, 40–2, 48, 49, 57,
 58, 62, 75–80, 86, 87, 95, 97, 98,
 107, 114, 118, 122, 131, 140,
 144, 153, 154, 159, 165, 166,
 170, 171, 173, 182, 196
 An Evil Cradling 9, 12, 15, 16, 21,
  24, 26, 30, 40, 42, 48, 49, 57,
  58, 76, 77, 79, 80, 86, 87, 95,
  98, 107, 114, 122, 144, 170,
  173, 196
Kelly, Noel 96, 97, 114
Kemp, Martin 81, 88
Kholmyansky, Ephraim 186, 204
Kilby, Jane 5, 22, 23
kill 6, 19, 27, 31, 34, 58, 118, 128,
 133, 151, 164, 165, 176, 178,
 181, 186, 190–2, 199
killer 10
killing 7, 65, 93, 104, 128, 134, 190,
 191, 193
Kinsella, Thomas 198, 208
Kinsey, Christine 71, 85
Knauft, Bruce 18, 30
Kress, Gunther 16, 29

L
Larmore, Charles 21, 30, 195, 207
Lebanon 6, 7, 24, 25, 35, 42, 43, 49,
 50, 58, 76, 98, 99, 122, 143, 185,
 203, 204
Lefebvre, Henri 17, 29
LeFevre, Karen Burke 67, 84
Lejeune, Philippe 15, 28
Lentin, Ronit 31

Levine, Caroline 9, 14, 26, 28,
 89–92, 95, 108, 111
Levine, Jerry 40
Libman, Ben 90, 109, 110, 111
Llansteffan 8, 17, 18, 43, 47, 69, 73,
 127, 142, 143, 154, 170
logos 18
Lowdon, Claire 89, 90, 109, 124,
 141
Lydda 183, 185, 186, 202

M
Ma'ale Adumim 186–8, 204, 205
Maguire, Anne 107, 118
Mahesh, V. 112, 193
Mahon, Derek 25, 175
Maunsell, Jerome Boyd 90, 110,
 111
McCann, Colum 8–10, 12–20, 26,
 27, 30, 48, 51, 61, 64–7, 75,
 83, 90–4, 107–12, 122–4, 130,
 133, 135–6, 140–1, 144, 146–7,
 150–1, 161–3, 167–73, 191–3,
 196, 207
 Apeirogon 10, 12, 15, 16, 21, 26,
  30, 48, 51, 61, 64–7, 83, 89–95,
  107–12, 122, 123, 131, 140, 141,
  144, 146, 147, 150, 169, 170–3,
  192, 193, 196, 207
McCarthy, John 40, 79, 98
McGuinness, Martin 132, 145
McMonagle, William Gerard 'Gerry'
 133
Montefiore, Simon 180, 201
Mookherjee, Nayanika 5, 23, 92, 111
moral 3, 13, 20–1, 32, 49, 63, 73–4,
 96, 108, 193, 195–7
morality 20, 196
morally 81, 198
Morris, Jan 80
mother 1, 31, 32, 33, 105, 150, 155,
 160, 163, 164, 177, 180

Index

Mraffko, Clothilde 177, 199
Mundye, Charles 45, 46, 60
Murphy, Dervla 8–10, 12–20, 26, 48–9, 61–2, 80–2, 87, 88, 100, 101, 103–5, 115–18, 122–7, 136, 139, 141, 142, 147, 148, 163, 164, 172, 196
   A Month by the Sea 9, 12, 15, 16, 21, 26, 49, 61, 80, 81, 88, 95, 98, 100, 101, 108, 115–17, 124, 141–2, 147–8, 172, 196
Murphy, Kevin 93, 112

N

Nablus 17, 137, 138, 148
Naidoo, Kumi 176, 199
Nasar, Hammad 195
Netanyahu, Benjamin 37, 39, 55–7, 66, 83, 94, 172
novel 10, 15, 18, 48, 50, 63–5, 67, 89–90, 92, 95, 106, 107, 123, 150–1

O

occupation 28, 39, 48, 54, 61, 64, 75, 81, 93, 94, 101, 112, 119, 123, 124, 166, 167, 189–95, 196, 198, 205–7, 214
Oddo, John 68, 84
Oosthuizen, Ann 73, 85
Orringer, Julie 90, 109
Osmond, Osi Rhys 7–10, 12, 13, 16, 18–20, 24, 25, 27, 43–8, 58–60, 68–73, 84–6, 94, 122, 127, 137, 142, 143, 148, 152–9, 167, 170, 171, 178, 188, 196, 197
   Ymateb 7, 10, 12, 16, 19, 21, 27, 46, 48, 69, 72, 142, 196
O'Sullivan, Tina 97, 114
Ó Tuama, Seán 198, 208
Oz, Amos 149, 166, 169, 173, 180, 201

P

pacifism 10, 20, 203
pacifist 188
painting 27, 43, 45, 47, 71, 73, 95–6, 107, 127
Palestinian Islamic Jihad 102
Pappé, Ilan 38, 39, 56, 57, 195
pathos 18
Patten, Pramila 102, 103
Paul, Joanne 12, 28, 50
peace 7, 10, 20, 27, 42, 58, 65, 80, 106, 117, 132–5, 189, 192, 201
place 1, 4–7, 16–18, 22–3, 32–3, 35, 43–5, 47, 59, 70, 72, 80–1, 93, 97–8, 100–1, 103, 107, 121–48, 149–50, 153–5, 158, 163, 166, 170, 175, 182–4, 187, 189, 191, 197
PLO 6, 24, 42, 58, 61, 99, 131, 137, 183, 187
poem 32, 45–6, 50, 59–60, 66, 76–7, 121, 123, 145, 155, 175–7, 179, 198–200
poetry 45, 47, 59, 71, 77, 98, 123, 177, 198
Postill, John 17, 29
prison 6, 11, 32, 34–6, 52, 62, 78, 79, 123, 149, 150, 153, 154, 161, 168, 172, 191
prisoner 10, 11, 18, 32–5, 36, 52, 58, 79, 123, 137, 163, 171, 172
proof 14, 17, 18
prosimetrum 15, 77, 78, 80, 98, 107
PTSD 31, 50, 106

Q

Qalandiya 17, 128–30, 139, 143, 144, 163

R

Rabin, Yitzhak 183
Rafah 17, 56, 103, 136

Ramallah 19, 89, 94, 105, 128, 149, 162, 163, 182
Ranta, Ronald 187, 205
Reed-Danahay, Deborah 12, 13, 28, 29
refugee 6, 17–18, 81, 93, 99, 121, 126–30, 139, 140, 143, 144, 148, 155, 163, 179, 182–6, 196, 202–4
refusenik 6, 11, 204
Regan, Stephen 77, 78, 87
review 16, 40–1, 71, 77, 89–93, 107–8, 124, 196
Reynolds, John 37, 55
Reynolds, Nedra 67, 83
rhetor 13, 67–8
rhetoric 8–9, 11, 16, 19, 31, 48, 67–8, 92, 107, 131, 176
rhetorical 9–10, 12–13, 15–20, 31, 63, 67, 93, 107, 123–4, 136, 139
rhetorician 7, 68, 95, 122, 197
Richter-Devroe, Sophie 101, 115
Robbins, Joel 18, 21, 22, 29, 39, 56, 57, 195, 207
Roberts, Adam 189, 193, 195, 206, 207
Roberts, Lynette 45, 46, 60
Ronald, Kate 67, 84,
Rooney, Sally 63, 64, 82, 83, 95
Rumsey, Alan 18, 30, 169
Rye, Gill 66, 83

S
Said, Edward 15, 136, 148, 204
Salmon, Adrian 90, 110
Sandomir, Richard 81, 88
Sansom, Ian 90, 110
Sartwell, Crispin 7, 8, 25, 26
Schmertz, Johanna 67, 84
Schwalm, Helga 15, 28
Schwarz, Daniel R. 48, 60
Secor, Marie 16, 28, 29

Seurat, Michel 40–1, 57
Seymour, Dermot 95–7, 113, 114
Seymour, Tom 195, 207
Sharpe, Christina 4, 22, 23
Shawa, Laila 98–101, 105, 114, 115
shooting 33, 129, 130, 133
shot 1, 33, 129, 133, 135–6, 142, 151, 161, 191, 197
Shrayer, Maxim D. 176, 199
Simpson, Edward 19, 30
Sinwar, Yahya 36, 53
Skoulding, Zoë 46, 60
Smith, Greg 5, 23
sociography 3, 5, 22, 23
son 22, 54, 73, 122, 199
Spielberg, Steven 48, 61, 108, 118
Steadman, Donna 90, 109
Steedman, Carolyn 4
suffering 6, 18, 19, 22, 30, 37, 48, 56, 57, 63, 81, 93, 147–74, 176, 178, 190, 207
suicide 6, 10, 19, 20, 43, 58, 89, 99, 100, 137, 148, 151, 161, 167, 168, 178, 182
Sutherland, Thomas 40
symbolic 8, 94

T
terrorist 6, 10, 42, 136, 162
testimony 1, 3, 11–16, 19, 21, 31, 39, 41, 69, 73–5, 80–2, 107, 176, 178, 195–7
Thomas, Dylan 43, 59
Thomas, R. S. 72, 85, 158, 170, 171
Thomas-Corr, Johanna 89, 109, 118
Tilche, Alice 19, 30
time 1, 2, 6, 10–15, 19, 22, 30, 31–62, 63–7, 69, 72, 76–81, 89, 91–2, 95–100, 118, 122, 128, 130–3, 136, 142, 154, 158–9, 161–6, 169, 175, 177–9, 181, 183, 190, 191, 195

Toha, Mosab Abu 177, 200
Toohey, Elizabeth 90, 110
trauma 1, 3, 17, 18, 30, 32, 50, 58, 63, 66, 83, 103, 106, 117, 127, 149, 159, 162, 168–9, 176, 189, 196–8, 208, 214
travelogue 9, 15, 80, 107–8
Troubles, the 21, 32, 50, 77, 97, 106, 117–18, 144, 175, 181–2, 191

U
Underwood, Alexia 177, 200
UNRWA 99, 104, 126, 128, 139–40, 143–4, 148, 172, 183, 185, 203–4

V
van Creveld, Martin 194
van den Hengel, Louis 16, 28
van Eck 95, 112, 113
van Leeuwen, Theo 16, 29, 93, 95, 111, 113
Vicary, Sam 72, 85
Vidmar, Iris 175, 198
violence 1–5, 7, 10, 21, 23, 28, 31, 37, 39, 58, 64, 76, 92–4, 100–6, 115–17, 127–8, 133, 167–9, 176, 177, 181, 188, 194, 199, 208
visual 5, 8, 11–12, 16, 18–20, 69, 71–2, 95, 104, 176, 208
Vivian, Bradford 12, 28, 32, 51, 64, 74, 82

W
Wagner, Erica 92, 111
Waite, Terry 40
Wales 7, 8, 12, 18, 25, 27, 45, 46, 59, 60, 66, 68, 69, 72, 85, 137, 184, 192, 199, 203
Walzer, Arthur E. 10, 26
Watson, Ash 5, 23
Weekes, Omari 4, 23
Weir, Benjamin 40
Welsh language 7, 10, 23, 25, 27, 43, 71, 72, 73, 94, 170, 177
West Bank, the 8, 16, 35, 42, 43, 48, 65, 81, 93, 102, 116, 131, 135, 136, 141, 143–4, 149, 151, 172, 177, 185–90, 194, 205
Wilder, Laura 16, 29
Williams, Nerys 45, 60
Winik, Marion 108–10
witness 1, 5, 8, 11–14, 19–21, 28–9, 31–2, 39, 46, 48, 51, 57, 63–88, 96, 98, 129, 134, 150, 152, 154, 161, 164–5, 176, 191–2, 196–8, 208
Woroniecka-Krzyzanowska, Dorota 130, 144

Z
Zionism 80, 105, 179
Zionist 36, 39, 80, 105, 155, 160, 171